The Urban Negro in The South

BY

WILMOTH A. CARTER

NEW YORK / RUSSELL & RUSSELL

FOREWORD

The original document which provided the data for this book was a thesis, written at the University of Chicago, and entitled "The Negro Main Street of a Contemporary Urban Community." Leaving the specifics unaltered, but positing their alignment with socio-cultural emphases of the southern city, the study was made into this book, *The Urban Negro in the South*, in 1961. This reissue duplicates the first edition. The book was a result of research undertaken at a specific point in time, and even though a decade has passed since first publication, it remains historically nonrepeatable despite the empirically retestable status of its hypotheses.

While the ideas assembled here offer explanations for many patterns of ethnically-oriented consumer behavior, the aggregate research findings portray, in fact, a community study. The diverse and differentiated urban behavior patterns found existent in the southern urban community when the study was first undertaken continue to be of contemporary significance. Where the behavior patterns were found to revolve around racial or ethnic groups, both structured and unstructured observation have provided evidence for the variant forms of behavior within the city. These have in turn posited suggested lines of inquiry for studying the community. Additional lines of inquiry have been suggested by the effects of current trends in urbanization, suburbanization, decentralization of shopping centers, consumer behavior, and community relations. These, however, are both extensive and variant and necessitate an analysis outside the confines of this study.

At the time of first publication of the book, the "sit-in" movement had just passed through a significant cycle. Its impact on consumer behavior in the southern city appeared to have dimensions relevant to "the urban Negro" or "the Negro Main Street" but, in order not to distort the original study, "sit-in" implications are given as an appendix. The urge to update the study in the light of present trends was superseded by the urge to reproduce a viable sociological study, the very title of which was especially pertinent to the period in which the study was conducted. It seems equally appropos to retain the specific racial connotation given in the title, for this was the conceptual preference of those included in the sample population studied.

Acknowledgments must here be made to those persons in the Department of Sociology at the University of Chicago under whose guidance the study was pursued; to those authors whose ideas the writer may have unconsciously incorporated into her own; to those publishers now inoperative from whom source materials may have been selected, as well as those who have permitted use of certain quoted materials; and to the many persons interviewed in order to ascertain verifiable data for the original study. Gratitude must be expressed to Shaw University, the Department of Schools and Colleges of the American Baptist Convention, my father, sisters and brother without whose invaluable asistance publication of the findings contained herein would have been impossible.

Shaw University   WILMOTH A. CARTER
Raleigh, North Carolina
October, 1972

PART I

INTRODUCTION

ERRATA

Page 41, line 33	*for* West. *read* West.[1] *This reference appears as the first footnote* *on the following page.*
Page 44, line 8	*for* marketerers *read* marketers
Page 253, line 35	*for* An the onset of the movement, *read* At the onset of the movement,

Chapter 1

THEORETICAL ORIENTATION AND METHODOLOGICAL CONSIDERATIONS

PERHAPS one of the most illuminating statements ever made about the status of the Southern city is given by E. W. Parks. Says he, "Every possible forecast implies that the continued growth of the city, with a concomitant advance of industrialism, will tend to standardize our cities and make them more completely like all other American cities. But at present they remain a group apart."[1] More than two decades have passed since this statement was made, during which time the Southern city has undergone numerous changes, but still maintains a high degree of individuality which merits investigation. Among the factors that keep the Southern city in "a group apart" is its low percentage of varying ethnic groups and its high percentage of two predominantly racial groups. Because a city is both a physical mechanism and a population aggregate, possessing reciprocal relationships between the physical and human elements,[2] the human and spatial patterns of living within such an unwalled community are of significance in studying American culture.

Numerous studies have called attention to significant features of ethnic and racial groups within the United States, but there is a dearth of scientific knowledge regarding such groups inside the Southern city. As a unit of investigation the Southern city has been one of the neglected aspects of inquiries concerned with urban society. The present study proposes to help fill this gap through an investigative approach that provides basis for a descriptive analysis of the behavior of a racial group in a community that forms part of the urban South. Accepting the view that racial and nationality bonds tend to subgroup a city's population into various economic areas and to further subgroup into social divisions within the economic areas,[3] the Negro Main Street of a contemporary community offers a valuable framework for the

[1] Edd Winfield Parks, "Southern Towns and Cities," W. T. Couch (ed.) *Culture in the South*, (Chapel Hill: University of N. C. Press, 1934), p. 518.
[2] R. D. McKenzie, *The Metropolitan Community*, (New York: McGraw Hill Book Co., 1933), p. 213.

analysis of a segment of urban behavior. The major hypothesis posited by this study is as follows: Main Streets assume their character under the impact of urbanizing forces linked with social systems in which certain culturally-dominant values help mold the behavior of persons identified therewith. Where the identifying persons are racial groups and the culturally-dominant values racially oriented, the nature of relationships between racial groups finds overt expression in the construction of specific media through which to channel the group behavior. Special institutions and services become part of the media constructed to serve this end, and their functions form the integrative elements in the structuring of such media. Thus, the Negro Main Street becomes a constructed medium that symbolizes specific values, maintains specific institutions and services, and aids the identification of patterns of behavior arising out of a racially-oriented community.

The central problem of this investigation is to determine the nature of functions of the Negro Main Street in relation to dominant social values that form a nucleus for specific types of social behavior in the contemporary urban community. It is proposed to delineate the characteristic functions of the Negro Main Street by tracing the history of Negro business in the community of Raleigh, North Carolina; by studying the nature of Negro business and services under the impact of discrimination; by examining the formal and informal group characterizations that emanate from Negro Main Street participation; and by analyzing change in the Negro business world within the context of general social change. Guided thus by the previously-designated hypothesis relative to the origin and nature of the Negro Main Street, and the problem of determining what the functions of the street are, the study is organized into the following parts: 1) Growth of Negro business under the impact of urbanization; 2) The influence of discrimination upon consumers' use of space; 3) Styles of life and their reflections in group formation, action and thought; 4) Facets in social change.

Organization of the data of this study into the preceding categories tends to help structure specific findings and generalizations resting upon the following premise: accompanying the urbanization processes have been changes in the nature of racial accom-

[3] R. D. McKenzie, *The Neighborhood: A Study of Local Life in the City of Columbus, Ohio* (Chicago: University of Chicago Press, 1923).

modation and, since the economy of a people is a basic component of its culture, alterations in the nature of racial adjustment are nowhere more evident than in the economic sphere where patterns of consumption have been conditioned by measures of discrimination. It follows therefore that, if racial adjustment involves usage of discriminatory policies and practices, then any racial group of consumers will find means of expressing this in areas most pertinent to its way of life.

A series of questions is posited by the approach to the problem around which this study centers. Those of primary significance are: 1) What has been the impact of urbanization upon the development of the Negro Main Street? 2) What factors have influenced the evolution of the street? 3) How has discrimination affected the formation and functioning of the street? 4) What patterns of consumption are manifest in the institutions and services located on the street? 5) How has spatiality influenced the character and use of the street? 6) By what means are special types of groups caught up in the web of Negro Main Street activities? 7) What effect has the Negro Main Street produced upon intra-group attitudes and cohesiveness? 8) What racial ideologies have developed in relation to the Negro Main Street and how have these been modified through time? 9) What social significance attaches to changes taking place in the street?

This study aims to provide a framework within which to seek answers to the preceding questions. The specific assumptions on which the questions are based can be stated respectively thus: 1) Urban phenomena assume their characterizations from specific combinations of interacting forces within the urban environment. 2) Differentiation of urban areas into segmentalized sub-areas is functionally related to the indigenous development of the specific areas involved. 3) A society based upon superordinate-subordinate relations tends to develop social mechanisms through which to maintain such relation. Where the superordinate-subordinate interests are directed toward the control of relations between racial groups, the mechanisms of control are designed accordingly. Discrimination is one of the controls used in the economic sphere of relations between races. 4) An interdependence exists between the social characteristics of consumers, items of consumption, from whom consumption goods are secured, and the conditions under which consumption takes place. 5) Consumption on the Negro Main Street, whether influenced by custom, law, or preference, occurs within a racial context. Within this context institutionalized services of a bi-racial nature have formed a dichotomy with a well ordered pattern of relationships that indicates: what the Negro *can* consume from whites vs. what he *must* consume from Negroes; types of institutions in which he *can* consume from whites vs. those in which he *must* consume from Negroes; conditions under which he *can* consume from whites vs. those under which he *must* consume from Negroes. 6) Formal and informal associations form an integral part of urban life. Insofar as the associational life revolves around some particular urban phenomenon the associations develop a unique connection therewith. 7) In the process of adjusting to a changing social environment individualized segments of the group tend to focus their attitudes and aspirations upon a common goal. Striving toward achievement of the goal, whether consciously or unconsciously motivated, tends to unify the otherwise diverse individualized attitudes of sub-groups. The overt manifestation of this is seen in things individual group members say and do. 8) Changes in the nature of occupational alignments of particular groups evoke changes in status and bear a significant relationship to changes in the thought patterns of a community. The reciprocal relation between what people say and what they do tends to aid in the formation of ideas for developing lines of action within the existing social structure. 9) Social and cultural phenomena do not exist in a vacuum but are interrelated with other forces in a society. Thus, change in a specific phenomenon produces some effect upon the generic social structure and becomes a facet in whatever broader changes are occurring at the time.

No sociological research bearing directly upon the problem of this study has come to the attention of the writer, but several studies point up suggestive and implied ideas therefor. Among the most significant of these is *The Ghetto* by the late Louis Wirth. The ghetto, medieval and modern, is found to be an institution —a cultural community—developed and perpetuated by the traditions, habits, and customs of an ethnic group, the Jew. As a form of accommodation between groups it tends to become a symbol of subjugation, indicative of the role and status of the Jew within an urban center. The internal structure of the modern ghetto, typified in the Jewish community of Chicago, exemplifies the means by which a subordinate group functioning in a limited inner world adjusts to a larger outer world. The nature of oc-

cupational groups and extent of division of labor within the
structure of the ghetto manifest themselves in a "Main Street"
complex or business center with its cluster of institutions that
cater to the needs of the group within. Specific types of institutions organized around religious precepts, ritual, customs, dietary
laws, and communal life functions tend to crystallize into social,
psychological, and situational forms that give the ghetto its
character. When these factors are viewed within the context of
the urban economy, the ghetto becomes a significant social phenomenon demonstrative of the growth of a natural social area
through which an ethnic group is able to participate in the life of
a complex urban center, but at the same time to remain distinct and
separate.

Another sociological study with implications for the present
one is Albert Blumenthal's *Small-Town Stuff*. Unlike the preceding study which gives a descriptive analysis of the community
as a changing institution, *Small-Town Stuff* portrays a changing
culture in which community life centers around intimate personal
relationships. The community studied is called "Mineville," and
several ethnic groups contribute to its culture heritage, but no
group has numbers sufficient enough for it to develop a segregated area. Thus ethnic traits tend to become diffused or submerged and personal traits and relations take precedence over
others within the culture. Mineville's main street occupies an
important place in the persistence of the community, for its
businesses form the centers through which activities and relationships of the total community are molded, dispensed, and
controlled. Since all Mineville activities rest upon personal bases
—whether pertaining to formal group life, informal, attitudes,
roles, statuses, customs, institutions, or just the daily routine of
living—business centers with their operators and clientele become the media of exchange for the interlocking social relationships of the community. Even where social change is effected
through new media or changing relationships the very nature and
direction of the change rest upon personal factors. It is this type
of "small-town stuff" which is often transplanted in contemporary
urban communities.

Not only the nature, but also the intensity, of personal relationships form the nucleus of behavior observed in still another
study of an urbanized ethnic group. William Foote Whyte's
Street Corner Society shows how personal relationships based

upon a system of reciprocal obligations operate in structuring group and organizational features of the community called "Cornerville." While informal groups form and function through certain corners on specific streets of Cornerville, their intra- and inter-group relationships extend through the total community structure. The characteristic institutions of Cornerville—corner gangs, racket, police, and political organizations—all have their bases in personal relationships. A high rate of interaction between persons forming the membership of these institutions tends to furnish the motivating force around which institutional and group activities are organized. Analysis of the intensity of personal relationships is beyond the scope of the present study, but types and functions of groups identified with the community have some comparative value.

Another study of comparative value for the present one is Drake and Cayton's *Black Metropolis*, an investigation regarding Negro participation in the life of a Midwest metropolis. Since race relations tend to condition the nature and degree of Negro participation in Midwest metropolitan activities, they tend also to serve as pillars in the structuring of a Negro world inside the broader Midwest world. Evolution and perpetuation of the Negro world have been through a color line drawn by usage rather than law. The internal structure of the Negro community, shaped predominantly by residential segregation and occupational discrimination, maintains a set of institutions similar to those of other communities in form but different in content. While custom makes a line of demarcation between social worlds of Negroes and whites, vested interests of Negro businessmen, politicians, civic leaders and preachers tend to support the maintenance and continued existence of such. Just as the most overt expression of a color line in the Midwest metropolis is the establishment of a Negro community, so the most evident form assumed by the color line is the existence of a business center with main- and side-street institutions that cater to a Negro clientele. Key institutions of the Negro community—newspapers, the policy racket, and business enterprises—all reflect the system of the race relations and perform racial functions for the Negro. The Negro community of the metropolis, therefore, becomes one of the forces of social control that reinforces the color line drawn between social worlds. As race contact, economic necessity, and political expediency effect shifts in the color line the community becomes also a medium of social change. Such factors as these, though characteristic of the Northern metropolis, have their counterparts in the Southern metropolis, hence their significance for the present study.

Of general relevance to any study of the American Negro and his distinct economy is E. Franklin Frazier's *Black Bourgeoisie,* a sociological analysis of the behavior, attitudes, and values of the middle-class Negro. The "black bourgeoisie," rooted in what the author designates as a "world of reality," is shown as having objective existence in economic conditions in which occupational differentiation has given rise to a class of white-collar workers marginal to both the Negro world and the white world. While education is the principal force shaping the ideals and values of the black bourgeoisie, faith in the power of Negro business to remove racial stigma and solve economic problems of the Negro has helped envelop the Negro in a world of unreality. This factor, coupled with racial discrimination and segregation, has created an isolated social world of make-believe, in which the black bourgeoisie strives for social status, personal gratification, and escape from the contempt of whites. Resultant frustrations, insecurities, and inferiority-feelings are the prevailing traits of bourgeoisie personalities functioning within such a framework.

Since one of the business interests dominating the economy of the American Negro has centered around the practice of medicine, Dietrich Reitzes' *Negroes and Medicine* is also pertinent here. *Negroes and Medicine* shows rather concretely that patterns of medical care as provided by and for Negroes differ from community to community, with patterns in southern communities more nearly resembling each other than those in other communities. In the Southern community, where segregation in medicine is practically complete, some of the key factors influencing the pattern of medical care include the self-segregation of the Negro physicians; attitudes of older Negro general practitioners toward the younger Negro specialists; variations by social class in conceptions Negroes hold of the Negro physician; and the general pattern of race relations prevailing in the community.

Without direct pertinence to the problem under analysis in the present study, but with sufficient indirect implications to be mentioned here are the following studies: Harvey Zorbaugh's *Gold Coast and the Slum,* and Caroline Ware's *Greenwich Village 1920-1930.* Both involve divergent ethnic groups living symbiotically in given localities within two of America's largest cities.

Neither of the localities is thought of as a community, but each possesses a number of distinct characteristics arising out of adaptations to changing urban environments. Neither can these studies be taken as analytical explanations of behavior patterns of designated ethnic groups, but rather as descriptions of areas that abound in heterogeneity, contrasts, and extremes. One of the primary forces in establishing the contrasts and extremes is the fact that resident groups of the areas comprise varying proportions of native and foreign population elements, of conventional and bohemian behavior, of vice and respectability, of poverty and wealth, of organization and disorganization. The selective relevance of this to the present study is the fact that within such a locality framework as the preceding there tends to develop a rialto through which specific occupations and businesses give expression to dominant culture values of particular ethnic groups.

Two other studies that have taken indirect notice of the trade centers of racial and ethnic groups in urban metropolises are: Wu's "Chinatowns" (unpublished Ph.D. dissertation), and Harry Walker's "Changes In Race Accommodation In A Southern Community" (unpublished Ph.D. dissertation). Wu found that the development of a central trade area in Chinatown, a segregated community within the metropolis, tends to make life social for the Chinese rather than just symbiotic. Institutions characteristic of Chinatown, such as laundries, restaurants and novelty shops, tend to form a nucleus for the two circumferences that make the functioning of Chinatown similar to a metropolitan center and its hinterland. As a local trade area Chinatown performs numerous informal as well as formal functions. As an organized community it is a function of ways of earning a living in urban America, where occupational competition between whites and Chinese forced the latter to enter "parasitic types of business" with the character of luxuries. Since there's no competition in the exchange of luxuries, these have become firmly entrenched and identifying marks of Chinatown.

"Changes In Race Accommodation In A Southern Community" analyzes race relations in Durham, North Carolina, from the standpoint of community organization. Early structuring of Negro-white relationships in this industrialized community involved personal relationships in which each individual Negro was dependent upon an individual white person; more recent structuring shows movement toward more impersonal Negro-white relationships. One of the principal factors in the shift toward the impersonality of relationships has been the growth of a rather self-contained Negro community in which Negro business has become well established, Negro leadership has become the adjuster of race relations, and high degrees of race consciousness and racial solidarity have become evident. Because of the interconnections of established business enterprises of this tobacco-industry community and the capital-city community of Raleigh, the Walker study is particularly pertinent to the present one.

The Negro Main Street appears first and foremost as an economic matrix—shopping or service center—and an ecological area. But it is functionally a cultural area and social center as well, and acts as a psychological link in the racial bonds chained to the culture. It seems reasonable to take cognizance of the following related articles: "City Shoppers and Urban Identification: Observations On The Social Psychology Of City Life," Gregory P. Stone, *American Journal of Sociology*, LX (July, 1954) and "Beale Street, A Study In Ecological Succession," Robert W. O'Brien, *Sociology and Social Research*, XXVI (May-June, 1942). The former attempts to show, through data collected on shopping from consumer-informants in the northwest of Chicago, how individuals select, evaluate, and identify with stores they patronize, and hence become bound to the larger community. The latter article indicates the value of changes in the use of a street —by years, by days of the week, by day and night—to the study of a community. Whether considered as a street of shoppers and consumers or as an area invaded by specific types of people and enterprises, ecological processes have been at work in helping establish a Main Street for the Negro community.

Fictional materials cannot be said to qualify as authentic data for research projects. However, three works should be alluded to here because of their emphasis upon nominal items somewhat akin to those of the present study. One of these, Sinclair Lewis' *Main Street*, lays stress upon the traits and habits of singular personalities of Gopher Prairie with the ultimate effect of showing the universality and typicality of standardized small-town behavior. Ann Petry's *The Street* revolves around fictional characters but is a vivid portrayal of 116th Street as a Negro main stem of New York City and is nonetheless realistic. The street as depicted becomes desolate in winter from frozen debris and icy winds; is transformed into an outdoor living-room and bedroom in summer; is crowded with groups of men from morning until night depending upon their employment or non-employment statuses; and its key institution, "The Junto," serves as a social club for both men and women. Such implicit behavioral characteristics could thus convert any street into a virtual Main Street. Still a third fictional work is William Gardner's *South Street*, a story of three personalities but also a depiction of Philadelphia's Negro Mecca, the uniqueness of which resides in the closing of stores and clubs and roping-off of its area for an annual three-day celebration called "Spring Festival." Dancing, singing, eating, drinking, parading, speech-making, and meetings form the nucleus of behavior during the festival period. The story of *South Street,* however, abounds in numerous personality types with key functions in the Negro community. Because race tensions are reflected in characteristics of the street and activities of its clients, South Street becomes a mirror for viewing race relations in urban America.

In the preceding studies and works one notes that ethnic and racial groups in America tend to adjust to the urban web of life by means of group-oriented devices and techniques. The specific forms of adjustment have been by-products of the culture heritage and experiences of the particular group concerned. The nature and degree of interaction between in- and out-groups have resulted in the establishment of separate ethnic or racial social worlds in urban communities and/or social values expressed in variegated institutions and customs. Even where emphasis has been on personalities, rather than groups, acting along individual lines they have moved within some group framework. Both symbiotic and social relationships are evidenced in the methods of accommodation developed by and between groups and persons, varying according to the nature and degree of interaction. Thus, while personal relationships make up the consistent elements of behavior in some communities and natural social areas, impersonal relationships characterize others. Forms of adjustment to urban situations, motivational forces in adjustment, and the expressed and symbolic features of these are more readily understood through the culture compulsives, values, and interests of the group caught up in the adjustment processes. Trying to understand the behavior of ethnic and racial groups of urban America in the light of the foregoing factors becomes therefore a significant objective of the sociologist. Analyzing Negro Main Street behavior is an attempt to supplement such understanding, for the street—ethnically or racially delineated —turns out to be not just structural but functional, not static but a living thing.

The Present Study

Data used as substantiating evidence for the Negro Main Street study as portrayed in the subsequent pages of this document were collected in the community of Raleigh, North Carolina, and focused upon the functional use of East Hargett Street. As a research laboratory several factors are of interest about the city itself. Holding the title of state capital, it occupies a strategic geographical position, for it is located near the center of the state. Its areal limits cover 15.3 square miles, served by a network' of state and federal highways and some 100 trucking lines. Its trade-center function attests to its dominance as a metropolis, for it is used by populations of the surrounding seven small towns and numerous rural areas; within a 100-mile radius of the city resides 30% of the combined populations of Virginia, North Carolina, and South Carolina. Raleigh's function as a governmental center did not devolve upon it merely by usage, for it was created by legislative act and set in a forest as "the city of oaks" in 1792. Her status as an educational center is linked with the six colleges, three business schools, and three special schools established in the city. Her bi-racial population, numbering 65,679 in 1950 but an estimated 86,000 in 1958, is 72% native white, 27.2% Negro, and 0.9% foreign-born white. The city's cross-section population has made her more like North Carolina as a whole than any other city within the state.

It is within the structure of this urban community of the South, this trade-governmental-educational center, that the Negro Main Street phenomena are observed. Using the characteristics of the Southern city as given by Demerath and Gilmore Raleigh is typically Southern. They point out the following features as characteristics of the Southern city: [4]

[4] Nicholas J. Demerath and Harlan W. Gilmore, "The Ecology Of Southern Cities," Rupert B. Vance and Nicholas J. Demerath (eds.), *The Urban South* (Chapel Hill: University of North Carolina Press, 1954), p. 136.

It is a small city; a retail trade and market center serving a limited agricultural area; an educational center, government seat, factory town, or mining town.

It has a bi-racial population. The two races live in separate social worlds.

The central business section is the dominant core around which residential areas are arranged.

No "one and only" ecological pattern exists.

It performs "general urban functions" for both rural and urban residents, and "local urban functions" for the city's residents and its daily commuters, both sets of functions standing in mutual dependence.

Like many of the urban communities already mentioned Raleigh too consists of two separate social worlds—a Negro world and a white world. A part of the separation that distinguishes between the Negro and white worlds assumes the form of a Negro business world, confined in part to the street designated as the Negro Main Street lying close to the center of the city. Socially this world caters to the population that resides within the boundaries of a visible and an invisible Negro world. Negro Main Street is generic, universal, and typical in American culture. However, its differentiating characteristics vary from city to city. It often assumes the characteristics of an Auburn Avenue or Decatur Street as in Atlanta—Auburn being known for its first-class Negro bank, leading Negro daily newspaper office and fashionable night clubs, while Decatur is described by many as a street of "telephone-pole philosophers," "wine bibbers," and "fun seekers." The Negro Main Street sometimes becomes renowned because of its originality, as did New Orleans' Basin Street which "gave birth to the blues." It may be frequented by both Negroes and whites who vary their usage of the street by time of day and place, as in the case of Memphis' Beale Street, or it may be as crowded and devoid of white customers as Chicago's 47th Street. It may change from an area of desolation in winter to one of out-door living rooms in summer, as does New York's 116th Street, or even close all businesses to celebrate "Spring Festival" as does Philadelphia's South Street. It may be as small as the Negro area of "Southerntown," as limited in business as Charlotte's East Second Street, or as inclusive as Norfolk's Church Street. Whatever its individual characteristics regardless of regional location, Negro Main Street has become an institution within American culture. The specific Raleigh street observed, East Hargett, extends from Fayetteville (chief thoroughfare for the entire city) to Blount Street where natural and cultural boundaries set limits. McKenzie's insight into the development of metropolitan communities indicates that "the evolution of economic organization from village and town to metropolitan economy is but the extension and specialization of centralization of each of the dominant interests of life." [5] The Negro Main Street can be seen as a product of this kind of centralization and specialization. Centralized by location, specialized by structure, as well as function, and generalized by type, it represents an extension of dominant interests prompted by cultural values. Discovering the functions performed by the Negro Main Street of the contemporary urban community of the preceding type has induced the general orientation of this study.

As originally stated, the community in which Negro-Main-Street behavior is analyzed is not only urban but metropolitan and Southern. It is therefore necessary to indicate the definitive context within which the Negro Main Street concept is used.

As used in this study the *Negro Main Street* is defined as the principal sphere within which business activities are undertaken by and for Negroes. Business activities are taken in the broad sense to cover the exchange of goods and services. Thus, personal services, professional services, insurance and real estate are categorized along with retail stores.

Metropolis is used within the framework of definitions set by the United States Bureau of Census. The Census defines a standard metropolitan area as a county or group of contiguous counties which contains at least one city of 50,000 inhabitants or more. The county or counties must also possess certain characteristics that conform to the criteria for being essentially metropolitan in character and socially and economically integrated with the central city. The central city and metropolis thus becomes the large city, as well as the one that performs the function of integrating contiguous territory. Two groups of metropolises are therefore noted: the city of 50,000-100,000 and the city of 100,000 and over.

The South is used here within the framework of Odum's

[5] R. D. McKenzie, "The Scope of Human Ecology," E. W. Burgess (ed.), *The Urban Community* (Chicago: University of Chicago Press, 1926), p. 177.

Southern Regions. Odum classified states according to their possession of homogeneity in natural, artificial, technological, human, and institutional resources. He thus distinguished between two Souths, a Southeast and a Southwest. The eleven states of the Southeast include Virginia, North Carolina, South Carolina, Arkansas, Kentucky, Tennessee, Mississippi, Alabama, Georgia, Florida, and Louisiana. It is this South of which the city of Raleigh is a part as discussed in this study.

Community is used here in the generally accepted sense of embodying a local area in which an association of persons and groups live together and influence one another.

Much of the material collected for this study is from primary sources. Personal documents, an unpublished autobiography, interviews, and minutes of meetings of the city council were relied upon for supportive evidence about the history of many Negro Main Street phenomena. Secondary sources, such as compilations of city ordinances, private, public and local laws, city directories, industrial surveys, and monographs of the city planning division have furnished data regarding types, location, and changes in business enterprises.

Demographic materials embracing characteristics of the population and trends in urbanization have been compiled from data published under auspices of the United States Bureau of Census.

Statistical support for many of the qualitative aspects of the study has been secured through sampling devices. Since Raleigh has no official wards or census tracts, the most authentic count of population aggregates is by means of block statistics issued by the Housing Division of the United States Bureau of Census. Using block data, out of 16,166 occupied dwelling units in Raleigh in 1950, 4,069 were occupied by nonwhites and distributed over 271 blocks. When additions are made for new residential areas developed and incorporated within the city since 1950 the number of nonwhite dwellings increases to 4,350, distributed over 286 blocks. Blocks were thus divided into heavy, medium, and light categories and a random sample of blocks and dwellings taken in such manner as to provide a sample of 350 nonwhite dwellings. Nonwhites who were non-Negro were rejected. Three hundred and fifty household heads were then interviewed with a schedule, a copy of which is found in the appendix. Of the 350, 116 turned out to be males and 234 females ranging in age from 18 to 75 and over. Additional information came from 96 other interviewees, 28 of whom are Negro Main Street operators of business with 57.3 percent of the 96 consisting of males of middle age and over. While 68 of the 96 were depth interviews, those held with the 28 operators of business were limited to securing information about specified items pertaining to the business operated. Thus, a total of 446 interviews, involving young adults, middle-aged and elderly residents provided the basic data for the study. This phase of the study covered a period of approximately four months, May-August, 1958, the writer's role as interviewer and observer being aided by residence and participation in the life of the city.

To help interpret the findings of this study in the light of the functional attributes of the Negro Main Street, it is necessary to get a glimpse at the street's influencing community not only at the local level but also at the state and regional level, and this the ensuing chapter attempts to do.

PART II

GROWTH OF NEGRO BUSINESS UNDER THE IMPACT OF URBANIZATION

Chapter 2

COMMUNITY CHARACTERISTICS WITHIN A REGION-STATE PATTERN

THE community of Raleigh reflects in its make-up and development many urbanizing features of the Southeastern region of which it is a part. Especially significant in the urbanizing traits of the South have been the slow growth of the urban population, the large number of small cities, and the complete lack of cities ranking among the nation or world's largest.

It was a full century after the first census of the United States was taken before the South had more than 10 percent of her population residing in cities. When in 1890 the population of the United States was 35.1 percent urban, the South was only 13.2 percent. Continued slow growth brought the population of the Southeast to a 29.8 percent urban status by 1930, with a less than one-third urban population in 1940.[1] Possessing a high land-man ratio, the South has lagged in urbanization with respect to both number and size of cities, but has maintained its urbanwise growth. In the 1930-40 decade, when there was a decided decrease in urban areas of the United States, there was continued urban increase in the South. Between 1940 and 1950 the increase in number of urban places was most evident in states that have long been among the most rural of the nation, as table 1 indicates.

Urbanity is relatively homogeneous within the Southeast, for it ranges from 65.5 in Florida to 27.9 in Mississippi. Only two states, Florida and Louisiana, were more than 50 percent urban and only one, Mississippi, less than 30 percent urban in 1950, the range in urbanity for the eleven Southeastern states being 37.6 percent.

Of similar import in the Southeast is the large number of small urban places and the small number of large urban places. Out of 892 urban places in the Southeast in 1950, that is, places of 2,500 and over, 679 or 76.12 percent were in the 2,500-10,000 category; 213 or 23.88 percent were in the 10,000-and-over category, the distribution of this 213 being as follows: 20 or 9.39 percent in the 100,000-and-over group, an equal number

[1] Rupert B. Vance, *All These People* (Chapel Hill: University of North Carolina Press, 1945), p. 20.

and percent in the 50,000-100,000 group, more than twice that number, 49 or 23 percent, in the 25,000-50,000 group, and 124 or 58.2 percent in the 10,000-25,000 group. Even with the largest concentration of urban places at the bottom, between 1940 and 1950 there was a 5.9% decrease in number of places 2,500-5,000,

TABLE 1

Number and Percentage Increase of Urban Places of the Southeast, by States, 1950 and 1940

State	Number of Urban Places 1950	Number of Urban Places 1940	Increase In Number	Percentage Increase
Alabama	85	74	11	14.86
Arkansas	64	62	2	3.22
Florida	98	92	6	6.52
Georgia	106	99	7	7.07
Kentucky	74	68	6	8.82
Louisiana	72	66	6	9.09
Mississippi	54	53	1	1.89
North Carolina	107	88	19	21.59
South Carolina	83	60	23	38.30
Tennessee	71	64	7	10.94
Virginia	78	61	17	27.87
Totals	892	787	105	

Source: United States Bureau of the Census, *United States Census of Population: 1950*, Vol. I, "Number of Inhabitants," Chap. 1, U.S. Summary, Tables 16 and 24.

while the number of places 50,000-100,000 remained stationary and the increase in places 100,000 and over made an equal distribution between places of 50,000-100,000 and places of 100,000 and over.

In 1850 there were no cities of 50,000 in the South, and in 1860, when New Orleans was the only metropolis in the South, there were no towns of as many as 10,000 people in North Carolina, Florida, Mississippi, Arkansas, or Texas. By 1900 there were three cities of 100,000 and over in the South and by 1950 fourteen of the fifty largest cities of the United States were in the South.

North Carolina is typically Southeastern. Her reflections of the preceding urbanizing characteristics can be noted in her having only one of the 106 cities of the nation with population 100,000 and over; five of the nation's cities of 50,000-100,000, and hence six of the 168 standard metropolitan areas of the nation. The bulk of her 33.7 percent urban population is distributed over 107 urban places and highly concentrated in the most medium-sized places, as shown in table 2.

TABLE 2

Distribution of Urban Population of North Carolina By Number and Size of Places, 1950

Places	Number of Places	Population	Percent of Total
100,000 & Over	1	134,042	10.02
50,000-100,000	5	352,190	26.34
25,000-50,000	5	175,876	13.15
10,000-25,000	20	318,782	23.84
5,000-10,000	27	181,158	13.55
2,500-5,000	49	174,918	13.08
Totals	107	1,336,966	99.98

Source: U.S. Bureau of the Census, *U.S. Census, of Population: 1950.* Vol. I, "Number of Inhabitants," Chapter 1: U. S. Summary, Table 16.

One writer has indicated that the South is evolving into a region of metropolitan communities or areas of metropolitan culture, which are possibly the only distinct social, cultural, and economic units in the southern economy.[2] Among the factors contributing to this metropolitan growth are expansion in industry, trade, banking facilities, increase in service occupations, and attractions of physical attributes of the area.[3] Concentration of these urban functions in Southern metropolises has forced many of the Southern cities into positions of dominance, the functional relationship of a central city and its hinterland constituting the significant aspect of metropolitanization. The importance of this factor is stressed by Gras who defines the metropolitan economy as an "organization of producers and consumers mutually dependent for goods and services, wherein their wants are supplied by a system of exchange concentrated in a large

[2] Walter J. Matherly, "Emergence of the Metropolitan Community in the South," *Social Forces,* Vol. XIV (March, 1936), p. 235.
[3] *Ibid.,* pp. 314-325.

city which is the focus of local trade and the center through which normal economic relations with the outside are established and maintained."[4] McKenzie further establishes the functional nature of the metropolis by describing it as a constellation of centers, the hinterland of the central city being bound to it by economic ties rather than by mass participation in the local institutions or life of the city.[5] Whether resulting from general economic, governmental, military, or other functions the interdependence of central city and hinterland in the South has created a number of widely dispersed centers of dominance. Of 29 such centers in the South in 1950, centers with population 100,000 and over, 9 were in the southwestern states of Texas and Oklahoma.

Although the South is becoming increasingly more metropolitan in make-up, its centers of dominance are functionally different one from the other. Differentiation of southern urban centers tends to be based upon what Demerath and Gilmore have designated as "general urban" and "headquarters" functions. The dominant ones of these urban functions in the South include merchandising, education, transportation, and government, along with numerous mutually dependent "local urban" functions.[6] Functional uniformity in the urban South exists in the dominance of one function, the servicing of an agricultural hinterland, and diversification by means of shipping, retail shopping, wholesaling, professionalized and skilled service concentration—all contributing to the culturally distinct metropolitanism of the South and producing profound interdependence of central city and satellites.

Accompanying urbanization trends in the South, as in other regions, have been changes in the occupational structure. As the South moved from a 15.0 percent urban population in 1900 to 47.1 percent urban (by new definition) in 1950, a concomitant decrease occurred in the proportion of workers engaged in agriculture, forestry and fishing—from 61.6 in 1900 to 21.3 in 1950;

[4] N. S. B. Gras, *An Introduction to Economic History* (New York: Harper and Brothers, 1922), p. 186.

[5] R. D. McKenzie, *Metropolitan Community* (New York: McGraw Hill Book Co., 1933), pp. 70-71.

[6] Nicholas J. Demerath and Harlan W. Gilmore, "The Ecology of Southern Cities," Rupert B. Vance (ed.) *The Urban South* (Chapel Hill: The University of North Carolina Press, 1954), p. 136-7.

an increase in trade, service, and other industries—from 27.9 in 1900 to 61.1 in 1950; and an increase in manufacturing—from 10.5 in 1900 to 17.6 in 1950.[7] The comparable decrease and increase in the first two groups of industries respectively are illustrative of changing economic emphases in the South, and hence changes in population distribution. Manufacturing has changed more slowly but helps point up the nature of industrial changes nonetheless. When occupational shifts are noted within the changing industrial structure, borne out by 1950 census data, the following factors are immediately apparent: 1) marked increase in professional and skilled occupations; 2) decrease in farm and other laborers and domestic service; 3) unequal occupational distribution of women; and 4) increase in employed white workers and decrease in Negroes.

The impact of such occupational and industrial changes is well depicted in Bogue's statement that, "the South is moving rapidly toward an industrial and commercial economy which is organized around cities and metropolitan areas. This change in economic and social organization is requiring the South's population to redistribute itself in new patterns and to acquire new skills and take on new characteristics." [8] Changes in industrialization and concomitant occupational structures have altered the relationship of communities, of central or dominant centers to their hinterlands, of urban structure and function, of population distribution and concentration, of regional status and development.

But who are the people that live within and are affected by this urbanization pattern of the southern region? Though biracial in general population make-up, the Southeast possesses unique racial characteristics. It is more than two-thirds white and slightly more than one-fourth Negro, the average percentage of whites for the eleven southeastern states being 73.06 and the average percentage for Negroes 26.8, with other races constituting only a 0.14 average.[9] Interestingly enough, however, there is much variability in racial make-up between states but equal variability between races. The variation in native-white, for

[7] Lorin A. Thompson, "Urbanization, Occupational Shift and Economic Progress," Vance, *Urban South*, pp. 38-41.

[8] Donald J. Bogue, *The Growth of Metropolitan Areas, 1900 to 1950* (Washington: Government Printing Office, 1953).

[9] Data based on Table 59, U. S. Summary, "General Characteristics," 1950 Population Census.

example, goes from 92.6 in Kentucky to 54.2 in Mississippi and that for Negroes from 6.9 in Kentucky to 45.3 in Mississippi—an equivalent range of 38.4 in each instance.

In addition to being predominantly white, the Southeastern Region abounds in a population with only a slight excess of females (15,736,670 males to 16,047,057 females) with the percentage of males being 49.51 and that of females 50.49. Both males and females tend to be married, marital status averages for persons 14 and over for the eleven states being: single males 26.6 vs. 19.4 single females; married males 68.19 vs. 66.35 females; 5.19 widowed or divorced males vs. 14.19 females.[10] Moreover, the Southeast has a young population with low income and eighth grade education. The average age is 26.45 years, average school years completed 8.2, and average annual income $1,648.8, with individual state items summarized in table 3. Individual states do not necessarily duplicate the region but their comparable characteristics are reflected in the over-view of the region.

North Carolina has been an intricate part of the South's slowly evolving urban pattern but uniquely different with regard to metropolitanization. No one large center has overshadowed the state as has been the case with Richmond in Virginia, Charleston in South Carolina, Atlanta in Georgia, or New Orleans in Louisiana. Not a single city in the entire state had a population of 100,000 in 1930, only one had attained this status by 1940 and it remained singularly in this category in 1950. In 1940 two of the three cities with population of 50,000 in 1930 were still in the 50,000 category. Of the six standard metropolitan areas in the state the capital city was the only one that did not reach the 50,000-inhabitants category prior to 1950. Ranking lowest among the six central cities in 1930 and 1940, she managed to rise to fifth place in 1950 as is seen in figure I. Within these six cities reside 35.54 percent of the urban population of the state, but such concentration has been in process for a long time. Fraught with competition between cities, rent by sectional battles between eastern and western sections of the state, complacently reclining amidst the ease of the East and wealth of the West, and lagging in internal improvements, North Carolina cities seem always to have taken short paces rather

[10] Data based on Table 68, *U. S. Census of Population: 1950,* "General Characteristics of the Population," Vol. II.

TABLE 3

Characteristics of the Southeastern Region, by State,
Race, Median Age, School Years Completed
and Income, 1950

State	Race Percentage White	Percentage Negro	Median Age In Years	Median School Years Completed, of those 25 and over	Median Income In 1949
Virginia	77.8	22.1	27.3	8.5	$2,172
North Carolina	73.4	25.8	25.0	7.9	1,864
South Carolina	61.1	38.8	23.6	7.6	1,647
Georgia	69.1	30.9	26.2	7.8	1,644
Florida	78.1	21.7	30.9	9.6	1,950
Kentucky	93.1	6.9	27.0	8.4	1,774
Tennessee	83.9	16.1	27.3	8.4	1,749
Alabama	67.9	32.0	25.5	7.9	1,580
Mississippi	54.6	45.3	24.6	8.1	1,028
Arkansas	77.6	22.3	26.9	8.3	1,315
Louisiana	67.0	32.9	26.7	7.6	1,810

Source: *U. S. Census of Population: 1950*, Vol. II, "General Characteristics of the Population," U. S. Summary, Tables 59, 64, 67 and 84.

than rapid strides in growth. The small urban place, both in physical structure and in population, has been the rule rather than the exception. As metropolitanism develops a new type of metropolis emerges in the state—the small industrial central-city that dominates an agricultural hinterland.

Internal distribution of the population along similar lines in cities has made city after city within the state appear as replicas of each other. Business centralization, high residential concentration, and non-industrialization have been among the earmarks of cities, but decentralization of business, industrialization, and residential dispersion are currently upsetting the old and creating new patterns. Ranking 10th in population among the 48 states in 1950, but 44th in urbanity, North Carolina's 4,061,929 people are only 33.7 percent urban and only 11.97 percent metropolitan. Despite the increase in population living within metropolitan areas there has been a decrease in the proportion of Negroes in these areas, with highest concentrations in the most industrialized communities as evidenced in table 4. For the most part the more highly populated areas have been in the non-industrialized, non-metropolitanized eastern half of the state. The city of Raleigh stands approximately midway between the more industrialized West and the non-industrialized East within a state that reflects in many instances the features of an entire region.

TABLE 4

Population of North Carolina by Metropolitan City and Percentage Negro, 1950 and 1940

City	1950		1940	
	Population	% Negro	Population	% Negro
Asheville	53,000	23.5	51,310	26.2
Charlotte	134,042	28.1	100,899	31.1
Durham	71,311	36.6	60,195	38.8
Greensboro	74,389	26.9	59,319	27.6
Raleigh	65,679	27.2	46,897	33.7
Winston-Salem	87,811	41.8	79,815	45.1
Total	486,232		398,435	

Source: *U. S. Census of Population*, Vols. II, 1950 and 1940.

Unlike many Southern and North Carolina cities Raleigh's physical structure and raison d'etre were so planned that she was functionally a city from her very inception. Organized as state government headquarters in a county central between the Virginia line and South Carolina boundary, she was considered for some time as a city of streets without houses. One writer gives this account of her founding:

Raleigh was born a city. No wandering pre-historic cows laid out her streets and marked her thoroughfares. . . . Her name was ready two hundred years before. . . . Her charter had been granted in 1587 when Sir Walter Raleigh attempted a permanent settlement on Roanoke Island. . . . 'It was a town of magnificent distances, of unsightly bramble bush and briers, of hills and mo-

[11] Hope Summerell Chamberlain, *History of Wake County, North Carolina* (Raleigh: Edwards and Broughton Printing Co., 1922), p. 63.

rasses, of grand old oaks and few inhabitants, and an onwelcome look to newcomers' . . .[12]

Though founded as a city, Raleigh has never had a phenomenal growth record. One of the chief characteristics by which her regional and state status are reflected is her slow growth. No real or significant growth was evident in the city until after the Civil War. Prior to 1803 the city was almost devoid of residents, for up to that time not even the commissioners who made and executed the laws of the locality were required to live within the city limits.[13] Situated in the interior amidst infertile lands, unimproved roads, non-navigable streams, the city's only prosperity came with officers-of-state residing there, legislative meetings held there, lawyers attending court there, and wealthy families fleeing there occasionally from malaria.[14] With the planning and directing of internal changes the city began to grow, so that her population increased from 669 in 1800 to 4,780 on the eve of the Civil War. At the turn of the century she had 13,643 persons within her limits. From 1900 - 1930 Raleigh's rate of growth, when compared with the urban population of the United States or of North Carolina, was not outstanding; since 1930 it has been more rapid than that of urban North Carolina or the United States, showing a higher rate of growth than other large cities in North Carolina.

Political designs and conflicts appear to have been the major factors affecting the growth of the city. Prior to 1792, when a commission was appointed to select a permanent seat of government for the state, the state capital had been a city on wheels rolling from one city to another for meetings. Even after Raleigh had been selected as the permanent locus of government, her very existence was continually threatened by political controversy between the eastern and western sections of the state. Each city that was vying for the capitalship conceived of itself as a faster growing place because of its geographical and commercial position. The eastern section consisted of slaves and plantations and populous areas, while the west boasted of small farms and few slaves. By 1830 more than one-half the population of North Caro-

[12] *Ibid.*, p. 93.
[13] Moses N. Amis, *Historical Raleigh* (Raleigh: Edwards and Broughton, 1902), pp. 63-65.
[14] Kemp P. Battle, "Raleigh and the Old Town of Bloomsbury," *North Carolina Booklet*, Vol. II (Capital Printing Co., 1902), pp. 19-20.

lina was west of Raleigh, but the high concentration of Negroes then as now was north, south and east of Raleigh. Raleigh stood between the east and west—a target of political differences from which it was difficult to emerge—uncertain of her continued existence and unconcerned about her growth. She seemed content to move slowly and was unwilling to act until her primacy as a political and convention city was threatened in 1910, when action was being taken to move the capital to Greensboro where halls large enough to accommodate large gatherings existed. Fearing that she would shrink into a small town, because she had not kept pace with other cities industrially, citizens and officials hastily planned and erected structures to accommodate large groups and retain the city's cosmopolitan and convention status[15]—the beginning of a building boom which, though motivated by political as well as social and economic forces, no doubt had profound effect upon the subsequent growth of the city.

Though conceived in political designs, founded in political necessity, and perpetuated through political controversy, Raleigh has possessed a number of features that startle when taking cognizance of her slow growth. Her primacy as a state innovator in areas indicative of economic status is gleaned from such factors as the following: she had the first telephone exchange in the state, put into use in 1879; the first savings bank, erected in 1885; the first post office with first-class rating, received in 1900;[16] and the first public service in the consumption of electricity, effected in 1885.[17] Such communicative and service functions are usually among those making city life advantageous and thereby impelling much of the redistribution of population between urban and rural communities, but for numerous decades they brought little change in the status of Raleigh.

However, as political controversy subsided, internal improvements accrued, population grew, building booms flourished, and the impact of many social forces began to be felt, industrial and other changes developed. Some of these changes are reflected in the current economic profile of the city, which shows the follow-

[15] Josephus Daniels, *Editor in Politics* (Chapel Hill: University of North Carolina Press, 1941), p. 583.

[16] Writers Program of The WPA in North Carolina, *Raleigh, Capital of North Carolina*, Raleigh Sesquicentennial Commission, 1942, pp. 37-43.

[17] Archibald Henderson, *North Carolina, The Old North State and the New*, Vol. II (Chicago: Lewis Publishing Co., 1941), p. 377.

ing consumer potential: an estimated labor potential between 15,000 and 20,000, with approximately 33,000 employed in Metropolitan Raleigh as of February 1957 at an average wage of $60.87 per week; 60,985 employed in Wake County, 36,500 of whom are males and 24,485 females.[18] Statistics for 1950 reveal that women constituted a higher proportion of the labor force in Raleigh than in urban North Carolina or urban United States.

Aside from the high proportion of women in Raleigh's labor force, 40.1 percent in 1950, the potential consumers have a number of other characteristics. They are, among those 14 years old and over, 58.6 percent married; 98.7 percent of those 21 years old and over are native born; in educational attainment they compose, among persons 25 years old and over, 45.4 percent of those with education of high school or above; with regard to sex they are 48.8 percent male; in age make-up they have a median of 28.8 years; and racially they are 27.33 percent non-white.[19] A combined population of 12,015 distributed in seven surrounding Wake County towns supplements the consumer population.

With Raleigh industries covering textiles, food products, auto repair services and garages, construction and electronics; with North Carolina's industrial development showing 167 new manufacturing plants and 143 expansions between 1956 and 1957; with an estimated 875 retail establishments in Raleigh in 1956, a total retail sales amounting to $148,617,000.00, and approximately 144 manufacturing establishments in and around the city in 1957, the growth and development of the city became apparent.[20]

Fuller understanding of the city's potentialities can be gained perhaps from noting the central local functions thereof, namely, government, education, and distribution. The 6,912 persons employed by state agencies in the city and 1,000 employed by federal agencies[21] attest to her primacy as a government center. A total of six colleges, 24 public primary and secondary schools, 3 special schools, and 3 business schools bear out the educational center characterization. Combined daily circulation of 138,084

[18] Industrial Department, Raleigh Chamber of Commerce, J. R. Drummy (mgr.), *Industrial Survey of North Carolina*, 1958 Revised Edition.

[19] A. Ross Eckler, Deputy Director, Bureau of the Census, "Census Statistics for Local Use," Reprint of talk before Raleigh Advertising Club, Raleigh, N. C., November 9, 1954.

[20] Industrial Department, Raleigh Chamber of Commerce, *op cit.*

[21] *Ibid.*

issues of two locally-owned and published newspapers through 33 Eastern North Carolina counties, headquarters of three gigantic warehouses serving 178 super markets,[22] home office for three life and two fire insurance companies, and home or branch office for 15 major trucking lines support the city's claim to being a key distribution center.

In economic status Raleigh occupies a white-collar position, a characteristic of the town since the first state buildings were erected there and continually sustained through the high percentage of special occupations and employment of state, federal, county, municipal, and educational personnel. For both men and women in 1950 clerical, sales and kindred workers were the most important occupational group. In social status the city is predominantly middle class, not a single millionaire living within her boundaries or contributing to her industrial growth as in the case of her metropolitan neighbor cities. In educational status she surpasses other urban places in the state, census data showing a median of 11.2 school years completed by persons 25 years old and older, and 89.2 percent of her population 14-17 years old and older in school as of 1950.

Central location and state-agencies headquarters, even more perhaps than availability of space, have made the city a convention place and given it a cosmopolitan air. Badges, parades, and signs of welcome have thus become a part of the expectations of large segments of the population.

Although the resident population is sufficiently concentrated and stratified along economic and racial lines to produce segregated areas, no involuntary residential segregation can be said to exist. There are no laws, like those passed in the cities of Greensboro and Winston-Salem from 1911 to 1914, requiring residential segregation[23]—another unique trait of the community.

Equally as pertinent to the development of the city is the mobility of the population with respect to migration. The proportion of migrants in Raleigh in 1950 exceeded that for urban North Carolina and the urban United States, being 9.5 percent for

[22] *News and Observer* and *Raleigh Times*, "Golden Belt Market" Brochure.

[23] C. Vann Woodward, "Origins of the New South," W. H. Stephenson and E. M. Coulter (eds.) *A History of the South*, Vol. IX (Louisiana State University Press, 1951), p. 355.

Raleigh, 6.7 for North Carolina, and 5.7 for the United States.[24] While the population of the city grew in the 1940-50 decade, growth from migration came largely through the movement of whites. The heavy in-migration of the whites 20-30 years of age and out-migration of Negroes in almost all age groups helps ex-

Chart No. I

Number of Nonwhites Moving Into and Out of
Raleigh, By Age Groups, 1940-1950

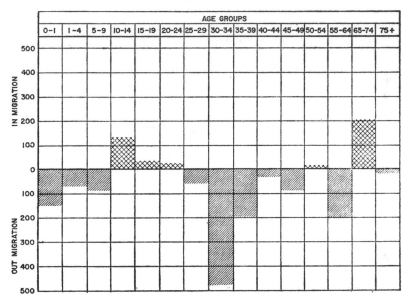

Source: *Raleigh Township Population Forecast*, Department of Planning,
City of Raleigh, North Carolina, August, 1953.
Legend: ■—Negro.

plain the bi-racial proportions of the population and carries numerous implications for Negro Main Street development. With the peak of out-migration for Negroes falling in the 30-35 year age group, and the proportion of Negroes in the population steadily decreasing, economic trends in the community can be assumed to

[24] A. Ross Eckler, *op cit.*

be associated therewith.[25] Trends in the out-migration of Negroes are shown in chart number I and their portrayal gives further insight into the nature of factors relevant to the regional-state-local urban pattern.

Generically then, the Raleigh community is but a reflection of a state, and the state of a region, growing slowly along urbanizing lines, emerging into metropolitan centers that dominate agricultural hinterlands, exhibiting a changing industrial and occupational structure, propelling a concomitant redistribution of its bi-racial population, and making available for consumption large percentages of population groups possessing differentials in economic and social traits. Specifically localized factors in the structuring and functioning of the community have given it distinct qualities of social significance to urban culture and society. Assuming, therefore, that any urban phenomenon receives its characteristic make-up from combinations of interacting forces within the environment, and recognizing the impact of somewhat remote urbanization factors upon rather immediate ones, the following generalization can be made: Negro Main Street characteristics have been produced through unique localized forces within a generic regional and state pattern. The unique or specific forces of the environment that have influenced the evolution of the street and structured its different aspects into a functional portrayal of local urban trends hold relevant positions within the urban scheme and are of principal concern in the next chapter.

[25] Department of Planning, Raleigh, North Carolina, *Raleigh Township Population Forecast,* August, 1953.

Chapter 3

Negro Main Street As A Portrait Of The Natural History Of Negro Business

THE original ground plan and organization of the Raleigh community, coterminous with the current downtown business area, expressed in itself a summary of the history of the state of North Carolina. Similarly, the structure of the community phenomenon known as the Negro Main Street is a functional expression of the natural history of Negro business. The structure and design of both the downtown area and streets contained in it have been outgrowths of the effects of numerous ecological and cultural factors. One of these factors is demonstrated in the manner in which the downtown area originated.

In constructing the city as a fixed political center, 400 acres of the 1,000-acre tract purchased as a state government site formed the core of its physical structure. With the six-acre Union Square (now Capital Square) in the center and four four-acre squares situated one each in the northeast, northwest, southeast and southwest corners of the city "for publick purposes," the remainder of the land was laid off in lots of one acre each. The original streets of the city radiating outward from Union Square in north, south, east, and west directions formed the nucleus of the set of streets extending over the entire land area of the city.

Superimposed upon this physical structure was a cultural one which carried historically significant political implications. This is symbolized in the names assigned to the streets and squares. The four squares, exclusive of Union Square, were named for the first three governors of North Carolina and the attorney general; the first eight streets were named for the judicial districts of the state; nine others were named for the commissioners elected to locate the government site, there being one from each of the eight judicial districts and one from the state-at-large; four were named respectively for the Speaker of the Senate, Speaker of the House, former owner of the land out of which the city was carved, and a cavalry officer in the American Revolution; the boundary streets were then designated as North, South, East, and West. Subsequent use of one city square as site of the governor's mansion, of another as site of state office buildings, and the two re-

41

maining ones as public parks, gives further evidence of the interaction of cultural and ecological forces in the development of the city.

The State House, erected in the center of Union Square, was not completed until 1794, two years after the founding of the city. The few stores and residences constructed at the time were located as near the State House as possible, extending southward from the State House more than in any other direction. Thus in 1808 all the stores were on Fayetteville Street[2] and for more than a decade the same picture prevailed, as the following statement indicates:

In 1822 Fayetteville Street was lined on both sides with wooden buildings ordinarily of small dimensions and moderate value. Nearly all the stores were on that street south of the State House and north of the Court House.[3]

Location of the Governor's house at the corner of Fayetteville and Hargett Streets added to the comprehensive all-purpose functions of what became the chief thoroughfare of the city. When in 1813 a site was selected at the foot of Fayetteville Street on which to build a more commodious home for the governor and the home complete in 1816 Fayetteville Street—which stretched in full length from the State House to the Governor's Mansion just outside the city limits—was described as the "principal or rather only street in this clean little country town."[4] The emphasis of the day with regard to architecture and structure was upon orientalization, and Raleigh's State House had been designed accordingly but was so situated as to look both east and west. Nevertheless, the chief thoroughfare of the city developed neither to the east nor west but to the south. Reasons given for this are:

The bulk of the population was in its southern and eastern portions, because settlers had worked their way up the Neuse and

[1] Moses N. Amis, *op. cit.*, pp. 23-29.
[2] *Ibid.*, p. 71.
[3] "Early Times In Raleigh," Address delivered by the Hon. David L. Swain at Dedication of Tucker Hall and on the Occasion of the Completion of the Monument to Jacob Johnson. Compiled by R. S. Tucker. (Raleigh: Walters, Hughes and Co., 1867), p. 13.
[4] Hugh T. Lefler, *North Carolina History Told by Contemporaries* (Chapel Hill: University of North Carolina Press, 1934), p. 198.

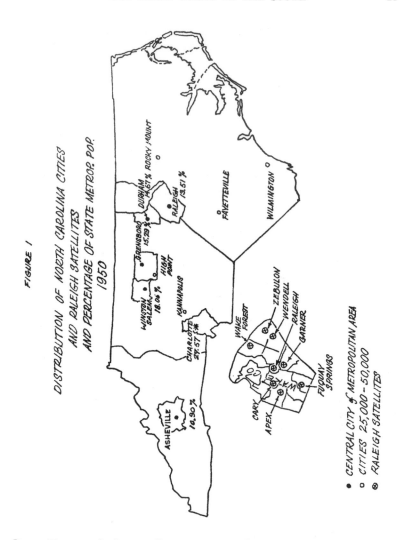

FIGURE 1

DISTRIBUTION OF NORTH CAROLINA CITIES
AND RALEIGH SATELLITES
AND PERCENTAGE OF STATE METROP. POP.
1950

● CENTRAL CITY ♀ METROPOLITAN AREA
○ CITIES 25,000 - 50,000
⊗ RALEIGH SATELLITES

Cape Fear and their tributaries. Merchants and mechanics, by getting locations on the street, received the advantage of the trade coming in on both the Smithfield and Fayetteville roads. . . . County authorities naturally located the court house on the same street so as to accommodate the majority of their constituents. . . . The great mail route from North to South ran by way of Petersburg, Warrenton, Raleigh, and Fayetteville, then to Georgetown and Charleston in South Carolina. . . . Tavern keepers and others seeking public patronage selected their business stands along this highway. . . .[5]

Opening onto the only road then leading to the old established towns of Fayetteville and Smithfield, Fayetteville Street became the inter-urban link—the thoroughfare along which business institutions located as attractions to in-coming marketerers and travelers. For more than a half-century the business section of the city remained confined to Fayetteville Street. By 1860 the only stores east of that street had been erected on Hargett Street. Thus, Hargett, later to become dominated by Negro business, was the first one outside of Fayetteville Street to form part of the functional business area.

As the city grew from an enacted framework of streets and government buildings to a crescive one of residences, stores, and office structures, a generalized pattern of institutional arrangements developed. Homes, hotels, saloons, taverns, boarding houses, and other business institutions were indiscriminately situated on Fayetteville Street, the lower part of the street retaining this feature until the late 1940's. The positional factor motivating location of the earliest institutions seems to have been to situate close to the State House, which became the center of activity for the city. The State House not only housed the varied branches of government, but it also served as town hall, conference chamber, lecture room, theater, and ball room. Its attendants included therefore officers-of-state and officers-of-city, city people and country people, residents and non-residents, natives and strangers.

Such institutions as were found interspersed with homes along the main thoroughfare were those catering primarily to a large transient population. As has been previously indicated, the transient population exceeded the resident population for many years after the founding of the city. It was only natural that expansion in the business area should follow first along the Hargett Street thoroughfare, for this was the next street cross-cutting Fayetteville Street just beyond those surrounding Union Square. On

    [5] "The Early History of Raleigh, the Capital City of North Carolina," A Centennial Address by Kemp P. Battle, October 18, 1892 (Raleigh: Edwards and Broughton Printers and Binders, 1893), p. 45.

Hargett, as on Fayetteville Street, the first institutional arrangements fell into a generalized pattern with business and residences interspersed. Establishment of the city market on Hargett in 1800, where country people could bring their commodities for sale and city people could have easy access to them, meant further extension of the generalized institutional pattern.

Gradually the generalized pattern began to give way to a specialized one. Specialization, however, did not mean growth of special districts for finance institutions, service institutions and the like. More specifically it meant greater separation of state office buildings, retail and wholesale business, and residences, as well as replacement of the general store by drug, grocery, dry goods, jewelry, book and other stores. By 1840, for example, when the city market was moved from the center of East Hargett Street, the saloons and barrooms that had developed around it had made of the street a specialized area by the name of "Grog Alley," while Wilmington between Hargett and Martin, an adjoining locality, was known as "Cologne." The State House, destroyed by fire in 1831 and rebuilt as the Capitol in the period 1833-40, paved the way for more concentration of state institutions around it and hence more specialized institutional arrangement.

Though impelled by the force of constant local change, Raleigh's business center made few enduring growth transitions until after the Civil War. With buildings constructed out of wood, businesses crowded together in one block, and little available fire insurance for protection, the fires of 1816, 1821 and 1831 practically devastated the business area on Fayetteville and Hargett streets. A drought in 1826 and heavy emigration from 1820 to 1830 brought astounding reductions in the population, hence further stifling growth. A number of major events in 1840 brought prosperity to the city and started another upward growth trend. Included among these were completion of the State Capitol, the first passenger train, a convention of persons interested in the manufacturing business, and opening of the first public schools of the state. A decade after these innovations, in 1850, Raleigh's population had doubled. In 1853 prosperity was sufficiently evident for the first state fair to be held there, and in 1857 growth warranted extending the city limits for the first time. Then came the Civil War and once again growth was arrested. The period of Reconstruction marked a new era for business and other institutional growth of the community, during which time the increase in the population and the changed status of the Negro influenced business and occupational developments.

What happened to the Negro in the South from 1619 to 1865 was generically the same in all localities. For comparative purposes then mention might be made of the Negro's occupational status in the southern economy before and after the Civil War as characteristic of the Raleigh community of that period. Prior to 1860 economic circumstances formed the chief criteria for social stratification. Thus, in North Carolina the socio-economic divisions of society resulted in the following pyramided classes: 1) The planter aristocracy or gentry; 2) Small slave-holding planters and farmers, small merchants and manufacturers, and lesser officials forming the middle class; 3) Small farmers and mechanics; 4) Landless tenants and laborers known as poor whites; 5) Free Negroes; and 6) Negro slaves.[6] The one class in this group that was without an acceptable place in the social structure was the free Negro. He was forbidden by a law of 1826 to trade with slaves; a law of 1830 voided any marriage to a white person; an act of 1831 prevented his preaching or exhorting in public, and a law of 1860-61 hindered his hiring or having control of slaves, though some owned them.[7] Though circumscribed in movements and activities, in almost all cities of the Ante-bellum South free Negroes comprised the artisan class of workers. They, along with a few selected slaves on plantations, were the barbers, blacksmiths, butchers, carpenters, shoemakers, mechanics, tailors and textile workers, and keepers of restaurants, cafes and hotels. The half-free status of the free Negro forced his loss of much of the local trade in these businesses even before the Civil War; the number of Negroes in business after the Civil War did not far surpass the number so engaged before the war; only after the South's recovery from the devastations of the war did the Negro begin to engage more actively in the business world, and even this was on an experimental basis until after the 1890's and doomed to failure when whites began to exploit potentialities of the Negro community as a trade area.[8]

[6] Hugh T. Lefler, *History of North Carolina* (New York: Lewis Historical Publishing Co., 1956), pp. 412-423.

[7] Fred A. Olds, *Abstract of North Carolina Laws.*

[8] J. H. Harmon, Jr., Arnett G. Lindsay, and Carter G. Woodson, *The Negro as a Business Man* (Association for the Study of Negro Life and History, 1929). pp. 3-16; 90-91.

A decade after the Civil War there were 31 Negro businesses in the Raleigh community concentrated in the same artisan and craftsmen's lines as indicated above. Hargett Street had already become a business street by this time, but businesses operated by whites predominated. Negro business, however, was downtown business rather than neighborhood, for 19 of the 31 Negro businesses were scattered along Fayetteville, Hargett, Wilmington, and Exchange streets—the heart of the business area.

During the latter part of the nineteenth century a number of factors point toward the emergence of a broader and broader Negro business world. In 1875-76, for example, there were only six barbers in the entire community and all six were Negroes, two of the six barbering for Negroes and four for whites. The barber group increased to eleven between 1875 and 1888, but all remained Negro. Three years later the number doubled, two of the twenty-two barbers being white, thus beginning in 1891 the introduction of a competitive group that was eventually to upset the pattern of a long-standing occupation.

In the same 1875-76 period all "eating houses" and huckster stalls were operated by Negroes, while the number of Negro blacksmiths exceeded the number of white blacksmiths, with an equal number of Negroes and whites as harness makers and saddlers. Variation in type of business operated by Negroes came with the advent of these: two Negro newspapers, an undertaker, and two additional graded schools in 1880 (one graded school had been established in 1855 but was then in complete charge of white teachers from the North and another, the East Raleigh School, held at the old Fair Grounds, had been established in 1878—the only one not held in a church)[9]; one attorney and five saloon keepers in 1883; one bakery, two boarding houses, one contractor and builder, one upholsterer, one fish and five meat market operators in 1886; a billiard room, dyeing and cleaning establishment, and furniture dealer in 1887; a hotel, physician and surgeon in 1888; and the first Negro dentist in 1911-12.

The years 1880-90 show fairly wide dispersion of Negro business over several downtown areas, but little variety in types of business, as seen in table number 5. Barbers, boot and shoe makers, butchers, hucksters, fish and meat dealers, and restaurant operators constituted the bulk of persons engaged in trades or

[9] Raleigh *City Directory, 1880-81* (Raleigh: Edwards, Broughton and Co.)

businesses. The very nature of these businesses, serving both Negro and white customers, accounted in part for their location on downtown "front" streets rather than back ones. Moreover, this was a period of non "Jim-Crow" and little forced segregation, for more Jim-Crow laws were passed in the 1890 period than at any other time. When, however, comparison is made between the number of businesses located on Wilmington versus Hargett Street one readily notes the former as having the higher concentration. But this was also the period of attempted group ventures in business operated concurrently with small individual businesses. Grocery stores operated by such groups as the Brick Masons and True Reformers, occupational and fraternal organizations, exemplified this effort. They seemed, however, to be lacking in elements necessary in the business struggle for existence and were short-lived. Explanation for this may reside in the nature of the occupational and fraternal groups in control rather than the grocery business itself. One rather illuminating account in this line follows:

In 1882 the brick masons had a grocery store, but that was on Wilmington Street and didn't last long. That was the only group venture I remember, all the others were individual ventures . . . my daddy was a brick mason and didn't run a business, but he was important because of being clerk of the court. He tried to teach me the brick mason's trade but after he died I gave it up, told my mother I wasn't going to follow that because all I'd do would be lay the brick and some white man would still be over me doing most of the important work and I wanted to be on my own . . . When I was ten years old I was taking up the brick mason's trade . . . when my daddy died I went to doing something I could work on when it rained and weather was bad; had to help support my mother . . . A brick mason didn't get but $3.00 a day in 1873-4 when we moved from Hungry Neck to Oberlin.[10]

Though the number of Negro businesses was still small during this time, if by location and concentration of these one could posit the existence of a Negro Main Street, then Wilmington Street was primary and Hargett secondary and continued such into the first decades of the twentieth century when Hargett supplanted Wilmington as the primary business location.

The 1890 period shows a significant increase in Negro business,

10 Personal interview.

entrance into still other occupations, and regaining control of many skilled crafts in which the Negro lost out after the Civil War. Thus in 1891 the Raleigh community had among Negroes 17 brick masons, 34 carpenters, 32 draymen, 19 mechanics, 4 painters, 8 plasterers and whitewashers, 6 printers, 16 shoemakers, and 2 tinners. The professional field broadened also with more lawyers, physicians, ministers, nurses, and teachers. The co-existence, however, of 275 "colored" washerwomen, 361 servants, 42 seamstresses, 113 porters, and 349 laborers—all listed in the *1891 City Directory*—must not be overlooked as suggestive of the chief occupations of the Negro. At the onset of the twentieth century many of the trends in Negro business started in the 1890's became fairly fixed statuses leading more and more into stationary downtown locations.

Prior to World War I Negro business seemed more widely dispersed over the downtown area than at any other time. Although similarity of location tended to characterize offices of lawyers and doctors, for the most part the most overt evidence of such was noticeable in the location of restaurants and barbershops. Since Negroes had a monopoly over the restaurant and barbershop business, location of these may have been based on individual selection, availability of space, or proximity to other lucrative businesses. Nevertheless, the fact remains that many of the restaurants catering to both Negro and white customers were either in basement or upstairs areas of buildings rather than on the ground floor. So prevalent were these among the types of businesses in which Negroes engaged that they became almost trademarks of the eating folkways of the day. Elderly residents' conceptions of early Negro businesses tend to point up this factor. As one resident stated it,

There were a number of restaurants on the back street. Wilmington St. was called Back Street and Fayetteville St. was called Front Street. Back Street was lined with Negro restaurants. Of course whites ate there; they could eat in colored places although colored couldn't eat in theirs. Then too, there wasn't as much segregation then as now. Many white folks went to the colored places to eat because they liked a particular mammy's cooking.[11]

Another commentary on the eating folkways of the day is given thus by an elderly native of the city:

[11] Personal interview.

Restaurants were mostly operated by Negroes. Tables for whites and tables for colored were all in one room. All entered the front door. In the N. H. Adams Building, corner of Martin and Wilmington, a Negro man had a restaurant downstairs. Jack Winston had a restaurant up over the saloon on Wilmington St. He was colored. Negro women waited tables but had few other jobs. Negroes lost out in business because they didn't have much business sense.[12]

A similar conception is indicated by another resident in these words:

Mandy Dunstan used to have about the biggest restaurant; they didn't call them cafés in those days. All the country whites ate with her. Her restaurant was down under the city market. She had a steady trade of whites. Colored ate there too but her biggest trade was white. All ate together. I don't remember any such thing as segregation in those places then and I've been here for 91 years, was born right on this same land January 10, 1867.[13]

The locational pattern was even more obvious in the case of barbershops. Negro barbershops for whites were all situated on the city's main thoroughfare, Fayetteville St., and all but one in basements. The one exception was the renowned Otey shop in the Yarborough Hotel. However, location was not the determinant of type of business engaged in. Nor was type of business the causal factor in location, but location of business seemed always to bear some relationship to the racial and status group to which the business catered. Where the occupational group was composed solely of Negroes and they served both white and Negro customers in the same physical plant a mutual downtown, front-street business location developed. Such was the case with butchers and dance bands. But where Negroes served both races in separate physical plants distinction was made through location. A rather vivid portrayal of this is seen in the statements which follow:

I've been barbering here for 32 years, barbered in a shop for whites for eight months mainly to learn how to cut straight hair. . . . All our trade when I was at the white shop was high class. The different shops for whites have different classes of white

[12] Personal interview.
[13] Personal interview.

customers. We did not wait on anyone but the upper class—doctors, lawyers, professors and that type. The real drawing card was the name of the shop or man who owned it. The shop I was in was the one old man Otey had had, and just the name Otey meant you got the best. All the Negro shops for white trade were on Fayetteville St. and in the basement of some store at that, all but Otey's, and there wasn't a basement there for them to be in. The colored shops for colored trade were mostly on the ground level, all but Sam Harris when he was on Wilmington St., but they are all in colored areas, none on Fayetteville St. There were no signs indicating which were for colored and which for white, you just knew them by location.[14]

So striking was the locational pattern of barbershops that one resident exclaimed:

Willie Otey had a barbershop in the old Yarborough House Hotel, and it was not a basement shop either! It was right on the main street and on the ground floor. Of course it was for whites, but many of the barbershops for whites were operated by colored in basements of buildings. Henry Otey was Willie Otey's son, had worked in the barbershop with his father and took it over when he died. He was the last colored to have it, and then it was turned over to whites. The few white barbershops left now that are operated by colored are in basements. When these shops flourished the aristocrats wouldn't go to anybody but colored. They had their own special barbers and went to them at special times and on special days. As I recall they brought a white barber here from some place else and put him in the shop there under the Masonic Building at the corner of Fayetteville and Hargett, and after that a number of white barbers began to appear.[15]

Closely connected with physical location as a distinguishing feature of business were the traditionally understood differences in enterprises. As one resident stated,

There were no signs indicating colored or white barbershops. Negroes just knew who the barbers were that had only white trade, aside from the fact that most of the white shops were on Fayetteville St. and the white shops were finely equipped. Until recently colored barbershops had almost nothing in them.[16]

[14] Personal interview.
[15] Personal interview.
[16] Personal interview.

Further historical significance of the locational pattern of early Negro business lay in what might be termed derivative business. Derivation in this sense, however, refers to subsequent and more-recently-developed businesses formulated through ideas and support received from earlier businesses. One such establishment is an educational institution which had made it the "business of the state" to train Negroes for many business fields. The statement of another resident helps clarify this:

All laws used to be made right in the Yarborough Hotel. Shepard used to stand out in front and wait for the various legislators to come out and then beg for his school over in Durham. It was only a high school then, but by begging and getting so many state appropriations look what he made out of it. It's now one of your leading colleges.[17]

One of the principal derivative businesses among Negroes must be traced back to a major opinion-forming and news-gathering institution—the barbershop. To the Otey barbershop is attributed the real origin of one of the most successful businesses among Negroes in the United States, as gleaned from the following excerpt:

General Julian S. Carr, W. T. Blackwell and Washington Duke undertook in 1880 to insure for Durham just as good a barbershop as W. G. Otey operated in the State Capital thirty miles away. The barbershop explains Duke University and the N.C. Mutual Life Insurance Co., the biggest organization of its kind in the world.[18]

The Otey shop existed far in advance of subsequent ones in the industrial city of Durham. Merrick started there as a bootblack, learned barbering there, and advanced from bootblack to barber, then finally moved to Durham where he opened barber shops for both whites and Negroes and through them received the Insurance Company idea. As told by contemporaries, the story runs thus:

Buck Duke gave John Merrick the best tip he ever got. He

[17] Personal interview.

[18] Jonathan Daniels, *Tar Heels: A Portrait of North Carolina* (New York: Dodd, Mead and Co., 1941), p. 124.

knew Merrick had acquired three barbershops for white people and two for Negroes. 'John,' said Duke under John's razor, 'why don't you hunt up a better job?' 'Organize an insurance company and make every dinged nigger in the United States pay you $25 a year.' Duke gave the suggestion, General Carr lent some money for the enterprise, Merrick, the barber, was its leader. Help came from Dr. Aaron McDuffie Moore and Charles C. Spaulding.[19]

From bootblack to apprentice, to full-fledged barber, to business operator and owner, to founder of business with established branches in the capital city—this is not alone the biography of a man, Merrick, but the history of several key Negro businesses, more especially the insurance business. Originally organized and incorporated in 1899 as the N.C. Mutual and Provident Association, under the motto, "merciful to all." the object of the corporation was to furnish relief to widows and orphans, those injured by accident, and the dead in need of burial. But it is no wonder that the organization became "big business" and spread throughout the nation, for the corporators embraced within their own ranks men with varied business interests and experiences. The corporators were John Merrick, A. M. Moore, J. E. Shepard, W. G. Pearson, and D. T. Watson of Durham; T. O. Fuller of Warrenton; E. A. Johnson and N. C. Bruce of Raleigh.[20]

As the twentieth century developed, the nature and location of Negro business began to evidence a number of changes. Restauranting and barbering for whites, leading Negro businesses of the nineteenth century, began to decline. Many white property owners ceased renting space to Negroes for business purposes. Jimcrow laws began to tighten, segregation became more enforced, the Negro business world began to contract to Negro customers and clients, and the majority of Negro business began to migrate to one street—East Hargett. By the second decade of the twentieth century East Hargett had became the hub of the Negro community. Only one business establishment remained on Wilmington Street and one on Fayetteville. But this Negro street has never been an all-Negro street. Some whites have always operated business there, some for Negroes only and others without regard to race. The designation "Negro Main Street" derives from the predominance of businesses operated by and/or for Negroes, as

[19] *Ibid.*, pp. 126-7.
[20] *Private Laws of North Carolina*, 1899, Chapter 156.

TABLE 5

Downtown Location of Negro Business By Specific Streets and Years, 1880-1891

Business	Wilmington Street						Hargett Street						Other Downtown Streets					
	1880-81	1883	1886	1887	1888	1891	1880-81	1883	1886	1887	1888	1891	1880-81	1883	1886	1887	1888	1891
Attorneys	0	0	0	0	0	0	0	0	0	0	0	0	0	1	1	0	0	0
Barbers	2	3	3	4	5	1	0	1	1	1	2	0	4	5	4	5	6	1
Billiards	0	0	0	1	1	1	0	0	0	0	0	0	0	0	0	0	0	0
Blacksmiths	1	1	1	1	1	0	1	1	1	2	0	1	0	0	0	1	0	0
Boot & Shoe Mfg.	0	1	3	4	2	2	1	3	3	2	1	0	0	0	5	0	0	0
Butchers	0	0	0	0	0	0	0	0	0	0	0	0	3	5	0	7	4	3
Cabinet Mkr.	0	0	0	0	0	0	0	0	1	1	0	0	0	0	1	0	0	0
Confectioners	0	0	0	0	0	0	0	1	0	0	0	0	0	0	0	0	0	0
Dry Goods	0	0	0	1	0	0	0	0	0	0	0	0	0	0	0	0	0	0
Furniture Shop	0	0	0	0	0	0	0	0	0	0	0	0	0	0	0	0	0	0
Grocers	0	1	0	1	0	1	0	1	1	1	0	0	0	0	2	0	5	0
Harness & Saddles	0	0	1	0	0	0	1	0	0	1	1	1	0	0	0	0	0	0
Hucksters	0	0	0	0	0	0	0	0	0	0	0	0	2	2	2	4	3	3
Livery Stable	0	0	0	0	0	0	0	0	0	0	0	0	0	0	2	0	0	0
Markets	0	0	0	0	0	0	0	0	0	0	0	0	0	0	6	2	2	0
Restaurants	0	3	5	6	4	2	0	1	1	0	1	0	0	1	1	1	1	0
Saloons	0	2	0	0	0	1	0	0	0	0	0	0	0	0	0	0	0	0
Undertakers	0	0	1	0	0	0	1	0	0	1	0	0	1	1	1	0	0	0
Upholsterers	0	0	0	1	0	0	0	0	0	0	0	0	0	0	0	0	0	0
Totals	3	11	14	19	13	8	4	8	8	9	5	2	10	15	25	20	21	7

TABLE 6—*Number and Type of Business Operated on East and 30th Street, By Race of Operator, By Decades, 1900-1959*

Type of Business	1900 N	1900 W	1910 N	1910 W	1920 N	1920 W	1930 N	1930 W	1940 N	1940 W	1950 N	1950 W	1959 N	1959 W
Personal Services	2	2	2	2	6	1	11	4	12	7	11	9	8	7
Professional and Semi-professional Services	0	0	1	0	7	1	14	1	13	0	10	0	13	0
Business Services	0	0	0	0	1	0	1	0	2	0	2	2	2	0
Repair Services	0	0	0	0	1	0	1	0	0	0	1	2	1	1
Automotive Service	0	0	0	0	0	1	0	0	0	0	0	0	1	1
Eating & Drinking Places	4	3	1	1	0	1	4	2	3	4	3	1	3	2
Food Stores	1	6	0	6	1	6	0	3	0	2	1	2	0	1
Clothing & Department Stores	0	0	0	2	2	8	0	2	0	5	0	7	0	5
Furniture & Household	0	0	0	1	0	4	0	6	0	5	1	3	0	4
Ice & Fuel Dealers	1	0	0	0	0	0	0	0	0	0	0	0	0	0
Finance, Insurance, Real Estate	0	1	0	1	2	0	7	0	6	0	6	0	6	0
Communication & Transportation	0	1	1	1	4	2	1	0	5	0	3	0	0	1
Recreation & Entertainment	0	0	0	1	0	1	1	1	3	1	2	2	0	1
Craftsmen's Places	1	8	1	2	1	5	0	2	0	0	0	0	0	0
Other Retail Stores	0	1	1	1	2	1	2	1	2	1	2	2	3	0
Manufacturing	0	0	0	2	0	0	0	0	0	0	0	1	0	0
Wholesale Trade	0	1	0	0	0	1	0	2	0	2	0	2	0	1
Miscellaneous Places	0	2	1	2	3	0	4	2	5	0	6	0	8	0
Totals	9	25	8	22	30	32	46	26	51	27	48	33	46	23

Source: Directories of the City of Raleigh, North Carolina.
Legend: N—Negro operated.
W—White operated.

FIGURE 2.

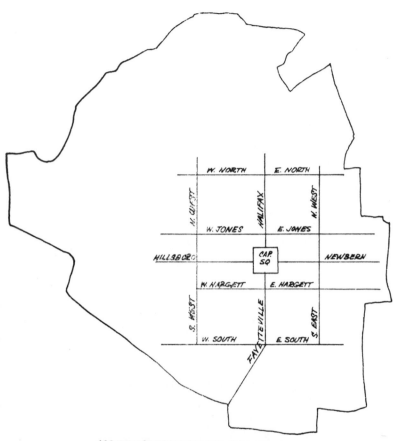

LOCATION OF EAST HARGETT ST. IN REFERENCE TO OTHER
DOWNTOWN BUSINESS STREETS

well as types of businesses necessarily located there. A summarized list of the number and types of these is given in table 6,
and the relationship of the street to other downtown streets in
figure 2.

Prior to the 1920's Negro business, except for barber shops with
white customers and the one dry goods store, was by no means
stable in location. Continual movement from one location to an-

other seemed more the rule than the exception. The frequency of movement is indicated in the following excerpts:

J. W. Ligon, who became principal of the school, had a newspaper, *The Union Reformer,* with office in 1917 on Wilmington Street; he moved to Hargett St. in 1920.

Harris' barber shop was on Wilmington St. first and then moved to Hargett. Doctors Delaney, Roberts, and Edwards had offices upstairs in the Hoover Building and then moved to Hargett St. in 1923.

P. T. Hall had a restaurant on Wilmington St., moved to the Arcade on Hargett in 1921.

Frank Constance and Jimmy Taylor had a pool room on Wilmington St., moved it from there to the Arcade on Hargett, then they split up and Jimmy moved back to Wilmington St., then came back to Hargett St. up there where the New York Café is, finally bought the building down below the Arcade where the pool room stayed until destroyed by fire.

Walker's barber shop was first at 117 Hargett St., then moved down to Lightner Building. He and old man L. fell out and he moved back to 117.

The Elks Home started out in the Lightner Building on Hargett St. It moved from there to the 200 block of Wilmington St., from there to the 500 block of Wilmington St., and from there to the 300 block of Cabarrus, then bought in the 600 block of Davie.[21]

Despite the shifts in location of business, however, one rather noteworthy locational factor shows up, namely this: Once Negro business had become dominant on Hargett Street it tended to remain there, the opposite of the trend on Wilmington Street where once the number of Negro businesses began to decrease the trend continued until only one business remained. Beginning in 1910 the steady decline in number of Negro businesses on Wilmington Street was accompanied by an increase in the number on Hargett Street, and the steady increase on Hargett brought Negro and white operated businesses to equal numbers in 1921-22, the Negro businesses exceeding the white ones in 1923-24. After reaching a peak in 1925 a slight decrease set in but businesses remained numerically high, as shown in figure 3. White businesses that were

[21] Personal interview.

established on the street prior to the invasion of Negro business tended to remain, while those that came later stayed only temporarily and then moved on. Although Negro business establishments were originally dispersed over a wide area, they were gradually compressed into a narrower area, and the main street area that extended formerly over the two long blocks from Fayetteville to Blount Streets contracted to one block. Location of the bank in the middle of the first block just off the city's main thoroughfare, however, has acted as linking agent between the lower part of the street and the real core of the city. Consequently physical isolation has not enveloped the area. Statements of a resident who moved to the city around 1912 are illuminating in this respect:

Actually in the teens the key Negro business was on Wilmington Street. It wasn't until the twenties that Hargett Street became the center of Negro business. The Negroes didn't own any of the buildings they were in on Wilmington St., none but Mr. Hoover, but they owned most of the places on Hargett St. When I first came to Raleigh the only white places on Hargett St. were Tucker's Furniture, Raleigh Furniture, Montague Building, and a clothing store whose name I don't remember. The Tuckers bought that place there where the New York Café is now just so they could put Jimmy Taylor out; they got mad because he had a pool room there beside them.[22]

Another resident who established his home in the city in 1919 says of the street:

. . . there have always been a large number of whites on the street operating business, but most of them have been in the upper part of the block. There have been more changes in the upper part of the block than below; it's easier to lose up there. The whites move there and try it for a while and don't do so well so they move on out, but the businesses that have been in the lower part of the block have really made the money and they have stayed rather permanent . . . the buildings have remained about the same on the outside but inside they have changed a whole lot, that is, with regard to tenants . . . some of the people who have had businesses there have moved from one spot to another but remained on the street. The peanut vender, for example, used to be across

[22] Personal interview.

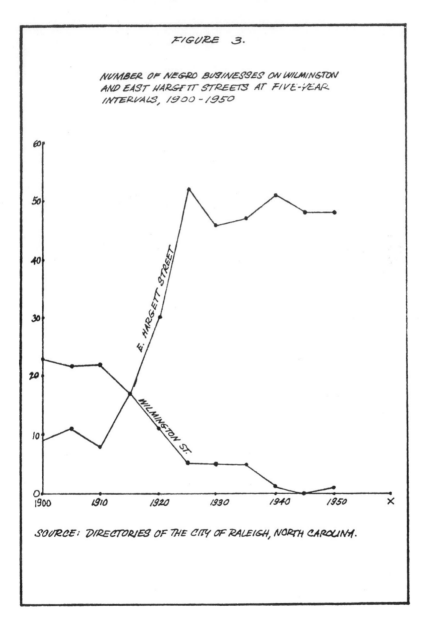

FIGURE 3.

NUMBER OF NEGRO BUSINESSES ON WILMINGTON AND EAST HARGETT STREETS AT FIVE-YEAR INTERVALS, 1900-1950

SOURCE: DIRECTORIES OF THE CITY OF RALEIGH, NORTH CAROLINA.

the street until he felt he needed larger space and when Robert-
son's Appliance moved (or went out of business) he got a chance
to move in there . . . Hargett St. is still the hub of the city. Everybody has to go there once in a while if nowhere but to the bank.
And many of those who don't do any banking there get their
checks cashed there at one time or another.[23]

The real establishment of East Hargett as a Negro business
street is attributed primarily to one man. Personal business interests, real estate investments, and extenuating circumstances combined to convert the efforts of this one man into a fixed location
for the operation of Negro business. After completing his formal
training and teaching for a short while he worked as contractor,
undertaker, wood dealer and garage owner. Opening business on
East Hargett Street in 1911, the life story of this businessman
outlines much of the history of Negro enterprise. A part of that
story is told in the ensuing explanation which he himself gives:

I came here in 1898 as a student at Shaw, and of course a student
doesn't know too much about the business of a town, but there
were no real big businesses when I came. Negroes did practically
all the brick work at that time and whites did the carpentry.
There were few Negro contractors. I think this was because of
the unions, but I don't know that this was the reason. Negroes
never were in carpentry as much as in brick work. Negroes did
the plastering too. There were few cafés. Negroes did all the
barbering for colored and white, but since then whites have taken
it over. There's only one white barbershop run by Negroes now.
As for the reason for this, the trend is for whites to grow more
envious, no that's not a good word, maybe I should say more
self-conscious of what Negroes were getting out of barbering. The
wealthiest Negroes in Raleigh were barbers. One of these was
Otey. He had one of the best cared-for families, was well off, and
made his money barbering. His father before him was a barber.
In the third generation of barbers the family dropped out. That's
one of the failures of Negroes: they don't raise successors to their
business and after their death the business goes; the children are
too anxious to sell out and blow the money.

Every Negro who wanted to go into business in Raleigh wanted
to get on East Hargett St. because we had built it up; everybody
who came to Raleigh felt he hadn't been to the city until he had

[23] Personal interview.

been to East Hargett St., and that's really the way this Negro business street got started. I really started it, and I'm not bragging, for I didn't intend to do business there at first. I intended to have business on Fayetteville St. The *News and Observer* had moved out and left an old building there on Fayetteville St. across from the Sir Walter Hotel. I went to Josephus Daniels and asked him if he wanted to sell it. He said he would sell for $10,000. I got ten men and formed a company, each of us put up $100 to get the $1,000 needed for the down payment. After we got in we borrowed enough for a new building. I then made a proposition to my company asking that I have an office on the front and my funeral parlor on the back. Brittan Pearce was the man who kicked this. So they wouldn't let me have my funeral parlor there. After they ruled me out I went and found an old shop owned by an old white man. This was where the Lightner Building now is on East Hargett. He said he had to move and wanted to sell the place. Judge Winston was handling it, so I went to him and asked about buying. He said he would sell for $10,000. with $500. down payment, don't remember the other terms but I paid so much a month. I rolled the wooden building to the back and used it until I built the new building; went back to Winston and borrowed from him to build this new building. So, I pulled out of the company and eventually all the others pulled out and let Berry O'Kelley have the property on Fayetteville St. O'Kelley finally sold it, that's the way he used to make so much money. The Negroes had no place to do business before so I gave them a place.

When I started in business on East Hargett St. (was doing contracting before that but not on Hargett) there was only one building in the whole block that belonged to Negroes and that was the Odd Fellows Building. That's where the shoe shop and barbershop were. The next colored business was a saloon run by Capt. Hamlin and Hoover. When saloons were closed Hamlin went into the drug store business and Hoover went into the clothing business. When I built a new building on the street N. C. Mutual had bought where the bank is now. I built the bank. Then most all colored business tried to come into the block. This was between 1921 and 1930. I built the Arcade for a hotel and office buildings together. I really built it because my wife got tired of me bringing so many of my friends to the house to stay, but there was no place in town for them to stay. The hotel used to be the main entertainment place in the city. It has never been the same since Mrs. Hall's death. She used to run it. As to how I acquired the place, there was an old white boarding house there, that is, it was for whites. It was put up for sale. Hudson-Belk was going to buy it, they didn't have anything but a little place and wanted a larger one. They ran the bidding up to $21,000, so I got it for $21,000. I got it and borrowed $75,000 to build the building. Had to put up that much and my building across the street (The Lightner Building) to get it. That's the most money any Negro has been able to borrow at any one time. I don't believe there's been another in the state to get that much of a loan at one time.

When I got sick the doctor said I had to give up business if I expected to live. I had three in college at the same time. Figuring out how I was going to meet those bills and my payroll is what gave me these gray hairs. So I had to get rid of the business. The Insurance Co. wouldn't lend me but one-half the value of my property. They said they would let me have the money I needed, but when they offered the loan at one-half the value I figured I could get more than that, so I decided on a private sale and just gave it up. That was about 15 years ago. I stayed on for a while and just paid interest until it got so I could not have a funeral there because of the parking problem. That's when I negotiated for the present Funeral Home my boys operate on Smithfield Street.[24]

Once East Hargett Street had become established and recognized as the main street for Negro business, it tended to portray through its dominant features a number of specific trends and tendencies other than locational ones. Any comprehensive explanation of the evolution of the street and its businesses must take these into consideration. Many of the occupations at which Negroes worked did not culminate into established business enterprises on the main street. Nevertheless, they form significant chapters in the history thereof because of their influence upon other specified types of business. One of the most inclusive views pointing up such factors is given by a resident of the community, who says:

I came to Raleigh in 1919 as a veteran of World War I. When I came Negroes had charge of most all the transportation, and that included taxis and drays. Now the whites have about 60% of the taxi business and about all of the dray business. I started to work in the post office in 1921, and at that time Negroes did all the parcel post work with their drays, that is, they delivered packages and did any transportation work the post office had to be

[24] Personal interview.

done. Of course the federal government has charge of that now, but it was different then. Draying was a good source of income for Negroes. 15 of the 16 carriers in the post office were colored at that time.

Negroes did practically all the barbering then too, and many of the shops were run for whites. Colored did all the street work too. They may have had a white foreman, but the colored did all the work. And they had charge of all the sanitary work (too dirty then for whites to do).

Negroes did a lot of construction work then too, they did about all the carpentering, bricklaying, and plastering but have gradually been edged out by the whites. We just don't have any Negro carpenters now. We have increased our number in bricklaying and decreased in plastering. The bricklayers and plasterers were the first integrated union group here. They've been integrated for 25 years I know.

During the years 1926-28 Negroes did all the landscaping in Raleigh. Everywhere you went, and I carried mail all over town, you saw Negroes doing the yards. All out in Hayes Barton and these other exclusive sections the Negroes did the landscaping, but now the nurseries have taken it over.

In most of these jobs the Negroes lost out because, as I see it, they haven't kept pace with the changes that have been made. For example, in the days of the horse and wagon it was easy enough for Negroes to do the transportation, but when the automobile came into vogue they needed to change and they wouldn't replace the horse and wagon with trucks so they lost out. One man did, that was Ed. Tate. When he died he had a whole fleet of trucks.

Women have never done much in Raleigh. They have been continuously domestic workers and teachers. About the only change that has taken place with them is that not many of them do laundry work any more. They used to do laundry work at home, some of them still do laundry work, but in the laundry not in the home. When I came here a Mrs. Roberts had a millinery shop up on Hargett Street but she was about the only woman then in business of any consequence. There have been a few women since who have ventured into some kind of business, such as the Yellow Rose Tea Room, but it hasn't amounted to much.[25]

[25] Personal interview.

In indicating what has happened to the previously all-Negro businesses, or occupations over which Negroes had a monopoly, another resident says:

The cleaning and pressing business used to be all colored and now that's white. The shoe shine was all colored until an old Greek, Gus Russell, came here and built up a cleaning and pressing and hat-blocking business from a shoe shine parlor. I guess that was over 50 years ago because it was when I was small and I am 58 now. There were a number of Negroes who had stalls in the old city market there where Montgomery Ward's is now. At one time the Carolina Power and Light Co. employed Negroes to do almost all their work, now they have only a few and all they do is the heavy work.[26]

The manner in which the Negro began to lose his monopoly over the shoe shine, cleaning and pressing businesses illustrates how certain socio-cultural forces have influenced the development of Negro business. Such ethnic groups as Jews and Greeks seem to have frequently gained control over businesses and occupations that were formerly engaged in primarily by Negroes. Occupational displacement of native groups by newcomer ethnic groups has been a familiar pattern in urban America, as has the entrance of many ethnic groups into occupations and businesses considered non-competitive with whites. Since many Negro businesses have been types in which native whites have had little interest, it is readily understandable how the small, independent, inadequately stocked, underdeveloped business of Negroes have often been displaced by business operated by ethnic groups. Such displacement is perhaps even more prevalent in the Southern community where industry is lacking and the number of ethnic persons insufficient to support a separate ethnic world based upon business that caters to in-group patronage. Being apparently motivated by economic rather than ethnic or racial factors, and portraying business insight relative to the location and nature of business to undertake for such, has no doubt influenced the development of business operated by ethnic groups and, in turn, displaced many businesses operated by Negroes.

Negro history is most often replete with the usual, commonplace, ordinary, or customary pursuits of Negroes within economic

[26] Personal interview.

realms. But Negro Main Street history carries much that is unusual as well—unusual in that they were businesses or occupations that Negroes were entering for the first time. A few cases in point may suffice to illustrate this. For example, John E. Williams served as clerk of the Superior Court from 1881 to 1885, and his son remarked of his position:

C. D. Upchurch was director of the court and he put daddy in there as clerk, he was right there in the office with the whites. Whites were nice to colored in those days. I used to have to carry daddy's lunch to him when court was going on. They had colored policemen when I was a child, put them in after the Civil War the same way my daddy was made clerk of the court—somebody who knew you just asked you to serve.[27]

During the same period a woman ventured into an old "male business," but a new business for females. In 1883 she was barbering and in 1896 she was dressing hair. Her shop, listed in the City Directory as Sarah Collins, eventually became the leading barber shop for Negroes under management of her husband whom she taught to barber before giving up the trade herself. The unusualness of this venture as indicative of the role and status of women is noticed in the statement below:

Sarah Collins was my uncle's wife. She was a barber and taught her husband how to barber. Don't know how she learned the trade so early but she did, and after her husband learned the trade, well, she faded out of the picture and left the shop to him. At first she worked in there right along with him but later she became just a housewife and dropped out of the business. Not many women were ever on the street. Only two or three, aside from the three oldest beauticians of the city who have continuously had their places there, operated businesses there and not many women were seen walking up and down the street as casually as the men. Of course they would come through on Sunday or some time like that just to get the approval of the men. Mrs. T. operated a tea room there, but few Negroes have had thriving cafés there anyway. The man who has the New York Café turned it into a white café and lost money, so he went back to feeding Negroes.[28]

[27] Personal interview.
[28] Personal interview.

Two of the persons who belonged to the group in unusual businesses earned titles of colonel and captain in the Spanish American War. After the war they went into businesses that still bear the imprint of their names. One of these, Colonel James Young, became "the" Negro politician of the day, aside from working at the undertaking business and having a clerkship and office in the post office. The other person, Captain Hamlin, opened saloon, billiard, café, and drug store businesses, but also worked as clerk in the post office.

Another unusual type of venture was Hoover's Cash Department Store, no similar business having developed among Negroes since the store closed. Operation of this store from its inception to the retirement of its owner at age 75 was most intricately interwoven into the conscious formation and functioning of a Negro Main Street. Unlike many other businesses already described, this one survived long enough for both old and new generations to remember it. Its struggle for survival is depicted thus:

When he (my father) was in the department store my mother worked there right along beside him and so did we, my sister and I, even though we were small. We worked after school and all day on Saturday. In those days we had to compete with the Jews on Wilmington Street. The stores opened at 7 in the morning and stayed open until 7 in the evening. Some of the Jews were selling the same things we were. The stores on Wilmington St. stayed open on Saturday until 12 o'clock at night, but the Fayetteville St. stores didn't. The Wilmington St. stores didn't belong to anything like a merchants bureau, so they could control their own hours. When you really made your money was after the Fayetteville St. stores closed. The Jews sold ready-to-wear and piece goods too, had it behind a dark counter. In those days, you know, the stores had these long counters with stools in front of them and rows and rows of shelves behind them. You could sit on the stools and pick out your goods from where you sat . . . Our customers were both white and colored. About half of the patronage came from the country. The farmers didn't raise much tobacco. Cotton was their real crop and when they'd sell cotton they'd come in and buy bolts of material, especially unbleached muslin, to make clothes for the whole family. Families were large then, there were no automobiles, boys and girls stayed on the farm, so when the family came to buy this made a large number of persons to buy for. And on Saturday they would come and bring their lunches and sit around and eat and nurse babies right in the store.[29]

One of the customers of this store accounts for its long life in terms of the owner's personal reputation and social participation. He notes that,

Hoover's store prospered because it was independently owned. When he opened his dry goods store he was outstanding in the community. He was well known among the lower classes and country people because he used to run a bar and they patronized him. Then too, he had served in the legislature and built up quite a reputation, so he had his own following of customers. Then again, Hoover's store was on Back St. and most Negroes, except for teachers and a few others, had to buy on Back St. . . . the truth is that Front St. stores didn't care to wait on Negroes. You could go in for something and a man could be doing nothing but talking to a friend and you'd have to wait until he stopped talking before he'd wait on you.[30]

Negroes had long been shoemakers but before the opening of Turner's Shoe Store they had not been sellers of brand-named shoes made by large firms. This unusual venture had also a unique history, as told in the following account:

The shoe store my father had on Hargett St. belonged to John T. Turner, Brittan Pearce and Berry O'Kelley . . . The store was organized around 1907 or a little earlier. I was a boy at the time. I took over after my father died and ran the store until 1931. The depression caught me. My father was a tight business man, didn't have more than $200-$300 credit on the books when he died, but when I ended up I had $7,000-$8,000 on the books. I went in with the big idea of building up a huge business and let all kinds of people have credit and couldn't collect. I was too soft; daddy was a success but I wasn't. It took a lot of money to open up that type of business because you had to deal with shoe companies and they wanted thousands of dollars at one time. We carried the American Gentleman and Lady's Shoe, made by Hamilton-Brown Co. of St. Louis—the very best. Guess that's one of the reasons Negroes didn't go into this business more—too much money. We would have had a really big business today if the depression hadn't caught me because we were doing well. Had a few white

[29] Personal interview.
[30] Personal interview.

customers but most were Negroes. Other Negro businesses too
had white customers, except eating places. Whites have always
used Hargett St. as far back as I can remember . . . I got a
chance to sell the business and sold to a Jew, needed the money
and at that time Jews came through buying up all the stock they
could get, probably sold it to some big firm. It's too bad I couldn't
have stayed on in business because that was the only one of its
kind in the South at that time.[31]

The history of Negro business is, moreover, the history of a
privileged few operating several businesses simultaneously, ven-
turing into something new when failure beset previous undertak-
ings, making the business a family affair, and receiving financial
support from whites. The constancy of this pattern shows in one
man's operation of "Peoples Drug Store" and the "Ideal Café" as
concurrent but separate businesses; in another's shift from huckster to saloon keeper, to department store operator, as well as
alderman and legislator; in the upgrading of one person from
groceryman to preacher to school principal, and of another from
barber to dentist; in one man's simultaneous shoe store and undertaking business participation; and in instances where the sons
operate barber shop, and shoe store businesses through the second
and third generations.

But these were the patterns of earlier generations whose fathers
were white and aided them in getting established in business, for
early Negro business and businessmen seemed always to be
backed with finance from whites. Of such widespread knowledge is this in the community that references are often made to
particular individuals and families and the means by which they
gained their financial backing as well as occupational status.
Some of the statements which attest to this are given below:

C. Y. worked in the post office under his father. Of course his
father was white. He held a clerkship office.

J. W.'s father couldn't do all he wanted to for him legally, so he
called him one day and gave him a locked suitcase and told him
it was not to be opened until after he was dead. When the old
man died and the son opened the suitcase it was packed full of
paper money. Naturally the old man was white.

The M. boys were fairly well off at one time. They owned the

---

[31] Personal interview.

building where Western Union used to be. It was given to them by their father who was white. The boys were fair-complected. They sold the building and left town, but wouldn't sell it to Negroes.[32]

Business, education, family ties, and financial support are all intricately interrelated and overtly manifest in one of the most frequently cited case histories in the community, a part of which is summarized below:

The Fraps Building was owned by the Ls, that's where they had the drug store on the front and upstairs was office space. When the drug store was moved to Davie and Blount the building was carried down and put on the property the Ls owned there. It was the same building on a different spot. The Ls owned a lot of property anyway because their white father left a lot to them. He had sent them to school and set them up in business. He was a L. Actually the children were Cs, that was the mother's name, but all of them went in the name of L. Old man L thought more of his nigger children than his white. He came from Chatham County, that's where he met the C woman and brought her to Raleigh. He never married her but took care of her and the children. Many is the time I've seen him ride by on a hot day and see his daughter, the L boys' sister, walking and pick her up and take her home. When she married Dr. C, I was one of the participants, right around in the house where the YMCA is now, and old man L was sitting right there beside M's mother when she got married. It looked funny but nobody thought anything about it because everybody knew the situation. When J.L. died a lawyer who was handling his business told me he was worth $37,500 on the books, that's ¾ actual value; it would be more than that now. J was the oldest and he was in charge of everything, was administrator of the old man's property even over his white children. He included his brother T in on everything he did. M and E got their shares too, but E never did do much, he was just a man-about-town, while J and T were both druggists.[33]

Though this was the pattern of an earlier generation, it must not be assumed that all such practices are past history. Many survivals of personal Negro-white relations in business are a part of contemporary history of business as well, a very able description of which follows:

[32] Personal interviews.
[33] Personal interview.

Negroes used to do well in many businesses here cause they had white fathers. D.S. used to have a taxi stand on Hargett but closed it and went into another business, and now he's operating a filling station . . . a white man owns it but he runs it. He'll always make it because he's a mixed breed. White people help the mixed breed more, even put them up in business. When I came to Raleigh 49 years ago the city was full of half-white folks. Most of them are dead now. The insurance agents, salesmen, and other such folk used to go to these colored folks' houses sometimes early in the morning to collect. They came and went right in the bedrooms or anywhere in the house. You got a lot of crossing then until the young Negroes got mad and started shooting, cutting and fighting about their women. That broke it up. Even so, some still go with white men. In these businesses where you see colored girls working and the boss is white she has to be dishwasher, food server and concubine. The cafés are especially like this. I know one woman who worked in the café there on Hargett St., the one for colored run by whites, and she handled all the money and was being paid well. The man began making passes at her and she asked him what he was going to pay her to be his concubine. She told him he hired her to do the dishes and serve food but she'd pull off her apron if he wanted a concubine, only thing she had to know was how much he was going to pay. She didn't stay there but two weeks. Her husband took her away. Even the policemen talked about getting the man, and I told them there was no need for that, that even policemen get killed sometimes.[34]

Where Negro-operated business caters to a white clientele, that which may otherwise be considered non-respectable is often appreciably dignified and made respectable through cultural acceptance. Insight into this type of behavioral tendency shows up in the excerpt which follows:

The whites had a red-light district on one side of the street there where Crosby-Garfield is, and the colored had theirs as close to them as they could get, the reason being they could get more money out of white men. It was absolutely no secret about Negroes and whites being blood kin. Everybody knew old man L was the L boys' dad, and Judge W stood by J the same way. And of course the mothers of these children are always provided for. I told a white friend of mine recently, as much a friend as you can say a white man is for a white man isn't a real friend—he'll eat

[34] Personal interview.

you up when you're alone and ignore you when he's with others—
anyway, we were discussing integration and he said he was afraid
of it. I told him the reason he was afraid was that they'd been
crossing the back fence so long, now it looks like we are going to
open the front door and walk in.[35]

While this type of pattern and attitude have pervaded and affected the development of Negro business from an historical
standpoint, their influence on Negro Main Street business in
Raleigh has been more indirect than direct. That is, the overtly
non-respectable types of businesses, such as prostitution, have
never flourished on the street, and yet, Negro women as para-
mours of white employers inside the respectable businesses operated on the street is a pattern that does exist there. The latter,
however, becomes a highly personal and individual matter operating in many respects similar to the personal relationships that
existed between Negroes and their white relatives.

But securing aid from white relatives or employers has included more than financial assistance for establishing legitimate
business or gaining patronage for the illegitimate. Ofttimes it has
meant getting help in buying property or extending civil rights
and getting protection for the entire minority group. When, for
example, Negroes tried to purchase the Odd Fellows Building,
the first owned by and used for Negro business operations on the
main street, the purchase was made by a white man. As one
elderly resident cited the situation, "They wouldn't sell it to Negroes so a white man bought it and turned it over to them." Similar tactics were used to make public transportation facilities
available to Negroes and thus extend the marketing and consumer area of the community. Such extension and interdependence of racial groups, based upon personal relationships, is evidenced in the statement below:

B. O. started Negroes riding buses around here, that is, inter-city
buses. They used to not let colored ride and the people in M had
no way to get into Raleigh or any other place. All they had at that
time was the train, and if you went from one place to another you
had to ride the train. B.O. went to buy a bus ticket and they
wouldn't sell it to him, so he got a white person to buy it for him,
probably one of the Ts cause he was kin to the Ts anyway. They

[35] Personal interview.

bought the ticket, he took it and got on the bus and they put him
off and he started a lawsuit from that. He was vice president of
the bank and owned a lot of real estate in Raleigh but had his
biggest business at M.[36]

Another factor in the evolution of Negro business mirrored
through the main street has been the shift from businessmen as
figureheads or fronts for white business to actual managers and
owners of their own businesses. The principal businesses in which
figurehead statuses were originally most noticeable were undertaking and the practice of law. Although one of the leading undertaking establishments never had to make the shift from front
to real, in its origin and development it was beset with competition from without and conflict from within, the opportune factor
which prompted establishment of a second funeral parlor by another group. The person credited with the founding of the second
funeral establishment started as a front but laid the foundation
for one of the most substantial businesses of the community. Part
of the history of these institutions is related in the excerpts which
follow:

When I opened my funeral parlor the whites had all the funeral
business. Big fellows like O'K worked against me. They were
heads of lodges and controlled the lodge folk. The laws said
when someone died to call the head knocker, etc. and the whites
were paying these colored to get the business. I had all that to
fight . . . In the undertaking business whites used everything
second-hand for Negroes. They used to use mules for Negroes'
funerals instead of horses, and second-hand hearses when automobiles came. When I took all the Negro trade one white man
was catering to the best colored and the po' whites. I didn't want
whites, never buried but a few whites in my life. The whites put
two businesses into operation for colored. H's still exists because
C. J.Y. was the head of it. When the whites started fighting each
other, one undertaker stopped burying Negroes and the others
had to do the same or lose white trade. Now colored bury all the
colored.[37]

Regarding the second establishment this account is given:

The Raleigh Funeral Home was organized by Jim Young (called
Colonel). It started out with ten stockholders, knew them all at

[36] Personal interview.
[37] Personal interview.

one time but have forgotten now who many of them were. The main ones were Jim Young, John Turner, and Maurice Watts (Dr. Watts's father). Before this Col. Young worked for Brown, a white undertaker, by getting Negro bodies for Brown and Brown giving him a commission. Another man, Strickland, was burying all the country Negroes and poor white folks. Brown buried the big Negroes, the Masons, Odd Fellows, etc. Then these ten men formed a company, Brown was behind it, by getting the head of the Masons, head of the Odd Fellows, and one man from each of the larger churches to form the company. When they got ready for a funeral Brown would send down a hearse and everything they needed. Negroes soon found a white man was behind it . . . D. H. went to embalming school, came and worked with the business and finally got control of it after Young's death. They went into it to run —— out of business, went all over town saying they were going to run —— out . . . the main thing was they hated to see an outsider come to town and make good.[38]
Daddy was in the funeral business at the same time he was running the shoe store. By this time D was coming up and they hired him to work there, and two others of us were there too. I took daddy's place when he died, got all his stock. The other fellow and I weren't interested in the business and it started going down. I just wasn't interested, but that's the business I should have gone into. Since then I've seen my mistake, but at that time I just had no interest in the business and the other fellow didn't either. D was smart, he saw what was happening and how he could get control of the entire business so he just stuck around and worked and kept his mouth shut. The other fellow said to me, 'I'm going to sell him my stock,' and I said, 'if he can take the business and make anything out of it he is welcome to it'; and that's how he walked into the business. Not many people know what really happened, but that's how he got it.[39]

While the number of Negro lawyers in the community has been rather small, traits of the practicing lawyer and community attitudes toward him have undergone as many changes as in the case of the undertaker. Most often the early lawyer was either a front for some white firm or a figurehead attorney and an actual common laborer. Views of three residents given below are in agreement about such situations.

[38] Personal interview.
[39] Personal interview.

We have more lawyers now who actually practice. In the earlier days the lawyers ran for white lawyers, you'd hire a Negro and when time came to pay you had to pay a white lawyer, come to find out he was working for the white man. They didn't have confidence in themselves earlier, but now they are actually practicing and doing well; only one runs for whites.

The colored have been sold out so much by colored lawyers that they didn't have much faith in the colored lawyers. D. P. Lane (Dr. Lane's grandfather) was a lawyer, and he worked for Montague. Montague made his money out of loans to Negroes, and Lane was the one who negotiated the colored loans and lent to Negroes for Montague, and now no colored can even rent in the Montague Building right in the midst of colored business.

A lawyer has never been successful here. The only successful one was Johnson and he made his out of real estate. He had about a hundred houses, was teaching law at Shaw, and had an office in the post office. He was the wealthiest man in the state. Negroes had no faith in a Negro lawyer, thought a white juror would always be swayed by a white lawyer. That has changed in the last 30 years. We've had several lawyers but they made their living out of pressing clubs and the like.[40]

The history of Negro business reveals again the manner in which numerous individuals have become successful business men independently of aforementioned factors. While some are better trained for their work today than previously, many are still untrained and uneducated but are rated in the community as successful businessmen. Success in this instance is measured by type, size, and permanency of the business, in addition to living conditions. The key to this success is most often the kinds of factors indicated in the excerpt which follows:

In many of the Negro businesses the wives are the brains behind the business. The men have built the business up but have no education; they have some business sense but can't do the necessary things when it comes to records and bills and that type of thing. . . . E. S. can't read or write unless he learned recently. His wife does all the finger work. When he gets a bill he has to pay he just lays it aside until his wife goes over it and tells him about it. When his men come in at night to check in they give him their envelopes and if she isn't there he lays them aside, each

40 Personal interview.

one to itself just like you'd do a bank book until she comes and checks them. He can remember who gave him which envelope but he can't do anything about it. She does all his secretarial work. She herself is a school teacher. Yet he has run a —— business for some 30 years. That's what most of these nigger men do, hire them secretaries who can do the finger work. B —— is the same way with his —— business. And E-F's just as bad with his —— business. But that's more than the younger men will do. All they want to do is gamble and have a good time, while the older ones have felt that they had to build up some kind of business.[41]

Equally as influential in the history of Negro business and its main street development have been attempts to form corporate businesses whose failure rates have far exceeded those of individually-owned businesses. One of the oldest in this group was the Peoples Savings Bank, incorporated 1909 with the corporators B. O'Kelley, J. H. Love, T. L. Love, L. B. Capehart, Brittan Pearce, G. A. Edwards, J. E. Hamlin, Walter Harris, A. W. Pegues and C. W. Hoover, but which never functioned.[42] Others included in this list were the Progressive Real Estate Co., in operation from 1913 to 1928; Capital Building and Loan Association, 1922-31; *The Independent*, a newspaper, 1917-22; the Orgen Printing Press, whose camouflaged name spells Negro backwards and whose original operators still boast of the fact that many whites did not know they were buying a Negro paper; the short-lived Business League, organized in 1921; Fidelity Clothing Shop, existing from 1924 to 1932. All of these were Negro Main Street businesses, and their short periods in operation demonstrate the lack of long-lived group ventures among Negroes. Invariably it was some of the same group of business-conscious men who started each of these businesses, and invariably lack of cooperation, inadequate techniques of operation, internal strife, and "get-rich-quick" methods ended them. A leading resident says of one of these businesses,

The Progressive Real Estate Co. lost out from bad management. L.C., J.E., C.W., L,, and old man L, and some others were all in it. I did some building for them. Of course they were all taking cuts here and there where they could, like getting enough

[41] Personal interview.
[42] *Private Laws of North Carolina*, 1909, Chapter 223.

lumber to sell some or build something for themselves when they went on a job. W — — has been the only one in the bunch who has been in on all the business started but didn't have sense enough to get anything for himself. All the others got their share.[43]

The lack of cooperation among business men and between business operators and consumers is seen as an outstanding hindrance to the growth of business, borne out by these statements:

In 1921 Lightner, Edwards and I started a league to promote business among Negroes. People complained that we tried to run everything, so we bowed out and Negro business didn't really show its head again until the bank came in 1923.

Another thing about Raleigh Negroes is that they haven't done any business on a cooperative basis, that is, in any kind of business association. Individually they do very well but won't work together in any way. A man'll put up a store and improve it the way he wants to and make good, but when you ask him to join a business organization he won't do it.

The chief attempt at organization among Negroes was the Co-op store. That really could have been a thriving business but it failed, and the main reason it failed was lack of Negro patronage. We had over a thousand stockholders and couldn't get 500 of them to patronize the store. We didn't put in any second-grade meats because we knew Negroes would say we had inferior goods, from the beginning we tried to offset that argument. But Negroes still didn't patronize us. There was an Alec White who was butcher at Cox's market, and he was supposed to be very good. The Negroes kept saying we ought to have a butcher like Alec White, so I went to the board and finally convinced them that we ought to hire Alec White and see if that would get the patronage. We brought him to butcher at the store but the Negroes still didn't come there. Finally we were told that we didn't have a butcher we had a meat cutter. Alec White had butchered at the white store but became just a meat cutter when he came to us. One day I met a fellow who was a stockholder and he said to me, 'Don't you all mess up my money down there at the Co-op.' I asked him did he belong to it and he said yes. Then I said, 'Don't you ever buy any groceries?' and he said, 'Yes, I buy at the A & P.' I told him I had never seen him in the Co-op store and he said, 'I've never been in it but I got a hundred dollars worth of

[43] Personal interview.

stock in it.' We tried one time taking the names of all the people who came there to buy, asked them to just write their name and address, and the Negroes got insulted and said they'd never come back again. What we were trying to do was get a list of all the stockholders who bought there, but the Negroes swore we were insulting them, that they didn't have to do that anywhere else and they weren't going to do it for us. I have often thought about the situation at the Co-op and wondered what else we might have done to make a go of the place. I'm convinced now that what the Negroes really want is a white man; best way to prove that is look at the thriving business the store does now with this white man as owner. I'm not so sure but what the thing for us to have done was hire a white man to run the store. Negroes just prefer the white man it seems. The group that patronized us the least was the intelligent, upper-class Negroes—the school teachers. I lost a lot of money in the store and several others did too . . . but I don't regret the money I lost. We tried to offer jobs to Negroes, and the very folks who were teaching our boys and girls to be clerks, etc. wouldn't send us a single person to work. I don't regret what I lost because I wanted to convince myself that Negroes could do the job as well as whites if given the same chance, and I found that they can. The sad thing is that we haven't learned to patronize each other. We even made our prices a few cents cheaper than other stores, trying to get patronage but it didn't work. We still have a lot to learn. We aren't as ready as we think we are.

Take the real estate company Negroes used to have, it was doing an excellent business. When old man L. was head of it, W., L., S., and several others turned a number of raw deals, then slipped out and left old man L. holding the bag and he had to pay off $10,000, but those are the things they don't tell.[44]

The Fidelity Dress Shop, operated by one man but owned by a group of stockholders, with many out-of-town customers who had orders mailed or delivered to them, offers another illustration of how failure seized business beset with mismanagement, etc. In the words of a customer,

Take the clothing store M —— F —— had there on Hargett St., that could have been an excellent business but they started wrong. A group of men controlled it; they'd go out and get people to buy shares, saying they needed stock. Many people took out shares but when they went to the store there wasn't any stock and the money was gone, so nothing to even buy stock with.

[44] Personal interview.

I know this for a fact . . . you see, they started wrong in the first place. They went in there to profit off the country people, but they started too late to fool the kind of people they were aiming at. There are as many school teachers, for example, among the country folk as there are among city folk proportionally speaking, and many were already too far advanced to be fooled like M — — and those thought.[45]

Just as failure in many corporate forms of business has been an influential factor in the development of Negro operated enterprise, so has individual ownership produced an impact thereon. Individually-owned businesses have had life spans greater than corporate businesses for the most part. Even where businesses have started out on a partnership basis their failure rates have tended to surpass those individually owned, one of the major factors in failure resting most frequently upon personal elements. Personal aspirations have tended often to becloud business operations to the point of either forcing the closure of the business or necessitating its continuance under individual management. Residents of the community most often view business failure as personal failure, the latter resulting from improper use of business ethics as well as making the business a means to personal ends. Quite illustrative in this instance has been the manner in which conflict between partners in one of the most lucrative of Negro businesses, undertaking, forced a change in the structure of the business and at the same time affected the personal relationships and social expectations of the personalities involved. The specific situation in this involvement has been explained thus:

L. tried to make all the money after he got started. One time he and daddy had an undertaking business together. Before that L. had one by himself but it was sorta shoddy. He was burying people for nothing practically. He asked daddy to go in with him because daddy was a society man and that would help him. At that time daddy was the head of a society called the Raleigh Union. . . . It was kind of an insurance-like that paid $115 when one died and taxed each member 15¢ when one got sick. The members came and looked after you. Daddy was a good business man but had no training. He arranged for L. to get the $100 out of the $115 the society paid when a member died; he thought the $15 ought to be given to the family to help pay for medicines and the like. This was a big jump over what L. had been getting,

[45] Personal interview.

cause he was burying for almost nothing, but he got greedy and wanted it all and started taking the whole $115. He even went so far as to take food, furniture, and anything a family had if they couldn't pay for a burial. So he and daddy fell out. Daddy saw he wasn't going to do right, so he pulled out and went into another funeral business, the one D. has now. L. has never had much good luck since that, his business started going down until he lost about all he had. Right now he has people rooming with him that he would never have even thought of speaking to in his heyday.[46]

So significant have been personal elements in shaping the history of Negro business that residents never fail to trace many current successes and failures of business back to specific individuals. The one person credited with contributing most toward the development of the Negro Main Street and its businesses is also blamed for its failures or shortcomings. Trends in business development are almost invariably portrayed so as to reflect personal influences. One resident says, for example:

L. used to be *the* man-about-town, wore fine clothes every day and stayed dressed up; reared his children like they were rich; had one building paid for when he mortgaged it for another and that's when he began to lose out because he finally lost both of them. It don't pay to live above your means. Now his house is about to fall down on him in the inside, and he has just about anybody rooming with him, drunkards and everybody else. Look at what he could have had if he hadn't lost his farm out where this new development is now. . . . Some of these Negroes here have made some money in business, of course they used trickery, etc., but most of them lost what they made. Dr. C. carried the lodge under for $47,000 when he was grand master and never made a dime of it good. He had all that fine home, nice building, and a lot of property, but when he died had sold his home even and was living right behind it in a small house. It just don't pay to do people wrong, you can make the money but you can't keep it.[47]

It must not be assumed, however, that all of the personal factors which affected the survival of business came from within the business structure itself, for many of them had origins in racial or

---

[46] Personal interview.
[47] Personal interview.

social forces that went beyond the realm of the economic. One such factor was the credit squeeze. The credit squeeze is ofttimes used by creditors as a means of controlling personal aspirations of Negroes and keeping them within the limits of socially approved behavior in a society where white dominance is a constant value. Again this becomes evident in the tight squeeze placed upon a leading Negro Main Street figure. A resident describes its use thus:

L. could easily have been the richest man in the city. He used to be able to borrow any amount of money he wanted, just walked into a bank and said how much he wanted and got it. When he built the L Building it cost him very little in comparison because he used the material from the old post office that was being torn down at the time. And after he did so well with that he thought he could successfully do another. He paid $22,000 for the lot on which he built the A——, and the building cost $100,000. He borrowed this from Durham Life. He did all right until he let John Love get him mixed up in politics. He ran for mayor of the city and made the white folks mad, and after that he couldn't borrow a dime. He had paid it down to $13,000, and a few days after he ran for mayor Judge Winston (he had borrowed the money for him) sent for him and told him his man wanted his money. He only gave him a couple of weeks to get the $13,000, and after that he couldn't borrow any more anywhere. I knew he was moving too fast though. I was head of the Progressive Real Estate then and I could see from what he did in that that he was going too fast. He had an eye for business but undertook too many things at one time. Letting John Love talk him into running for mayor was his undoing.[48]

While the person involved in this credit squeeze recognized the potency of the same, he saw his individual aspirations as mythological rather than real, and racial rather than personal. He says of the situation,

One time Dr. M. T. Pope, Cheek, and I ran for mayor, commissioner of safety, and commissioner of public works. There was nothing real about this, we knew we wouldn't win, and even if we had won we knew the whites wouldn't let us administer, but we just wanted to wake our people up politically. That did stimu-

[48] Personal interview.

late them to the point of voting. About all I lost was some money.[49]

Just as whites put the credit squeeze on Negroes to restrict their activities to non-competitive realms, at least non-competitive with whites, so Negro businessmen used a counter squeeze on other Negroes as a means of aiding the rapid growth of business. Although the inter-racial credit squeeze produces an ultimate effect upon all social realms, it is sensed most keenly by the businessmen to whom it is applied. The intra-racial credit squeeze on the other hand affects business and non-business groups alike. A case in point is related by a resident thus:

We had a Building and Loan when I came here but those in it couldn't work together. They had the capital and the borrowers, but the Negroes handling it were class-conscious; they wouldn't lend money to the lower classes but let a teacher or somebody like that come to borrow and they had no trouble getting a loan, and they are some of the worst people when it comes to paying back . . . they charged exorbitant fees that not everybody could afford to pay. In 1927, for example, I went to Mr. L., who was the head of the Building and Loan, and asked to borrow $600 to buy a house. He had to take it up with the board, but they approved and I was to pick it up at a certain time. When I went to get it, he had signed the contract for 6 per cent interest and other fees before, I had to go talk to him before I got it. Well, just before he handed it to me he asked me what was this money worth to me, and I told him it was worth the 6 per cent interest. He said, 'You know that's no money during these times, we have to charge more or we wouldn't make anything.' I told him I had signed the contract and agreed to pay what they had asked. He said, 'No, this ought to be worth at least $100 to you and if it isn't you can't get the loan.' Well, I paid the $100 extra because I figured I wasn't really losing anything. See, what I was going to do was buy a house that another man had offered to sell me. It had been appraised at $1,500.00 and that's what he wanted for it, but I told him I couldn't pay that. The house remained empty for a while and people kept breaking in it and stealing the fixtures, so he wanted to sell it because he couldn't seem to rent it. He kept on coming down on the price until one day he asked me what would I give him for it and I said $600, and he told me I could have it for $600 if I paid him the next day. That's why I was so anxious to get the money then and figured I wasn't really

49 Personal interview.

losing anything, so paid the $100 extra, but after that I didn't fool with them.[50]

Having thus posited the assumption at the outset that differentiation of urban areas into segmentalized sub-areas is functionally related to the indigenous development of the specific areas involved, a multiplicity of factors can be seen as influencing the evolution of the Negro Main Street as a segmentalized urban sub-area. The most essential of these factors have been the following: 1) Method of founding the community; 2) Location and structure of specific areas, streets, and institutions; 3) Changing occupational and business alignments accompanied by shifting locational patterns of key businesses; 4) Establishment of a fixed business location via individual endeavor, competitive ventures, simultaneous and successive enterprise attempts, and personal assistance of whites; 5) Shift from fictional to actual and successful businessmen status; and 6) Effect of personal aspirations and influences upon the impersonal *modus operandi* of business. We may thus generalize at this point and state that the origin, location, and growth of the Negro Main Street emanate from trends in the ecological organization of business augmented by certain culturally permissive factors within the supporting community. One of the most totally permissive factors in Southern culture has been discrimination. It is expedient to investigate the effect of discrimination upon the formation and functioning of the Negro Main Street, the nucleus of the next chapter's discussion.

[50] Personal interview.

Part III

INFLUENCE OF DISCRIMINATION UPON CONSUMERS'
USE OF SPACE

Chapter 4

THE NEGRO MAIN STREET AS A SYMBOL OF DISCRIMINATION

HAVING delineated the manner in which the Negro Main Street assumed its general characterization as a specifically located business street; having traced its genesis and growth as a mutually dependent element in the evolution of business; and having noted the manifold factors affecting the functional specificity of the street, the question arises as to what motivational force may have conditioned such formation, characterization, and functioning. While the answer may appear obvious for a Southern community in which the social dichotomy rests upon superordinate-subordinate patterns in race relations, the particularized value of this cultural force is far from being self-explanatory. The force itself seems to have been discrimination, the social value of which was most keenly sensed in the period 1880-1890 even though the ideological sanctions for it rested in the social arrangements that functioned during slavery.

In defining discrimination as "the unequal treatment of equals, either by the bestowal of favors or the imposition of burdens," Hankins indicates that discrimination permits prejudices, or differential emotional reactions towards individuals, to operate; that it alters the competitive power of those presumed to possess a freely competitive status; and that a social group uses discrimination against opposed groups or individuals in an effort to maintain itself or achieve its purposes.[1] In the society discussed here two larger social groups are involved, Negroes and whites, but it is the latter whose discriminatory policies are so directed against the former as to aid the promotion of a separate, non-competitive business world in which Negroes cease to threaten the status of whites. Nor did this spring into being at once as a culturally permissive social value. It is instead the result of a series of developments in which status distinctions have been sharpened by the stages through which discriminatory usages have passed.

Status distinctions in North Carolina, even prior to the Civil War, were somewhat different from those in the majority of

[1] Frank H. Hankins, "Social Discrimination," *Encyclopedia of Social Science*, Vol. XIV.

Southern states. In 1838 Judge Gaston rendered a decision declaring North Carolina inhabitants to consist of two classes, citizens and aliens, with slaves forming part of the alien class and free persons of color helping to make up the citizens class.[2] Emancipation of the slaves conferred citizenship status on large numbers of persons formerly classed as aliens, but instead of making for equality between status groups it led to more limitations on the rights and liberties of the new classes of citizens and sharpened the lines of distinction between Negroes and whites. Old laws affecting Negroes were repealed and new ones enacted; new definitions for Negroes were developed, making a "person of color" any Negro and his issue to the fourth generation, even when one parent was white in each generation; and a double standard of racial morality was enforced by revising criminal laws and making assault with intent to commit rape upon a white woman a capital offense only if committed by a person of color, otherwise an aggravated assault—punishable by fine and imprisonment.[3] The push for white supremacy became uppermost. The force of law was applied to the customary separation of Negroes and whites in public conveyances, and cries went up from the *News and Observer* charging that the presence of Negroes in public office was "Negroizing Raleigh."[4]

Thus, by the end of the nineteenth century so intent had one social group become upon subjugating the other that the Negro was without his franchise, had lost his former protection from Northerners, labored under unequal economic opportunities, and had to live by a racial etiquette that set him aside as a subordinate caste. Meanwhile, however, aided by the Freedmen's Bureau and Northern whites who saw the economic salvation of the Negro as residing in education, the Negro made advances in education that later proved to be one of the mainsprings of Negro main street business. The oldest Negro college of the South had been founded in Raleigh in 1865 by Henry Martin Tupper, a chaplain in the Union Army. Acquiring its present site in 1870, and incorporating under the name of Shaw University in 1875, the school became one of the most potent community influences in

[2] J. G. DeRoulhac Hamilton, *Reconstruction in North Carolina* (New York: Columbia University, 1914), p. 152.

[3] *Ibid.*, pp. 153-4.

[4] Hugh T. Lefler, *History of North Carolina* (New York: Lewis Historical Publishing Co., 1956), Vol. 11, p. 691.

the development of the pseudo-separate economy of Negroes. Practically all of the early professional men at work in the community received their training at this school. Many came from communities scattered throughout the nation just to go to school and took permanent residence there afterwards. The first class was graduated by the school in 1878. The first class in medicine came out in 1886; the first in law, 1890; and the first in pharmacy, 1893.[5] Outlining the progress of the Raleigh community in 1899 the *News and Observer* stated:

Raleigh may well be termed the Athens of North Carolina for she has in her borders more of the state's educational institutions than any other city. Prominent among these is Shaw University, established for the education of the colored race. Her students have become prominent in the ministry, law, pharmacy and medicine and in the Third North Carolina Regiment of the United States Infantry called out during the Spanish-American conflict the following Shaw men are found: Colonel James H. Young, Adjutant E. E. Smith, Chief Surgeon J. E. Dellinger, Assistant Surgeons M. T. Pope and W. W. Alston, Captains J. J. Hood and J. T. York.[6]

Along with the educational factor and its relative influence on the development of business institutions of the community must be mentioned another type of pertinent force, the political. Though of shorter duration, it more immediately affected the total social world, not just the Negro, and was perhaps for that reason more circumscribed. The inadequacy of Negroes in political realms during Reconstruction is most often proffered as sufficient reason for the differential treatment of, or discrimination toward, Negroes. The fact that they were Negroes was frequently enough to justify the biases aimed at the Negro's political activities. In mentioning the Negro in politics in North Carolina, for example, it is rarely noted that between 1895 and 1899 four of the ten Negroes in the General Assembly had college degrees; that two others had been to college and taught though they were without degrees; that one had two academic degrees, had founded one school and been principal of two; that one was a lawyer; that

[5] M. W. Williams and George W. Watkins, *Who's Who Among North Carolina Negro Baptists*, 1940, p. 44.

[6] *News and Observer*, Twentieth Century State Edition (Raleigh), August 24, 1899.

one was owner and editor of a Raleigh newspaper; that one was business manager of a newspaper; and that the majority of those in the Legislature were not inexperienced politically, for they had been political office holders prior to their election to the Assembly.[7] The more usual notation instead is reiterated under the caption in the monumental Twentieth Century edition of the *News and Observer:*

The Passing of the Negro in Politics
White Men Will Rule

The white people of North Carolina will never again submit to Negro domination nor that the Negro shall rule the white man in any part of this state. This was the decree of Nov. 8, 1899 . . .

While the whites were busy developing discriminatory policies around pleas for supremacy of whites and inferiority of Negroes, Negroes erected a rationalized value system upon business and services where whites were not desirous of competing with Negroes, and hence less inclined to instigate sharp racial distinctions. On the other hand, interracial group interests moved along a color line that distinguished between Negro jobs and white jobs; that made room for the employment of more white women and thereby necessitated more racial segregation—the most overt manifestation of discrimination.

With laws passed to separate the races; with many citizens pointing to the virtues of the old-issue Negro under the old social system and the lack of these in the new-issue Negro; with Negro leaders stressing work, thrift, and education as the means of solving the Negro's economic problems; and with the mounting number of professional Negroes in the community without free social and economic opportunities, development of parallel institutions in a separate social world was a necessary concomitant thereof. Whether Negroes wished it or not, there was no mistaking the intentional policies of whites in channelizing Negro interests into a separate society, for at the Negro state fair held in Raleigh in 1901 the recently inaugurated governor of North Carolina, Aycock, said in his address:

The law that separates you from the white people of the state socially always has been and always will be inexorable, and it

[7] Hugh T. Lefler, *op. cit.,* Vol. II, p. 690.

need not concern you or me whether the law is violated else-where. It will never be violated in the South. . . . We are willing to give our energies and best thought to aid you in the great work necessary to make you what you are capable of and to assist you in that elevation of character and virtue which tend to the strengthening of the state. But to do this it is absolutely necessary that the race should remain distinct and have a society of its own.[8]

By the 1920's, when the Negro Main Street had become a fixed social phenomenon in the culture, the color line was as rigid as it had been in the 1880's and 1890's. The growing rigidity of caste had heightened the social distance between Negroes and whites through expressions of discrimination in the form of segregation. The major forms of racial segregation have been found by John-son to embrace the following: 1) residential areas; 2) educational, recreational, and other public institutions; 3) quasi-public or privately operated institutions under public control, such as rail-roads, streetcar and bus systems, and hospitals; 4) private busi-ness establishments, such as hotels and restaurants; and 5) other private commercial and professional services, such as department stores, mortuary establishments, and doctors' offices.[9] To this list might be added a sixth form, the Negro Main Street, whose cul-tural existence tends to be a result of discriminatory policies and practices manifest in the preceding forms of segregation.

Although color line and segregative distinctions have cut across all areas of social behavior, the areas in which discrimination has had the most noticeable effect in producing separate or parallel businesses and practices for Negroes are these: 1) Customer treatment in downtown businesses; 2) Burying the dead; 3) Edu-cational institutions; 4) Occupations and employment; 5) Render-ing professional services; 6) Recreational facilities; 7) Using public facilities; and 8) Political activities and proceedings. De-tailed analyses of each of these areas of discrimination and its specific influence on the development of the Negro Main Street would necessitate a study devoted to this alone. Nor is it feasible to discuss these separately with regard to the methods of dis-crimination used in each. More pertinent here is the total effect

[8] Archibald Henderson, North Carolina, The Old North State and the New (Chicago: Lewis Publishing Co., 1941), Vol. 11, pp. 440-41.

[9] Charles S. Johnson, Patterns of Negro Segregation (New York: Harper and Brothers, 1943).

discrimination has had on the formation and functioning of the Negro Main Street, an understanding of which rests upon a knowledge of how varied discriminatory techniques have been used in the preceding areas. It is the latter factor that claims our attention at this point.

The techniques of discrimination which have appeared to produce the most profound effects on the Negro Main Street, as evidenced in the business institutions and services found there, can be subsumed under five categories: 1) Custom; 2) Gentlemen's agreements; 3) Institutional arrangements; 4) Private bequest designations; and 5) Legal and political devices. These categorical techniques of discrimination, used to implement the normative patterns of behavior involving Negro-white relationships have eventuated into what Linton designates as "a design for living." The interracial "design for living" within the community has been sustained primarily through custom, so appropriately defined by Hertzler as the imperative folkways or culturally inherited usages with the rightness of time and weight of generations behind it.[10]

Despite the moral and temporal sanctions which custom has behind it, however, it has not always been sufficiently imperative to accomplish the objectives of the society. Thus, the remaining discriminatory techniques listed above have been used as complementary devices in the reinforcement, and even legalizing, of practices that have given form to the way of life of which the Negro Main Street is symbolic. Variation in the intensity with which a particular discriminatory technique has been used to implement a specific norm has been somewhat dependent upon the stage of the segregation-discrimination cycle in vogue at the time. Both factual and conceptual data give credence to the idea of a cycle in race relations corresponding to changes in practices of segregation and discrimination. The stages in this cycle can be presumed to correspond to four periods, namely: 1) Fluctuating lines of segregation but minimal discrimination; 2) Fixed lines of segregation and heightened discrimination; 3) Persistent lines of segregation but lessened discrimination; and 4) Sloping lines of segregation and less-obvious discrimination. Chronological dates for these may be arbitrarily approximated as follows: 1865-75; 1875-1910; 1910-1930's; 1930's to the present.

[10] Joyce O. Hertzler, *Society in Action* (New York: Dryden Press, 1954), p. 196.

The year 1865 is chosen as the point of origin for, when emancipation was proclaimed that year to North Carolinians, the status of the freedmen, a new social group, became an immediate issue of concern. Shortly after the freedmen had been advised not to congregate in towns a set of regulations was published for governing them, while they themselves circulated a petition requesting equal rights with whites and established a newspaper in Raleigh as their medium of expression.[11] This was likewise the period of Freedmen's Bureau operations in the community, of the establishment of private and special schools for the Negro, and of the organization of the Negro Baptist Church as a unit separate from whites. Such segregated institutions, however, were more the result of voluntary than forced action and relations between Negroes and whites remained rather amicable although a specific connotation was placed upon the Negro's status and roles. One writer summed up the situation thus:

Treatment of slaves in Raleigh was generally kindly and wise. Nowhere was there a more agreeable feeling between the races. . . . Nowhere were there better cooks, seamstresses, housemaids, mechanics and hostlers. When fires occurred the colored were always at hand and worked as hard, mounted as dangerous roofs, and were as much singed by the scorching flames as the whites. Throughout the war the colored were . . . true to their owners and after its close neither the unbalancing effects of emancipation, nor the heated discussions incident to politics, introduced any permanent ill-feeling between the races.[12]

Even Negroes themselves shared this feeling regarding the nature of race relations at that time. At a convention of Negroes held in Raleigh in 1865, one specifically designated as "not engineered by whites," an address was adopted which stated:

Born upon the same soil and brought up in an intimacy of relationship unknown to any other state of society, we have formed attachments for the white race which must be enduring as life, and we can conceive of no reason that our God-bestowed free-

[11] J. G. DeRoulhac Hamilton, *op. cit.*, pp. 148-50.

[12] Kemp P. Battle, "The Early History of Raleigh, The Capital City of North Carolina," a Centennial Address, Oct. 18, 1892 (Raleigh: Edwards and Broughton, 1893), pp. 73-4.

dom should now sever the kindly ties which have so long united us. . . .[13]

The harmonious relations existing between the races after the Civil War were still a part of the conceptualizations of many residents of the community during the period 1875-1910. Sensitive, however, to the many changes that occurred in relations in the course of the era, their conceptions are likewise indicative of the manner in which the fluctuating line of segregation and discrimination assumed its fixity. So inclusive and far-reaching were many of the changing policies and practices that older residents have retained vivid images thereof. A few of their conceptions are worthy of note in developing the imagery of the community for that period. The original lack of segregation is envisaged by one resident thus:

I was born in 1870 right there at 711 East St. . . . I began traveling different places and working in 1893. There was no Jim Crow on the train then, you could sit anywhere, no special cars for colored . . . And when the city market was there where Montgomery Ward's is the white and colored were in there selling right together. There wasn't any such thing as a separate colored section in the market.[14]

The influence of custom on the nature of race relations is recognized by another resident as follows:

When I was a child living out here at Apex my father used to bring me to Raleigh to the market, that's how I learned about Shaw University and determined to come here to school, which I did when I was 15 and have been here ever since. Finished Shaw in 1899. When we'd come to the market we would come one day with a packed lunch enough to last until the next day when we'd go back home, just fourteen miles away. We'd go to the camp house there on Wilmington Street above where the Episcopal Church is now and camp all night. This was one big room where whites and colored sat all night and swapped jokes until day, then went out to sell whatever they had brought to market, and the next day we'd head for home. . . .[15]

[13] Samuel A'Court Ashe, *History of North Carolina* (Raleigh: Edwards and Broughton, 1925), Vol. II, p. 1027.
[14] Personal interview.
[15] Personal interview.

A resident born in the community in 1867 recalls how changes in race relations began to develop:

The Legislature used to be half colored but as soon as whites got in power they got the colored out. Colonel Young's name was in the cornerstone at the Capitol until the Democrats got in power and took it out. Fuller used to be in the Legislature and many others. Negroes voted and put them in, but when whites got back in power they challenged the colored vote on the grounds of being able to read and write.[16]

The role of political forces, their extension to other areas of behavior, and their impact upon the production of a fixed line of segregation are reviewed by another resident thus:

The most prominent Negro in early days was James H. Harris who ran for the Legislature against Judge Fowle. That was in the days before the automobile. The Judge got up in public and said it made his blood boil to have a Negro running for such an office, and what did he say that for? The Negroes voted and Harris won over Fowle. The house I live in right now was bought from Judge Fowle. Dr. Scruggs bought it. Colonel James Young ran for the Legislature against Broughton and beat him. Hoover went to the Legislature too. In those days Negroes voted. There wasn't any feeling about Negroes then. I've seen those men up there in the Legislature put their arms around Colonel Young and talk just like he was one of them. . . . During Reconstruction Negroes had many privileges that whites took away just as soon as they got into power. For ten years after the war slave owners couldn't vote and Negroes could. Negroes ran the government until the states signed back into the Union. Then whites began trying to put the Negro back as close to slavery as they could. They passed a law saying Negroes couldn't vote unless their fathers had voted in 1896, so naturally that cut Negroes out. . . . I can remember when there was no segregation in drug stores and the like. You used to be able to go in any drug store and get what you wanted and sit down and eat it. There wasn't too much feeling then like now.[17]

The co-existence of different forms of segregation along with presumed forms of racial equality is described thus:

[16] Personal interview.
[17] Personal interview.

The Roundstep Bank there where Walgreen's is used to have a colored barber place down under it. And John Love had a drug store on the corner of Fayetteville and Davie Streets. It had as many white customers as colored. In fact, a lot of things were mixed then. I used to belong to a mixed church when I was young —the Congregational at the corner of South and Manley Streets. . . . Well, we had a white pastor though the majority of the congregation was colored. . . . I have never known any outright mixed congregation in the churches, that is, so far as sitting together is concerned. Negroes went to white churches, but always in the gallery. I wound up in the choir loft one time trying to get to the gallery of a white church.[18]

Changes in racial attitudes as related to changes in the use of community facilities helped tighten the segregation line in this resident's opinion:

In the earlier days there were no signs anywhere saying 'for colored.' You could trade anywhere. A store or shop became known by its name and people knew whose it was. In those days whites thought as much of colored as they did of themselves. Whites and Negroes lived in the same neighborhoods and in the same blocks all mixed up together. If you saw a place you wanted you just went on and bought it. The white school was up there where the city Auditorium is now (was called the Centennial), and the colored school was down in the next block where the Congregational church is. I reckon things started changing and making for more of this segregation business when whites and colored got so the children started fighting. I remember that right on that corner there by the Auditorium white and colored children used to fight every evening after school, so then they started the colored coming up on one side of the street and whites on the other. I believe that's when a lot of these changes regarding whites and Negroes began. When the dime stores opened up white and colored both ate together at the counters, then they started getting a lot of those rebel whites working in the stores and that changed. They used to have nice restrooms in the stores even, but later all they had for colored was old dirty places or no places at all. Now there are only a few places with nice clean places for colored. . .[19]

The recency of changes effected in helping freeze the line of seg-

18 Personal interview.
19 Personal interview.

regation is revealed in the comments of another resident who says:

. . . This hasn't been more than 35 or 40 years ago that the Centennial School closed and whites started moving out of this Negro area. I remember it because living right here my son couldn't understand why he couldn't go to that school, and he couldn't go to school at all until he was six years old.[20]

Such evidenced shifts in segregative policies persisted from 1910 to the 1930's, but discriminatory usages began to abate. Reduction in such usage was not apparent, however, until the 1930's when circumstances of the depression began to cause a deemphasis on the color of skin of customers. The persistence of segregated institutions during this period is evidenced in the Negroes erecting four new, and purchasing one old, of the seven buildings they own on the Negro Main Street; in the city's provision of a park in the community and a library on the main street for the exclusive use of Negroes; in the origin of two Negro newspapers, originally published on the Main Street; in whites opening on the street of a theater and a café for Negroes, both of which still operate there; and in the fact that the Negro bank, also on the Main Street, was one of the two banks of the city to remain open during the years 1930-1933 while six others were closed. Meanwhile, however, this period saw jobs once classified as Negro transferred to whites, accounts of Negroes made welcome in white-operated banks upon their reopening, credit accounts permitted in stores where Negro patronage was previously unwelcome, and Negro usage of professional services of whites discouraged. Segregation and discrimination with regard to restroom and eating facilities remained equally rigid in the downtown area during this period. However, this was less keenly felt because of the facilities which Negroes themselves had provided on the Main Street, then almost an absolute necessity for Negro usage.

So imperceptibly were many less-obvious discriminatory policies introduced that it is difficult to tell exactly when the present era set in. Nevertheless, it is fairly certain that during the 1930's instances in which Negroes were denied charge accounts at downtown stores became fewer; Negro women being asked to cover

[20] Personal interview.

their oily hair with newspaper or cloth before trying on hats became a rarity; denial of the privilege of trying on clothes was
almost non-existent; and fewer and fewer evidences of these and
similar factors were noticeable in the 1940's. The 1950's witnessed
the instituting of a restroom "for colored women" on the main
floor of one downtown store; of unsegregated restrooms in another downtown store; the supplying of linen service to Negro
barbers and beauticians and diaper service to Negro mothers;
serving Negroes in the same reading room with whites at the
State Library; the organization of interracial groups where individual Negroes no longer are invited as representatives of all
Negroes but many may join; and the housing in offices with
whites of Negro personnel serving in educational capacities in the
State Prisons Department. And yet, discrimination continues but
along less direct lines. In one downtown store salesmen are still
advised against serving Negro customers who are not "well
dressed"; one bank still advises Negroes who wish to open small
accounts to take them to the Negro bank which specializes in
such; a few sales people continue to refer to adult Negroes as
boys and girls; and Negroes eating with whites in downtown
stores is still prohibited. Insofar as these lines of segregation and
discrimination have been suggestive of "designs for living" in the
urban community of the South, they show influences not only
upon the formation of the Negro Main Street, but also upon its
ability to survive. And insofar as these "designs for living" have
been structured by discriminatory policies and practices, they
tend to function in a manner similar to "the persisting life activities" around which "every culture develops its institutional structure," as Lynd noted.[21] From these functional areas of living
numerous status-fixing codes of behavior have crystallized into
culture norms. Among the norms emanating from interactions of
Negroes and whites relative to the status-fixing codes the following have been most evident: 1) Outright denials; 2) Acceptance
with provisos; 3) Covert rejection; 4) Agreeable private arrangements; 5) Overt attention to an unequal-status philosophy; and
6) Ambivalent racial-messiah attitudes. The implementation of
these culture norms has tended to rest upon the usage of the
several techniques of discrimination referred to earlier. Each of
these norms is portrayed here in order to show further the extent

[21] Robert S. Lynd, *Knowledge for What* (Princeton University Press,
1939), p. 65.

to which its practical application has been symbolized in the Negro Main Street.

Outright Denials. The maintenance of a superordinate-subordinate pattern in some areas of relationships has been assured through outright denial of certain privileges to Negroes. The discriminatory techniques most effectively used for implementing the outright denial norm have been private bequest designations, legal and political devices, and certain institutional arrangements. One of the leading bequest designations has served as a deterrent to Negroes' usage of a public library for more than a generation, for when Richard Beverley Raney, owner and manager of the Yarborough Hotel, donated the Olivia Raney Library to the community in honor of his wife, it was a gift to "the white people of Raleigh." Chartered in 1899 and established in 1900, the stated purpose of the library was given as being "to establish and maintain a free library for the use, without any charge whatever, of the white citizens of the city of Raleigh." [22]

Rather keenly sensed by Negroes is the bequest technique of preventing Negro usage of one of the largest buildings, once owned by Negroes, on the Main Street. How this prohibition works is best related by a resident who attempted to rent the building. Says he:

. . . There have always been Negroes on Hargett Street and no objection to their being there. Of course there is one exception and that's the Montague Building on Hargett St. I rented it once, got a section on the third floor for a printing office. Adams and Terry were handling it, so I went to them and asked if I could rent that space, and they said yes, anyone could rent it who had the money and wanted it. I had been there about a month when they told me I would have to move, and I told them no, I was perfectly satisfied. Then he said some fellow had come by and mentioned seeing a Negro in there and said, you know Negroes are not supposed to be there ever because Mr. Montague put that in his will. They said they had searched the will and found that to be true. I told him to let me talk to the daughter because I knew her very well, and he said, 'No, my God, she's all right but her husband hates Negroes worse than snakes and he's administrator for the Montague property, and that would ruin us because they'd take away all the business we handle for them.' So he told me to just close up and leave my things there until I found a

[22] *Private Laws of North Carolina*, 1899, Chap. 65.

place to move. I could have beat the whole thing but figured it wasn't worth it since I was only going to be there until I could find a better place; then too, I talked to some of my friends about it and they advised me to go on and move out. Here about three years ago another fellow said to me, 'It's a shame for all that building to be there empty, we could make a nice hotel out of it, let's try to buy it.' So, I went to see the daughter about it and she told me I'd have to see her husband because he was administrator for the property. I went to see him and he asked me if I thought I had money enough to buy it. I told him I didn't know, that depended on what he wanted for it, but I was to decide whether I could afford to buy it or not. I told him it was empty and we could put it to use so it could earn some money. He told me it didn't need to make any money, that they have enough people in it to pay the taxes and that's all was necessary because Mr. Montague paid for the building in his lifetime and it had made its money even though it wasn't making any now. I still asked him how much he would take for it, and he said $65,000, but added, Even if you could pay that I couldn't sell it to you because no Negro can ever be in it, that was Mr. Montague's will provisions.[23]

Legal and political devices have been even more widely used than bequest designations in denying privileges to Negroes. The nature of behavior placed under legal control can be observed from types of laws passed that aimed especially at the Negro. In 1803, for example, free Negroes were permitted to vote but not live in the city without special permission; in 1831, as a result of the Nat Turner rebellion scare, Negroes were prohibited from preaching; in 1835 free Negroes were disfranchised; in 1875 separate schools were decreed for Negroes and whites, marriage between races banned, and secret political organizations prohibited; in 1899 the first "Jim-Crow" law was passed separating the races in railroad passenger cars, steamboats, etc.; in 1900 the "Grandfather Clause" to eliminate the Negro vote was adopted; and in 1907 the "Jim-Crow" law requiring separation of the races on street cars was enacted. One of the legal orders of the day that has variously affected many areas of life was a state law of 1899, revised in 1913, stating that, "No fraternal order or society or beneficiary association shall be authorized to do business in this state . . . whether incorporated under the law of this state or any other state, province, or territory, which associates with, or seeks

[23] Personal interview.

in this state to associate with, as members of the same lodge, fraternity, society, association, the white and colored races with the objects and purposes provided in this article." [24]

Legislation found its strongest support in the use of another technique of discrimination, namely: institutional arrangements. Denial of privileges in institutional areas, however, came more with regard to physical separation of the races and the use of inferior qualities or minimal amounts of goods and services for Negroes than in the lack of provision of a service itself. "Negro Divisions" of education, welfare agencies, public libraries, parks, hospitals, and cemeteries with locations in the Negro community have been among the institutional implementations of the norm of outright denial.

Acceptance With Provisos. Another cultural norm by which the community lives lies in the provisional supplying by whites of certain goods and services to Negroes. Explicit provisos whereby Negroes must use balconies, are permitttd to rent some public places or attend public gatherings, and may secure goods and services from whites under certain customary segregative and discriminatory procedures are often concurred in. Objection to such procedures can only result in non-patronage, for their use is generally an understood and acceptable part of the culture. Some of the specific uses of custom in implementing such provisos are mirrored in the reactions of Negroes to these culturally sanctioned techniques of discrimination which have varied with the increasing development of Negro Main Street businesses. Reviewing such developmental trends one lifetime resident comments:

I can remember Dr. Scruggs as the first colored doctor. Before they got colored doctors we had to go to whites. Dr. Peter Williams was another colored doctor. Dr. Hines was white but when he would go out of town he'd turn his patients over to Dr. Peter Williams to look after until he returned. . . . At first Negroes patronized the white fairs until they got their own, and then they patronized whites more than their own. The Negro fair continued until they built the new state fair grounds where they are today, and that hasn't been too long ago. . . . There weren't any such things as movies but there was a Metropolitan Hall and another but I can't remember the name. They used to have stage shows there. Traveling people would play for a week sometimes.

[24] *General Statutes of North Carolina*, 1943, Vol. 11, Ch. 58.

There was a gallery for Negroes, but then colored troupes would sometimes come there for a one-night stand and when that happened the Negroes would have the whole place upstairs and down. . . . There's more feeling now than there was then when Negroes were put out of something. . . . I sure was glad when they got a colored dentist here. Before that you had to go to the white and they weren't so nice to you. They would yank out a tooth without giving anything to keep you from feeling the pain. The colored dentists were nicer. Dr. Dunston was the first colored dentist, then Dr. Evans. When you went to the white you had to stand out in the hall until they'd let you come in and wait on you. Sometimes they'd be nice enough to give you a chair to sit on. And sometimes they'd tell you if you had anything else to do to go do that and come back in a half-hour or so. The doctors did the same thing until there were colored ones. The whites got nicer when we got colored dentists. It's sure nice now to have a waiting room with our own color where you can go sit. . . . In the drug store they sold drinks but if you got one you had to take it outside and drink it. I've seen lots of colored buy sodas and be told, you can't drink it here. I was a little girl and used to want to buy but wouldn't because I couldn't drink in the store. They used to sell a chocolate soda that I wanted so bad to know how it tasted but I never bought one until they got a colored drug store, and that's when Love's drug store opened. That was the first colored one. . . . There were no rest rooms for colored in the stores. You had to go to the colored restaurants for that. There was one place in the basement at the city market when the market was on Fayetteville St. but I never went down there.[25]

Custom is often utilized within a legal frame of reference to separate the races in such way as to give the appearance of equality of service in some institutions. Eating establishments in which Negroes and whites are both served, the only visible line of division being unobservable from the outside, are exemplary of this factor. Interestingly enough, the majority of such institutions currently surviving in the community are situated on the street that originally possessed an excessive number of Negro-operated restaurants and was the forerunner of the present Negro Main Street. Complete partitions are not used to separate the races within these, but the shelved cases of dishes and food items, strategically placed between two long counters with whites eating on one side and Negroes on the other, are sufficiently tall to

[25] Personal interview.

screen one group off from the other. Thus, the statement given below is as vivid a description of these places at the present as formerly.

. . . The Greeks had a number of eating places where white and colored ate but there was a partition running from the front back to the kitchen. Whites ate on one side and colored on the other. When you sat down you couldn't see over the partition but you knew whites were on the other side. Both colored and white went in a mutual front door. . . .[26]

Negroes have so internalized these culturally accepted provisos that the Negro personality is often viewed as passively accepting discrimination from whites while actively resisting it from other Negroes. Comments to this effect are most frequently heard in conversations between Negroes and, as evidenced in the commentary below, reactions to such customs are as prevalent today as they were in earlier days.

I remember once when Mr. E., and he was a minister too, went into —— grocery to buy some meat and got cut by the grocer because he told him what piece of meat he wanted. He saw what he wanted and showed it to the man, and he started cutting off the rough edge to give him, and he said, 'Mr. —— I want the inside not the outside.' The grocer reached out and slashed him across the face with the knife and said, 'No nigger tells me what he wants.' I went into Peoples' store right after I got married just to buy a few groceries, but I waited and waited until I got tired and then asked to be waited on, and he told me I'd have to wait until he got ready to wait on me. Even today some of the same things go on. If you go into a store you often have to wait until all the whites have been waited on, unless it's a Jew's store. The Jew rushes to you and has his salesmen do the same because he wants the money. But the white man would rather sell you the other thing every time. You go in and ask for one thing and he wants to show you something else, he'll say this other is cheaper or is a real bargain. These are the kinds of things Negroes don't talk about too much, they'll tell you they don't like to trade with Negroes because they don't rush to wait on you or want to sell you something you don't want. We don't see the things the white man does to us. Back when most folks had charge accounts in grocery stores one man went in Mr. ——'s grocery to pay his bill and get more groceries. Because he didn't have all the money the

[26] Personal interview.

man cut him, kicked him, and knocked him out the door, but the very next week he went right back to that same store. We just don't see what the white man does to us, but had that been a colored man who did that to him you would never have heard the last of it. . . . Whites talk real bad to Negroes sometimes and they take it and say nothing. I do a lot of notary work (as a J.P.) and have to go in these places where I hear a lot of it. And something else we do is brag on white physicians and knock the colored. When I was doing hotel work, worked as a bellhop for a short time but didn't stay in it because I couldn't bow to the white man so I made very little money, I had to go to the dentist for a bad tooth. Had to go to Dr. B. because he was the hotel's dentist. I got there early that morning and stood in the hall, there wasn't any place for colored to sit, and waited. He knew I was there but waited on all the whites who came before he attempted to see me, and then was going off without seeing me. I stood there until 12 o'clock and when he came out to go to lunch I asked him to please wait on me. He said he didn't have time but I kept after him and he said, 'All right, come on in.' The next time I told the hotel folks I was going to my own doctor. They said if I did I would have to pay for it myself, but I preferred paying and getting more immediate service and a place to sit in the colored doctor's office. . . .[27]

The limited discrimination described above, evidenced in the fact that white business and professional men accept Negroes as clients or customers but make them wait until whites have been served, cannot always be shown as having racial intent behind it, for limited discrimination is often directed at other types of status groups as well. It appears quite often where business and professional men who are themselves in search of status use prestige factors as means of gaining recognition for their business. In such instances the less important clients, those with the least prestige, are usually served after those with more prestige have been served. The very nature of Southern community heritage ascribes more prestige to whites than to Negroes. Whether prestige be based upon economic and or other values, the fact remains that many business and professional persons structure their businesses along prestige lines.

Where Negroes tend to be rather aggressive their reactions to the culture norm which makes provisional discrimination possible

[27] Personal interview: Negro Justice of the Peace.

follow varied lines of action. The informant quoted below, for example, takes notice of an often used reaction pattern. Says he,

I remember when I was about ten a group of us would go in that old Jew's soda shop there at the corner of Hargett and Wilmington and order sodas. He'd take all the caps off the bottles and we'd turn the bottles up to drink and he'd yell, 'You can't drink that in here.' We would drink big swallows, put the bottles down and run. We've messed up a many a soda that way, especially on Sundays after church. Spaulding got kicked out of a soda shop right there near the bank in his own building by going in there ordering a soda and drinking it there. He owned the building but had rented the place to this white man.[28]

The prevalence of Negro acceptance of discriminatory provisos in the realm of professional services helps explain the effectiveness of "the cake of custom" in insuring conformity to the norms of the community. On the other hand, because conformity to norms pertaining to many professional services has remained a matter of personal choice, accepting discriminatory provisos has tended to make segregation less complete in medical and dental practices than in many other areas. One physician notes this in indicating that even today "about half of the Negroes still have white physicians, we get that from the school records where the name of the family physician is given." [29] It is difficult to ascertain the reasons for the persistence of such practices where Negroes are in search of medical and dental care. Partial explanation may inhere in the greater number and variety of specialists among whites than among Negroes, although specialists are not completely lacking among Negroes. Some Negro physicians have specialized in such areas as pediatrics, gynecology, obstetrics, eye, ear, nose and throat treatment; some others engage in specialized practice merely because of reputations relative to their capabilities in specific fields, but the great majority remain first and foremost general practitioners. It is hardly likely that the large number of Negroes using services of doctors, however, are in search of treatment by specialists, hence other reasons must be sought to explain the persistence of the pattern mentioned here. One of the most often repeated explanations refers to price fac-

[28] Personal interview: Negro taxicab driver.
[29] Personal interview: Negro woman physician.

tors, the cost of medical and dental care being reputed to be higher when one secures service from a Negro than when the same service is secured from whites, as is shown in the statements below.

I am a dental technician, have been working at it for 21 years and haven't missed more than nine days of work in those 21 years. . . . I am working for a white dentist now, but have worked for colored. I worked for Dr. B. for a year and Dr. D. three months. That's how I really got started at the job. . . . About as many Negroes as whites use the dentist I work for, that is proportionally speaking. I think the main reason is that the whites are cheaper. A colored dentist will charge you $250.00 for the same work that a white dentist will charge you $150.00 for, I know what I'm talking about because I have worked for both. Any other dental technician will tell you the same thing. There are about eight colored dental technicians here, but all are working for white dentists. Some of the white dentists have separate chairs and facilities for colored and some don't. Sometimes you just wait until they get the others out of the chair and then they'll take you.[30]

Covert Rejection. Equally as significant as the preceding culture norms is that of covert rejection of Negroes from certain organizations, institutions, occupations, and services. Here gentlemen's agreements are most operative as techniques of implementation. These unwritten policies may often embody deliberate omissions, verbal contracts, parallel treatment, or implied interdictions, but all tend to be directed toward exclusion of the Negro from certain specified areas. Burying the dead was for quite some time one of the principal areas in which gentlemen's agreements became obvious, as well as being one of the dominant influences affecting the nature of Negro main street business. The following excerpts bear this out:

For a long time there were only white undertakers here. The main one was B. He got most of the Negroes. Many a time I've seen B. cry at a nigger funeral because that was good advertisement. . . . When the death rate was high the whites used to call in the Negro undertakers to help. The whites did most of the

[30] Personal interview: Middle-aged Negro dental technician.

work but there were some things they would have the Negroes do to assist.[31]

. . . After we opened these funeral parlors for colored . . . some of the colored would still go to the white and the whites would tell them to come to us, they'd even call us to come take a Negro body. I know L has gotten such calls because I have. The whites went so far as to tell the Negroes that they had trained us to take over and that we could do the job as well as they and for less money even.[32]

Although Negroes have been consistently among the low income groups, having them as customers or clients was for quite some time a steady source of income for whites. Since the whites for whom Negroes worked often advanced money for payment of their bills, Negro patronage was welcomed by whites. Those Negroes who were in position to assume responsibility for their own accounts were frequently members of lodges and other benefit organizations which made provisions for such things as burial fees. Thus, white undertakers not only welcomed but sought Negro patronage, arranged with key Negro lodge men to secure Negro business for them, and often established business strictly for Negroes as is shown in the origin of the funeral home described in chapter three. Since the men with power in the Negro community were not only the heads of lodges but key business men, placing the burials of their fellow lodge members under supervision of white undertakers was a source of income for them as well as for the white undertakers. As the number of white undertakers increased, competition for bodies became keener, and whites became more discriminating in their selection or encouragement of patrons according to status, social pressure began to force whites to relinquish Negro trade in order to retain white trade. One of the major results of this situation was that burying Negro bodies became Negro business and began to make the Negro undertaker a leading business man, as is indicated in the following account.

When I opened my funeral parlor the whites had all the colored funeral business. Big fellows like O'Kelley worked against me. They were heads of lodges and controlled the lodge folk. The

[31] Personal interview.
[32] Personal interview.

laws said when someone died to call the head knocker, etc., and
the whites were paying these colored to get the business. . . .
Strickland was burying all the country Negroes and poor white
folks. Brown buried the big Negroes, the Masons, Odd Fellows
and the like. . . I had all that to fight. And another thing I had to
fight in the beginning was that on the plantations whites would
call white undertakers when their "Niggers" died. They would
get a ten percent discount on the funeral. This discount was
charged to the Negroes for the next year. I couldn't afford a discount so I'd lose country trade, but when I found out this was
happening I got out and spread the news. . . then that country
prejudice where whites had to stand for the bills began to break
down. I sold them the idea of burial insurance and began to get
more business. . . The whites (undertakers) would use everything
second-hand for Negroes. . . mules for Negro funerals instead of
horses, and second-hand hearses when automobiles came in. . .
When the whites started fighting each other one undertaker
stopped burying Negroes and the others had to do the same or
lose white trade. Now colored bury all the colored.[33]

Unwritten pacts were just as binding with dentists and doctors
as with undertakers, as attested to in the ensuing statements:

At first there weren't any colored doctors, dentists, or lawyers.
Colored had to go to whites. They eventually broke from whites
after they got colored doctors, etc., but that took a long time.
Whites used to tell the Negroes to go patronize their own color;
they used to say, if Scruggs can't cure you I can't.[34]

After World War I when Negroes began to have their own businesses whites began to push them out of theirs. I remember the
dentist I used to have, there were no Negro dentists earlier, he
said to me, 'Well, when Dunston gets back from dental school I
guess he'll expect you all to come to him', and I said, 'Yes, I expect so'. That's the way they began to push the Negro into Negro
businesses.[35]

The community's first Negro dentist, Dunston, had operated a
barber shop with all white trade for many years. When he gave
up barbering to enter dentistry he was by no means a very
young man. Recalling how Negro colleges were begging for men

[33] Personal interview.
[34] Personal interview.
[35] Personal interview.

to enter the professions at that time, how barbering began to become a less-respected profession, and how occupational mobility was viewed within the culture, helps explain, as in the following comments about this first dentist, the extent to which gentlemen's agreements were made in the professional realm.

Dad's first trade, even in dentistry, was all white. The whites were coming to him and the Negroes were going to the white dentists. Eventually the whites called him into one of their professional meetings, in fact he went to the meetings but couldn't belong to the group, and told him that if he would refuse white trade they would refuse colored. He agreed but it didn't work because those Negroes kept right on going to the whites. They would ask them if they had been to Dunston but would still serve them, and some of these Negroes are still doing that, they just trust the white man more.[36]

These covert ways of rejecting Negro patronage were also used to circumscribe the occupational status of Negroes, to keep them in some types of jobs but release them from others to make room for whites. Again this was done through verbal contracts and implied interdictions. With regard to the use of these in government service, a retired postman remarks:

Within the post office there was a gentleman's agreement that the whites would do the clerking and Negroes do the delivery. I remember when I first tried to get a job there [started to work there in 1921] I was told that I could be delivery man but could not get a job as clerk. At least 90 percent of the delivery employees were colored and none of the clerks were colored. Now colored have about five percent of the clerical work and ten percent of the delivery work, so we've broken down the barriers of segregation that way.[37]

Jobs are sometimes made difficult to secure through the indirect application of pressures that make their attainment almost prohibitive. One of these pressures, felt especially where the competition for jobs is great, is often applied by making it difficult to attain license to engage in a business activity. Since the power to license is controlled by whites, the nature of business activities

36 Personal interview.
37 Personal interview.

engaged in by Negroes is likewise influenced by whites. This was no doubt a contributing factor in the Negro's loss of his monopoly over barbering, for as regulations for barbering began to be instituted and licenses required, Negro barbers began to decrease in number and to lose one of their long-standing sources of income. The application of similar pressures may also account in part for the Negro's inability to even secure token employment in some types of business activities. Awareness of such factors is indicated by one resident thus:

. . . I can remember when Booker T. Washington used to tell the Negroes to hold on to these manual jobs but Negroes were trying to get away from them. Then too, the whites stepped in and made it hard for Negroes to get licenses doing these jobs. It takes a Negro 2-3 years to get a license to practice some of these jobs. They always find some reason for not letting him have it, but the whites can get license without any trouble.[38]

By deliberate omission Negroes are often rejected from membership in organizations where "lily-white" values have usually dominated. Asked if any Negroes belong to the Merchants Bureau, for instance, the president said: "No Negro has ever applied for membership; if one applied and has a good reputation he would be treated just as whites are." [39] When the same question was asked of one chief executive at the Chamber of Commerce the reply was, "No Negro belongs and if one applied he would not be accepted." [40] A Negro businessman said of such omitted membership:

Negroes haven't tried to join. . . I guess too they're waiting to be invited to join. It's like the Undertakers Association. We were asked by the whites how we would feel about coming into the organization if asked. I told them to extend us the invitation and see then how we feel about it. The invitation has never come and we haven't bothered about it because we have a nice state organization of our own.[41]

In the case of a park and a hospital donated to the community

[38] Personal interview.
[39] Personal Document.
[40] Personal Document.
[41] Personal interview.

for the use of its citizens covert rejection of Negroes has been of rather recent origin. The park, an original eighty acres of land given to the city by a business man, Richard Stanhope Pullen, in 1887, has been made into a recreation center of some one hundred and fifty acres and numerous techniques devised to bar Negroes from using it. Building a park for Negroes has been the parallel device for diverting the attention of Negroes from use of this park. Similar tactics have been used in freeing Rex Hospital of Negro patients through aid to a hospital specifically for the use of Negroes. Provisions for the former hospital were made by an early citizen who, as manager of the first tannery in Raleigh, accumulated a large estate and after manumitting all his slaves at the end of his life, bequeathed the remainder of his estate to endowment of a hospital.[42] In 1891 the trustees of the hospital were "instructed to proceed to have built upon said lands devised by John Rex for the purpose two suitable buildings. . . one for whites and one for the colored indigent, sick and afflicted of said city", [43] and in 1893 the Manly residence on South Street was purchased for this purpose. An elderly citizen of the community, recalling the way in which such institutions were changed to service whites only remarked:

. . . Old Rex used to be a wooden structure. The land was given to the city for the citizens of Raleigh to make a hospital site. Just like Pullen Park it was for everybody and not just for whites. Nothing in the charter indicates that they are for whites, and at first Rex took care of colored as well as whites. It had a separate ward and separate entrance for colored but they went there. When they got ready to expand the city gave so much money to St. Agnes to provide for the colored and rebuilt the hospital with no provisions for colored.[44]

Private Arrangements. In numerous instances Negroes have seemed to maintain a psychic dependence on whites whereby arrangements made privately between individual Negroes and whites have had the sanction of the mores behind them. In this

---

[42] R. S. Tucker (Compiler), "Early Times In Raleigh," Addresses Delivered by the Honorable David L. Swain at Dedication of Tucker Hall, and On the Occasion of the Completion of the Monument to Jacob Johnson (Raleigh: Walters, Hughes and Co., 1867), p. 13.

[43] *Minutes of Raleigh City Government,* Dec. 4, 1891.

[44] Personal interview.

regard the explicit expressions of this dependence are but implicit manifestations of the nature of relations between the races at the personal level. One of the areas in which this is observable is again that of burying the dead. When the southern portion of the old city cemetery was used for the burial of slaves of whites interred within the same enclosure,[45] private arrangements for burial there were unnecessary. As long as minimal discriminatory practices prevailed Negro and white bodies could be buried in the same cemetery without special permission having to be privately granted, for this was part of the cultural norm. The general use of the cemetery is indicated by a citizen who says,

I was born here in Raleigh right over on Hargett St. next to the cemetery. They used to bury colored there as well as white. Mama has a child buried there. Don't know why they made it an all-white cemetery.[46]

But even in a cemetery, where arrangements are made privately between Negroes and whites it is possible for these arrangements to supersede law and for the norm to be wavered when the "VIP's" of the community do the wavering, for personal relations between Negroes and whites often assume the value of norms themselves. It is this kind of factor that makes the following report understandable:

Negroes used to be buried in the cemetery there on East Martin and Hargett. There's a Mrs. AHC whose husband is buried there and she is supposed to be buried there when she dies, right along beside her husband. She lives in Washington now but I have the papers in my safe signed by the mayor of the city in assuring that she will be buried there. Prof. L, who teaches at St. Aug. and is to be retired soon, is to be one of her pallbearers. I have all the details for the funeral right in my safe.[47]

Devising schemes for keeping a job is likewise one of the routines of living that has made private arrangements between Negroes and whites an important part of the interactional pattern. This permeates the behavior of many Negroes who work for whites and are so often heard saying, "Don't never let a week

[45] Kemp P. Battle, op cit., p. 97.
[46] Personal interview.
[47] Personal interview.

pass without getting an advance on your wages; always owe the whites and you'll always have a job 'cause he won't fire you 'long as you owe him." [48] But borrowing or securing loans from whites is only part of the devised scheme for maintaining personal relations. Having whites as savings depositories has ofttimes been a similarly utilized device, but a more infrequently used one among younger Negroes whose relations with whites tend to be less of a filial type, more impersonal, and more suspect. Although such behavior tends to be highly individualized and hence preferentially permissive, the sanctioned discriminatory principles upon which it is based permit no redress by Negroes who may be caught up in this web of relationships through deception. It is through the latter factor that implied discriminatory policies affecting the economic status of Negroes have been generally discerned. Many citizens of the community see this as a major contributory element in the loss of Negro-owned property—an extension of personal arrangements between Negroes and whites to the public acquisition of private property. A review of the situation as related by an elderly citizen indicates that,

. . . Negroes used to own all that property out on Newbern Avenue, from East St. back, and all that out on Person St. John Price lived on Person St. where the Southern and Seaboard Railroads are and he lost that property. Scott owned all the way back to St. Aug. Where Mary Elizabeth's Hospital is used to be owned by colored. Colored began to lose their property when mortgages came in. . . .

There used to not be any such thing as mortgages, and when they came in that's when many lost. Scott lost all that property he had to Mr. M. M was a big wholesale man and Scott let him keep his money for him; when he went to M to collect it M told him he didn't have any money belonging to him, and he couldn't do a thing about it. See, he trusted M because he had been keeping his money for him, but this time M gave him nothing. People used to have a lot of property because you bought by blocks. Colored owned that block where Hugh Morson School is. The man who owned it left and went to Ohio, the city kept up the taxes on it and got it for nothing. It was easy to watch the books at the Courthouse and see who didn't pay taxes. . . and that's how many folks would get property. The Montague Building on East Har-

48 Personal Document.

gett St. used to belong to colored. Montague got it by paying the taxes and now a colored person can't even rent any part of it.[49]

Overt Attention to the Unequal-Status Philosophy. The technique of custom has been variously used in many definitive situations that call attention to traditions regarding the unequal status of Negroes and whites. Keeping the unequal-status philosophy before the community as a constructed referent for racial behavior has meant the focusing of attention upon community-vested interests. The emphasis which the community places on the unequal-status philosophy warrants its classification among the principal culture norms producing an impact upon the Negro Main Street. Since the community is a white-collar, middle income, out-migrant town devoid of large industries, one of its vested interests is in maintaining sufficient workers for her middle class families and reserving as white jobs those that are more dignified and bring the highest income. Means of accomplishing these ends have employed both occupational leniency and stringency, but with the continually developing policies of discrimination nonetheless. The excerpts which follow explain some of the specific uses of these both previously and currently.

The city was lenient on Negroes when it came to taxes. A Negro could owe 14-15 years back taxes and they wouldn't foreclose on them, but they'd foreclose on whites in a second. They needed the Negroes too badly for workers to put them out of some place to live. Then too, most of the early Negroes were sired by whites. Take people like the T's, they didn't have anything though they turned out to be a pretty prominent family, but their father was white and he put them in that house and it has become the old home place. . . I've even heard my mother and father talk about their white ancestors, but some of these people don't discuss such. . . The first real awakening among Negroes came when one or two doctors got cars. Then Negroes started getting away from trades and trying to do other things. There were only a few things Negroes could do anyway. They could do all the dirty work such as clean stables. Whites would own the stables but they wouldn't clean them. A number of Negroes had stalls around the city market. Stalls were 10¢ a day at the market, they were raised to 25¢ a day in the 1920's. Negroes would be out there at 6 o'clock in the morning and stay until dark, they'd bring anything they had to

[49] Personal interview.

sell—it could be nothing but carrots or cabbage or anything but they'd come. . . All this was outside the market. I know because it was right there at our house. Inside the market many of them had fish stalls and meat counters, this was counted among the better businesses for Negroes. All the butchers were Negroes. Whites wouldn't butcher because they didn't want to touch bloody meat. . . Later on vegetable stands were added. Then whites began to replace Negroes in doing all this because the Negroes were making too much money for them. . .[50]

The thing that kept Raleigh down was no manufacturing. Negroes never could get in the factories because the white women said this interfered with their domestic service. They say that the Women's Club is so organized as to prevent Negroes from getting work in manufacturing. The biggest government job Negroes have. . . is mail carriers. I sorta get angry every time I go to town and see whites streaming out of those state offices and think that I have to pay taxes and yet my people can't get any of those jobs.[51]

A subsidiary part of an early philosophy that attempted to distinguish Negro jobs from white ones permitted Negroes to have the voluntary jobs but gave paying jobs to whites. Survivals of this are still felt in many areas where the better-paying jobs often reject Negroes. The precedent for these practices can be traced back to such shifting interests as the following:

There used to be two colored fire departments, the Bucket and Ladder Company and the Victor Company. I was a member of the Victor Fire Co. myself. These companies lasted until Sherwood Upchurch got on the board of aldermen, you know they used to have aldermen to run the city instead of councilmen and commissioners like they have now. Aldermen were elected from each ward in the city. After Sherwood Upchurch got to be alderman he fought to get the colored out of being firemen. They made the fire company a pay department to get the colored out. Upchurch said to me, 'Charlie, I know you're mad as hell with me but when it comes to pay, by God, I think it belongs to whites' . . .[52]

Another vested interest of the community which works to call

[50] Personal interview.
[51] Personal interview.
[52] Personal interview.

attention to the unequal-status philosophy is seen in the redistribution of the population. Interest in peripheral living near shopping centers with ample parking space tends to force the white population closer to the rim of the city and make the mid-city area more characteristically Negro. The reciprocal replacement of Negroes by whites at the periphery and of whites by Negroes at the center has been a means of easing Negroes out from desirable locations, differences in the assessed values of racial groups making this possible. Destruction of old residences at the periphery and the erection of palatial ones in their places tends almost immediately to alter the character of the area, while occupancy of old residences nearer the center of the city has a reciprocating effect. Thus, while movement may entail a change in economic status of both groups it still aids retention of a subordinate social status by Negroes. How this change has been effected is related thus:

Negroes used to own all the property in Oberlin. That was once a Negro village. Latta himself owned 200 acres on Oberlin. I went out there as principal of the school in 1916 and there wasn't a white person on any of that property, then whites began to pay high prices for the property. . . then they tried to run the Negroes out. I stayed out there eleven years and there were still no whites out there then. . . two or three citizens and the principal governed it. Later it was incorporated as part of the city.[53]

. . . Now not one eighth of Oberlin Road is colored. That was the most desirable property in Raleigh, for it overlooks Raleigh. . . Whites paid them (Negroes) good money for it, that's why they sold it. One fellow got 50,000 for his property. This excited the Negroes, they hadn't been used to paying over $4-5,000 for houses. It's hard to find a desirable residential lot in Raleigh, except Developments, and many white folks don't like to live in Developments. That's why they pay dearly for desirable property. . .[54]

Perhaps one of the most explicit uses of custom in perpetuating the norm that seeks to draw attention to the unequal-status philosophy lies in the forms of racial etiquette that prevail. Especially pertinent to Negro Main Street functioning have been

[53] Personal interview.
[54] Personal interview.

the conventions through which certain courtesies are extended to, and others exacted from, the Negro business man by whites. One of the forms these courtesies have assumed is in the assaying of status by modes of address, as thus indicated:

Hargett St. used to have the reputation it did because it represented the thought, activity, and money of the city. Nowhere in Raleigh except on Hargett St. were Negroes called Mr. and Miss, and whites catered to those Negro businesses there.[55]

On the other hand, courtesies exacted from the Negro have often meant giving personal care and attention to the white customer, as well as maintaining respect for the white man's value of time. This practice is repeatedly mentioned by those accustomed to regular white customers and is readily gleaned from the businessman quoted below:

I worked in a shop (barber) where the trade was white but didn't like it one bit. Whites always want you to do something special for them. They had their own mugs with their names on them and you'd better not make a mistake and use someone else's. Once they start coming to you they'll come back but always with the attitude, that's my nigger and you're supposed to please me. One day I had a guy in the chair giving him a shave, he claimed the razor was dull and asked me didn't I have another razor, I said, Yes sir, and he said, well use it because this one is dull. I laid the razor down then picked it right up again and honed it a little on the strap and went back to shaving him. I asked him if that one was any better and he said, yes, much. Now that was the same razor, I tried it because I didn't believe he knew. You always have to give them special treatment. One thing about a white man that's different with a Negro is the white man is always in a hurry when he comes to the barber shop. He'll come in and ask you how long it will take you to wait on him. You never tell him, but ask how long he can spare. If he says five minutes, or anything else, you say, 'Have a seat I think I can get you out in that time'. It actually doesn't take but a few minutes to cut a white man's hair but sometimes you fool around a little longer. You can actually cut more heads of hair and make more money working on white folks, but I can't stand having to give so much special treatment.[56]

[55] Personal interview.
[56] Personal interview.

But this type of courtesy implied another—that of being a gentle-man—and while it may have ascribed status to the Negro busi-nessman equivalent to that of other businessmen, by indirection it affixed his position above that of other Negroes. Description of this is given thus:

The most dignified business Negroes had in days past was barber-ing. That was in the days when. . . the barber was a gentleman. Watch F sometimes around his barber chair. He came up under CW and men like that who had barbered for whites, and the way you handled a customer, your quiet voice when speaking to a customer, showed dignity. There were certain marks of a gentle-man. . . and of course being a gentleman or a lady was the kind of thing that carried over into the caste system.[57]

A basic requiremment of the etiquette used to implement the unequal-status philosophy is that of carefully ascertaining one's racial identity. One of the greatest breaches of racial etiquette that is contrary to the culture norm is to mistake a white person for a Negro. Insults resulting from errors in racial identification of whites have ofttimes been used as personal means of evincing group antagonisms to Negro businesses that arouse competitive fears in whites. A case in point is noted in the early development of one of the most substantial Negro businesses on the Main Street, the bank. Describing the opening of the branch Mechanics and Farmers Bank and the opposition it faced from whites be-cause of Negroes transferring their holdings from white banks to the Negro bank, the former manager and cashier states that,

. . . the building was completed and the bank opened for busi-ness January 1, 1923. Deposits the first day amounted to $24,000. Early depositors included North Carolina Mutual with two ac-counts, one $5,000 and a savings account about the same. The late B. F. Montague (white attorney) deposited $1,000, and the Durham Life Insurance made a large deposit. . . In my enthusi-asm I sent out letters to a number of people listed in the city directory asking them to come in and make deposits in the first and only colored bank in the city. One white man got mixed up in the list, the city directory at that time used a c to indicate colored. Somehow a mistake was made and he was listed as colored, so he received one of the letters I sent out. He got mad

[57] Personal interview.

and came in and asked me what did I mean by sending him one of those letters, that he was a white man and not colored. I could obviously see that. I apologized and told him I was sorry for the error, that I was only trying to send letters to my people. That same man today is a staunch supporter of Mechanics and Farmers Bank. Many whites started kicking the bank. They said, 'They ought to close that damn Negro bank'. An employee of another bank made a discourteous remark about the bank and someone came and told me the name of the man who made it. I immediately sent him a note and sent a copy to the president of the bank saying: 'Dear Sir, I understand that you have made some unfavorable remarks concerning our bank. If there is anything that we are doing that is inconsistent with the principles of good banking, we would appreciate it if you will so advise us'. No reply to this was ever made, and that same man now praises the bank.[58]

Ambivalent Racial-Messiah Attitudes. Custom has undoubtedly been a major discriminatory technique helping keep alive acceptance attitudes of racial messiahs whose advocacies are attuned to the status quo. Those who propose avenues of action that might rapidly alter the existing designs of living tend to be culturally rejected, though often tolerated as spokesmen and threatened as social actionists. As long as one's advice and suggested program for racial development are in line with culturally-desired Negro behavior, then any Negro tends to become a racial messiah, no matter how temporary his self-appointment. Thus, a single functioning messiah has often received approval of his immediate action program and disapproval of the more remote one, or vice versa. Herein lies the ambivalence that motivates many of the acceptance-rejection patterns pertaining to racial messiahs.

From 1895 to 1915 the generally acclaimed racial messiah was the nationally-known figure Booker T. Washington. Washington's advocacy of industrial education as the solution of the economic problems of Negroes was quite acceptable to whites, for in essence it offered a compensatory system for continung to exclude the Negro from fields of endeavor that would necessitate competition with whites. Thus, when he spoke at the Negro Fair in Raleigh, in 1903, a news reporter commenting on his speech gave the keynote as "train yourselves to be good workmen"; and de-

[58] Charles R. Frazer, Sr., *The Uses of Adversity*, unpublished autobiography.

scribing his appearance he said, "He is light in color, wears no beard . . . hair cropped close, has the broad flat nose of the African . . . head and face large and massive . . . the general aspect of the man is that of strength rather than intellectuality." [59] A Negro's recollections of Washington and the Fair give some idea of the local acceptance of Washington as messiah. Says he,

I remember very well when Booker T. Washington was speaking at the Colored Fair. . . You know whites had amusements, various eats and everything at their fair but the Negro had little except some leading person to speak. I used to want to just slip into the white fair because it looked like they enjoyed themselves so. Anyway Booker T. told the Negroes at the fair to watch their jobs and watch their back fences. I didn't go along with all he said at the time, but I'm about to believe that he really knew what he was talking about. . .[60]

During the same period a local person who claimed to possess intuitive knowledge about the Negro's ambitions and attitudes undertook a campaign for redirecting these. His self-conception as leader, organizer, and social engineer led to a one-man crusade for education of the Negro in the name of Latta University. Whites' acceptance of the idea is verified in the facility with which he secured financial aid from them, while Negroes' rejection of his presumed interests is seen in their failure to provide students for the school. Both the acceptance and rejection attitudes are perhaps understandable from views given by Latta himself. Justifying and explaining his efforts he says:

The colored people, as a race, don't seem to have much ambition. . . if a colored man buys a house and lot, as a rule, it is just as high as he desires to get. . . those who have become lawyers, doctors and ministers don't seem to have ambition to want to accumulate anything more. . . It seems strange, yet it is true, they own Easy Street by heredity. . . When I started to erect Latta University colored people said it was too much for one man to do; called indignation meetings, said the governor of North Carolina wouldn't allow one man to do that much to solve the Negro problem. They called meetings for two years, had my name printed and circulated all over the city, saying I was a fraud and never would build an institution. . . Latta University

[59] *News and Observer* (Raleigh), October 31, 1903.
[60] Personal interview.

was incorporated under the laws of North Carolina, February 15, 1894; property for it was purchased in 1891 and the school founded in 1892. . . . I have been successful in investments in Durham and Raleigh . . . have borrowed over $100,000 in Raleigh and from the Merchants Bank there nearly $25,000; borrowed $30,000 from one man alone and set aside over $100,000 worth of property to pay the indebtedness of the school. . . [61]

Negroes' non-acceptance of Latta as a racial messiah did not continue to be so overtly manifest, and yet it neither changed to open acceptance nor to complete negation. In a manner of speaking both the Latta objectives and methods of attaining them were in line with the culture norms, for begging for education of the Negro in private schools that help maintain racial segregation has continued to be culturally accepted. Unlike the "Tuskegee Idea" of Booker T. Washington, however, the "Latta Idea" never reached fruition, the reasons for which are offered thus by local residents:

. . . Latta was a smooth character. He went North and begged for this university and got a lot of money for it, came back and built him a fine home out there on Oberlin. Most of his students were members of his family. . . He was a real crook but they didn't find it out until some of the folks who were giving these large sums of money to the school came down and investigated.[62]

Latta's University was all bogus, it wasn't even a good primary school. . . He had about 200 acres of land running all the way back to Dixie Trail, but he only had two wooden buildings and they weren't even good barns. The three or four students he had were members of his own family. He hardly had a fifth grade education himself. He started the place at a time when people were really giving to Negro education, so he raised a lot of money but it didn't go into any school. Nobody cared enough about what he was doing to stop him, they just ignored him and his efforts. Somehow he managed to get a number of teachers but had nobody to teach. Even during the '30's there was a man up there near the Episcopal Church who went out there every day, supposedly keeping the place open. He'd stay until around noon and come on back home. The Renaissance in education came

[61] M. L. Latta, *History of My Life and Work* (Raleigh: Orgen Printing Co.), pp. 60-61; 74-75; 84; 296.
[62] Personal interview.

around 1890, and there was no public high school in North Carolina until 1907. There were a lot of private academies, so that's why Latta could get away with his bogus deal so long.[63]

In more recent decades the would-be racial messiah of the community, an out-spoken and highly respected minister, sought through direct negotiation to help raise the status of Negroes. Disliked by whites because of his persistent requests and verbalized expressions about the rights of Negroes, he lived daily under threats made anonymously by telephone. Classified as a too-out-spoken rebel by Negroes, he never ceased to speak, to initiate movement, and to go without followers to request facilities, privileges, or rights for Negroes. With little expressed concern for his efforts, many Negroes scattered throughout the community have been heard regretting their manifest inappreciation for what he did for the Negro. Personally rejected by Negroes and whites, but superficially accepted for his ideas and efforts, his status as a racial messiah became most evident with his demise in the summer of 1958. His drive in behalf of the Negro was continued in the face of rejection because the basic interest thereof was in presumed agreement with existing culture norms. As one resident reviewed the situation he remarked:

One man who did more to get Negroes in some areas they wouldn't be in had it not been for him died this summer, and that was Father F. He really stuck his neck out for Negroes and got things done for them but always had to do it without their support. He was responsible for their putting in a separate rest room for teachers at Crosby-Garfield, even after all the plans had been drawn up; he got Chavis Park over here for Negroes by going out there and telling the whites, since Pullen Park was for all citizens and they were using government money to fix it up he was going to see to it that Negroes started using it more. He tried to get this precinct changed and put a Negro over it, and when they got in the meeting and votes were being counted all the Negroes who promised to stick with him voted with the whites. Had it not been for him some of us wouldn't be working right up there in the post office today. He is responsible for that too, and now there are ten Negro clerks up there, eleven Negro handlers, eleven Negro mail carriers, and two Negro mechanics. When JW and those first started having those big public dances they

[63] Personal interview.

didn't know a thing about how to do it. They went to Father F and he told them how and as soon as they learned and began making a little money they stopped even speaking to him. We are a funny people, we hate for you to know more than we do, and just as soon as we get 'in the know' we are going to show you up if we can.[64]

The foregoing analysis shows somewhat conclusively then that differences between status groups have always existed but that effects of the Civil War led to a redefinition of status groups which made them synonymous with racial ones. Pressing for ways of translating the ideology of white supremacy into "designs for living" brought growing rigidity to the lines of distinction between Negroes and whites. Lines of racial demarcation found reinforcement through discriminatory techniques often made manifest in segregation. Such discriminatory techniques as custom, institutional arrangements, private bequest designations, and legal and political devices used in areas affecting the most personal relations of Negroes and whites have tended to result in a number of culture norms. The Negro Main Street, a compensatory form of segregation resulting from discrimination in specified areas, and in line with certain norms, thus reflects in both its origin and continuation the very areas in which discrimination against the Negro has been most severe. This in turn accounts for the nature of consumer goods and services prevalent on the street, and the personal views which follow serve as summarized verifications for the racial, social, and spatial motivations giving structure thereto.

I used to notice how hard it was on women when they came to town and had no place to go to a rest room, so I said if ever I built I was going to remedy this. When I built the Lightner Building I had in mind making a nice place for women to go, so I put a rest room in there for them and everybody knew it was there. It didn't hurt my business any, it really made my building quite popular. . . I really built the Arcade because my wife got tired of me bringing so many of my friends to the house to stay, but there was no place in town for them to stay. . .[65]

. . . Negroes had to go to Hargett Street for both relief and refreshing. The stores had no rest rooms for Negroes, no drinking

[64] Personal interview.
[65] Personal interview.

facilities, and no place for you to eat even standing up. So if you were shopping you had to go to Hargett St. I can well recall that one of the ways my uncle got so much trade in the barber shop was that Negroes came there to go to the rest room and to leave packages. One of the ways Mr. Lightner began to get such a hold on the country people in his funeral business was that they would go to his place to use the rest room and leave packages. The barber shop and the funeral parlor were the chief places that had these accommodations. . . At one time all the dances were held upstairs in the Arcade. The most regrettable thing about the development there is that Mr. Lightner never was able to complete plans for the theater back of the Arcade. Lightner really made Hargett St. Almost all activity was centered in one of his buildings.[66]

. . . I think daddy went into business because he saw the need for getting Negroes to trade with Negroes, to spend with their own race. Even when I went in business it wasn't like now. Negroes did not have charge accounts at all the leading stores like they do now. Very few could get charge accounts. Negroes needed their own places and the whites would tell them to come to the Negro. Of course, Negroes are funny—they always have an excuse for not trading with the Negro. I've had them tell me 'I would trade with you but you don't have what I want.' I tried to get what they wanted, and other people went into business too to try to provide them the same things that whites had. Dunston quit barbering and went into dentistry not only to make a different living for himself but because there was no Negro dentist here.[67]

With these provisions made on and by the Negro Main Street, the next question posed pertains to how the Negro as consumer has reacted thereto, answers for which will be sought in the following chapter.

[66] Personal interview.
[67] Personal interview.

Chapter 5

NEGRO MAIN STREET AS AN INDEX OF
CONSUMER BEHAVIOR

THE series of physical, cultural, and social factors comprehended
in the origin and growth of the Negro Main Street give the street
a life-cycle appearance similar to that of the human organism.
After looking back upon the manner in which these factors helped
shape the nature of the street during its most formative years of
development, a glance at the present phase of the cycle becomes
imperative. Seeing the Street now as a fixed physical phenomenon,
a culturally-entrenched economic phenomenon, and a racially influenced social phenomenon, we can now view its characteristics
and functions as a market. The point of departure here is away
from the much-discussed Negro businessman, or Negro business
as such, and toward the functional relationships and social characteristics of Negroes as consumers within the confines of a local
market, the Negro Main Street. We need not therefore make the
focus of concern that of the often-cited success stories which
relate Negro achievements in business;[1] nor that of the frequently
felt need for Negro business to move away from separatism and
toward integration;[2] nor that of a newly developed black bourgeoisie in relation to Negro business;[3] nor that of the uniquely
portrayed myth and fact of Negro business.[4] For, insofar as fact
and reality coincide, the picture here will be the current situation
"in fact" relative to consumer behavior for which indices are
found in the Negro Main Street.

Factual relevance of the information regarding consumer behavior as reported here comes from a sample of 350 persons interviewed with schedule to ascertain their trading characteristics.
Selection of the sample, as discussed in Chapter 1, and the questions to which answers were sought, as found in the Appendix,

[1] Booker T. Washington, *The Negro in Business* (Boston & Chicago:
Hertel, Jenkins and Co., 1907).

[2] Robert H. Kinzer and Edward Sagarin, *The Negro in American Business*
(New York: Greenberg, 1950).

[3] E. Franklin Frazier, *Black Bourgeoisie* (Glencoe, Ill.: The Free Press,
1957).

[4] St. Clair Drake and Horace R. Cayton, *Black Metropolis* (New York:
Harcourt, Brace and Co., 1945).

give some idea of the inclusive nature and representation of consumers and their patterns of behavior.

Inseparably bound with whites to the urban, middle class, economic and political life of the community, but constrained to separate education, low income, unequal economic opportunities and social distance sustained by discrimination, the consumer wants of the Negro are not unlike those of any other consumer. Dissimilar to other minorities whose ethnicity and customs make consumer demands more understandable and easily supplied by businessmen of their own groups, the Negro makes no exceptional consumer demands and produces no specialty goods for consumption. When comparisons are made, however, between sub-groups of Negro consumers differences, as well as similarities, become apparent. Replies from the sample population, for example, indicate that the leading social want to which Negroes attach singular value is a home, an increasingly significant American value. Asked what item or service they would secure as first choice, provided they had sufficient money for that purpose, 65.1 percent listed a home, and a home remained first choice for both males and females, the percentages being 63.8 and 65.8 respectively. Although a car tended to be rated as second in value by both males and females, only a small percentage (26.7 males and 23.1 females) showed such interest, this conclusion being warranted by the data of table 7. Are the wants of Negroes thus different from those of other urban Americans? Is it possible for the needs and wants of Negroes as listed in table 7, to be satisfied by goods and services supplied by the Negro Main Street? Is one forced to secure certain desired consumer items from the street or is consumption a matter of personal choice? After one takes cognizance of these factors he is faced with the realization that Negro consumption, of whatever goods and services, is conditioned by factors over and above supply and demand. The most pertinent questions which arise at this point pertain to what is supplied by and actually consumed from the Negro Main Street itself.

Securing consumer items from the Negro Main Street is not so much a function of the nature of the consumer as a function of certain cultural trademarks. Likewise, the particular items of consumption available on the Main Street are by no means so unique as not to be found elsewhere, but the culture-brands placed on them are different. Inasmuch as the businesses located on the street represent to Negroes the better types of businesses, as will be shown subsequently, the goods and services they offer tend to be culturally of first-quality brands. But even these first-

TABLE 7

Items and Services Consumers Would Secure
If Money For Such Were Available,
By Number of Males and Females

Item or Service	First Choice Males	Females	Second Choice Males	Females
Bank or save	1	2	7	13
Business	4	2	2	6
Car	0	3	31	54
Church (give to)	0	2	1	3
Charity (give to)	1	3	2	5
Clothes	3	9	6	9
Education:				
For self	4	4	2	4
For children	1	2	6	20
Food	2	10	0	0
Home	74	154	2	9
Household items	1	8	3	21
Invest in bonds, etc.	0	2	10	11
More property	10	2	8	13
Pay bills	3	6	0	3
Provide for children				
and relatives	0	0	0	7
Remodel home	0	4	0	1
Travel	1	2	1	2
Miscellaneous	2	4	5	7
Don't want anything	0	1	1	1
Don't know what to buy	6	9	4	6
Unanswered	3	5	25	39
Total	116	234	116	234

quality brands are offered to consumers under the cultural trade marks of custom, law, occupational availability, and racial selection. Thus, the trademarks and brands take precedence over the consumer items themselves in labelling what can be secured on the street.

The trademark of custom, formulated out of the usage of discriminatory techniques discussed earlier, conditions the consumption of the greatest number of consumer items perhaps. Under this mark Negroes serve Negroes, and the goods they sell or services they render are in areas necessitating the most direct contact between customers. Consumer items in this category include the following: barbering and hairdressing; bury the dead by embalming, funerals, or burial association; concerts, lectures and institutes; dancing; debutante presentation; drug store services; fountain and lunch counter service; hotel, furnished room and boarding house accommodations; hospital service; insurance; legal counsel; medical and dental care; newspaper publication; notary and stenographic service; organizational membership—professional and social; real estate; recreation and entertainment; and office space for consultants performing public service.

One of the most significant things about these consumer items is that each has been offered, at one time or another, directly from the Negro Main Street, and the majority are still offered there though often duplicated elsewhere. A few variations are noteworthy, however. In the case of the presentation of debutantes, a private affair under private auspices, whether influenced by class-conscious motivations or white emulation, the Debutante Ball, like practically all significant innovations of Negroes, had its origin on the Main Street. It has become one of the big businesses sponsored by Negroes, net profits from which go toward scholarships for selected young women, one of the major economic emphases of social groups in the community. Though currently held outside the Main Street, its annually increased member participants relate it like any other item of consumption in a presumably free society to the Negro Main Street market. There has never been a hospital on the street but doctors with offices there have served to connect the two. Concerts, lectures, institutes, and dances are no longer held on the street, but the street is one of their chief avenues of advertisement. Even public dances sponsored by whites, though private and closed in dance-floor participation, maintain a consumer relationship to the street by always placing tickets there for sale to Negroes interested in spectator participation. Ambulance, embalming, funeral and burial association services and several successive newspapers all started

out on the street but have moved in recent years to other locations. The one weekly newspaper now published by Negroes is
primarily significant because of its coverage of "Negro society"
items. Many local functions of the paper are being rapidly replaced by the two dailies, published by whites, in which news
regarding achievements, leading events, programs, etc., of Negroes is continually covered; yet, the paper remains the chief
agent for communicating news of the Negro market to the Negro
world and thus retains its customary cultural trademark.

Another group of services and goods afforded by the Negro
Main Street is so implied or designated under the trademark of
law that if Negroes are to receive the benefits thereof then they
must be provided separate from whites. These embrace professional consultation in education and public welfare; eating and
drinking services; rest-room facilities; library accommodations
and services; fraternal or lodge membership and meetings. Although many of these are public services, they tend to be performed by and for Negroes in a manner similar to many privately
performed professional services. Making provision for them in the
midst of other available professional services is another way in
which the Negro Main Street has extended its list of items for
consumption.

Occupational availability is the trademark used for such items
as midwifery, baby-sitting, and domestic service. While midwifery
is becoming extinct and more and more difficult to secure, baby-
sitting is becoming more "professionalized" and less difficult to
secure. The fact that the only midwife and babysitters listed in
the 1951 city directory (the last year for which distinctions are
given between Negroes and whites) were Negroes means that
availability more than choice must condition the use thereof. Not
all domestic servants are Negro but the majority are, and these
are certainly the only ones available to Negroes. Neither of these
services is directly obtainable from the Main Street, but each
bears a consumer relationship thereto through its functions in
and for the Negro world.

Still another trademark which acts as a controlling force in the
consumption of items available on the Negro Main Street is that
of racial selection. This pertains to preferential selection of an
item from either Negroes or whites where both offer the same
goods or services for consumption though under different racial
circumstances. In some instances, for example, Negroes and

whites serve each other reciprocally, that is, both Negroes and whites offer the same items for consumption to both racial groups. Among the consumptive items that fall in this category on the Main Street are banking, dressmaking, fountain service, "without being seated," cleaning, pressing and tailoring, watch and jewelry repair and retail, hardware retail, and rental of space. On the other hand, some items made available by Negroes as specialty goods are carried by whites as convenience goods. These include Negro newspapers, cosmetics, hair oils, pressing irons for the hair, and such foods as pork chops and chitterlings. Then again, certain consumer items are made available to Negroes through Negro workers under all-white supervision. Such is the case on the street with the motion picture theater, one café, and two shoe shops. In this latter category two other services should be mentioned, namely: the selling of automobiles by one Negro who receives a commission therefrom, and radio broadcasting by another Negro whose job it is at specified hours of the day to handle

TABLE 8

Most Often Used Hargett Street Businesses,
By Number of Regular Users,
From Listings by 350 Respondents

Business	Number of Users	Per Cent of Users	Business	Number of Users	Per Cent of Users
Drug store	246	70.3	Lawyer	50	14.4
Doctor	175	50.0	Tailor	33	9.4
Bank	155	44.3	Beautician	21	6.0
Theater	138	39.4	Notary	12	3.4
Dentist	99	28.3	Photographer	12	3.4
Shoe shop	71	20.3	Justice of Peace	9	2.6
Hardware	70	20.0	Hotel	9	2.6
Barber	61	17.4	Jeweler	3	—
Café	56	16.0	Cleaner	2	—
Real Estate	52	14.8			

— Less than 1 per cent.

all matters of special interest to Negroes. These last items, though not directly connected with the Main Street, so encompass the entire Negro world that they automatically include the street.

These are the consumable items one finds so characteristic of the Negro Main Street, but the question is to what extent do Negroes actually use them?

Whether consumer wants or needs of Negroes can be satisfied through Negro Main Street businesses or not, the fact is that not all Negroes are inclined to secure goods or services from the street. But the fact that the vast majority of Negroes frequent the street and secure some item there at stated intervals is indicative of the function of the street as a reflector of consumer behavior. The nature of the street as a complementary one for consumers generally, but a primary one for a racial group against which discrimination in certain businesses is directed, may explain the patronage of some businesses more than others. By far the most extensively patronized business on the street, based upon the 70.3 percent of consumers listing usage thereof, tends to be the drug store whose consumer items include fountain and lunch counter service along with others. Fewer individual patrons, but similar patronage patterns, are shown in the 50.0 percent listing usage of the Main Street doctor, the 44.3 percent using the bank, and the 39.4 percent using the motion picture theater. The relative frequency with which the Negro Main Street businesses are used can be gleaned from table 8.

The above listings are by no means indicative of total usage of these or other businesses on the street, but of those most frequently used by specified numbers of persons. In the case of insurance, for example, usage is by no means correlated with frequenting of the street for this purpose since the majority of those using the business do so directly from their homes. One has but to stand for hours and observe and count the number of entrants into many of these businesses, as the writer has done on numerous days and at different hours, to realize that at least one-tenth of the passers during any one hour enter the drug store.

Such observation poses a question as to whether or not certain patterns of consumption might not be identified with the Negro Main Street in terms of frequency and regularity with which one trades there. The many window-shoppers coaxed by proprietors into the second-hand clothing store, girls from nearby towns attending movies between work and scheduled-bus hours, lines of children waiting for the movies to open on Saturday morning, country people going repeatedly into the same eating places, crowds streaming through the street on Saturday, the quietness of the street on Sunday, and the sudden emptiness of the street at varied intervals during the week—these are but indicative of some of the rhythm obtained in patterns of consumption on the street.

One of the first patterns that shows up is that Negroes tend to

TABLE 9

Frequency of Trading on the Negro Main Street,
By Time Periods and By Sex

Time Period	Number of Times	Number of Persons		Total
		Males	Females	
Per Week	1	26	80	106
	2	18	29	47
	3	19	7	26
	4	3	2	5
	5	1	6	7
	6	3	3	6
	7	14	5	19
Per Month	1	5	28	33
	2	7	13	20
	3	1	7	8
	4	2	1	3
	7	0	1	1
Per Quarter	1	1	8	9
	2	1	0	1
Per Year	1	1	5	6
	2	0	1	1
	3	1	0	1
	5	0	1	1
	7	1	0	1
	0	0	1	1
	9	0	1	1
Don't Know	—	2	0	2
Unanswered	—	10	35	45
Totals		116	234	350

be weekly traders on the Main Street, 2.3 times a week being the average for weekly patronage. Of the 216 persons giving weekly frequencies of trading, 38.9 percent are males and 61.1 percent females, yet the weekly frequency of trading by males exceeds that of females, averaging 3.0 times for males and 1.9 times for females. Individuals who trade on the street only a few times a month, quarter, or year are far fewer than those who trade weekly, a complete list of which is presented in table 9.

Unlike the shoppers of Beale Street whose cycle of mobility O'Brien found characterized by sharp contrasts and complete shifts in shopper-personnel, more regularity of patronage by the

TABLE 10

*Number of Persons Trading on the Main Street,
By Preferred Day and Part of Day*

Specified Day	Preferred Part of Day				Total
	Morning	Afternoon	Evening	Any Time	
Any Day	—	—	—	134	134
All Days	—	1	—	15	16
Special Days	—	—	—	—	—
Sunday	—	3	—	—	3
Monday	24	4	1	4	33
Tuesday	1	3	1	—	5
Wednesday	7	3	—	—	10
Thursday	1	1	—	—	2
Friday	18	12	4	3	37
Saturday	21	7	1	9	38
Two or more days					
Friday and Saturday	3	2	—	2	7
Others	2	2	—	23	27
None given as preferred	—	—	—	38	38
Total	77	38	7	228	350

same patronizing group tends to obtain on the Main Street. Beale Street is portrayed as one of Negro shoppers six days a week, white burlesque-seekers on Thursday night, farm hands during the day on Saturday, and cooks, maids, and factory-hands on Saturday nights.[5] Although both racial groups and all economic groups of Negroes are known to secure goods or services from

[5] Robert W. O'Brien, "Beale Street, A Study in Ecological Succession," *Sociology and Social Research* (May-June, 1942), Vol. XXVI, p. 434.

the Main Street depicted in this study, no such differences in time of securing these seems to exist as on Beale Street. One explanation may lie in the very nature of race relations, but most pertinent perhaps are the types of institutions on the street, location of the street, and motives of consumers.

Despite this weekly trading pattern, however, it can be seen from table 10 that, for the most part, those who use the Negro Main Street had just as soon go there at one time of the day as at another. Some 22.0 percent prefer going there in the morning, and 10.8 percent in the afternoon, but 65.1 percent have no preferred time for going. At the same time 250, or 71.4 percent, indicate no day or part of the day they are interested in avoiding the street when it comes to trading there. Some few, 9.1 percent, tend to avoid the street on Saturday but such a small group is hardly sufficient to make this avoidance pattern evident. The very negligible number of persons either preferring or avoiding patronage on the street in the evening attests to the inutility of the street as a night spot. Its consumer items are those used primarily by a day population, the largest night-consumer group appearing there on Monday and Thursday evenings in search of jack-pot fortunes at the motion picture theater where one has to be present to win.

But who are the consumers of whom such patterned behavior is descriptive? One of the first things to note is that the majority of Negroes tend to secure some item or service from the street at one time or another. Within the sample population only 43 (12.3 percent) persons consider themselves non-traders, while 307 (87.7 percent) are traders there. The social characteristics of these traders are made evident in the factors of sex, age, marital status, and occupation. Chi Square tests reveal that sex, age, marital status, and occupation tend to be more significantly related to trading on the street than do educational status, income, and length of residence in the community.

An observed Chi Square of 2.16, significant at the ten percent level, shows a degree of relationship between sex and trading on the Main Street. Numerically Negro Main Street traders tend to be females, but proportionally they are males. Of the 307 persons indicating that they trade on the street, for example, 65.5 percent are females and 34.5 percent males. However, 91.4 percent of the 116 males tend to be Main Street traders as opposed to 85.9 percent of the 234 females. Thus, while numerical count tends to reveal the street as one of female consumers, when proportional consumption is considered it becomes a market for slightly more males than females. The numerical excess of females is perhaps in line with what might be expected for a population such as that of Raleigh, whose 1950 census calculations show its nonwhite population to be 53.2 percent female and 46.8 percent male.

When the 340 traders and non-traders whose age groups are given are classified into categories of under 21, 21-30, 31-40, 41-50, 51-60, 61 and over, and a Chi Square test applied thereto a significant relationship is found to exist between age and trading on the Main Street. An observed Chi Square of 11.5 shows significance at the two and one-half percent level. One of the most readily ascertained facts about the street is that, while it is constructed for adult patronage, the male traders tend to be older than the female. Slightly more than one-half of the traders (52.2 percent) range between the ages of 21 and 40. Among the female traders 56.8 percent are in the age group 21-40, while among the males the bulk of traders, 52.4 percent, are 41 and over. While the proportion of female traders aged 21-30 is far in excess of the males, females of this group comprising 31.8 percent and males 16.2 percent, the proportion of males 61 and over is far in excess of females, being 18.1 percent for males and 9.4 percent for females. The group under 21 comprises only a small percentage (4.7) of Negro Main Street traders, thus making the street characteristically one of relatively young women and older men.

A Chi Square test reveals again that a relationship exists between marital status and trading on the Main Street. In this instance an observed frequency of 10.9 shows significance at the 1.0 percent level. Although a larger percentage of the male traders (77.4) tends to be married than the female (58.7), more than twice as many female traders (20.4) tend to be widowed as males (8.5), thus making the total married male trading group only 1.7 percent less than the total of married and widowed female traders combined (79.1). The distribution of Negro Main Street traders by age, sex, and marital status, shown in table 11, helps account for the labeling of the street as one of relatively young women, older men, and an excess of married men. This is not to say that single persons are completely absent from the street but that they are a numerical minority, the very nature of the street being partial explanation therefor.

Negro Main Street traders include those in non-worker categories, as well as those whose occupations are of a professional, skilled, or unskilled nature. An observed Chi Square of 11.3, significant at the one percent level, is indicative of a definite relationship between one's occupation and his trading on the street. Subsuming the 349 given occupations under the classifications noted in table 12 Negro Main Street patrons are seen to be

TABLE 11

Number of Traders on the Negro Main Street
By Age, Sex, and Marital Status

| Age Group | Male | | | | Female | | | | Total | Per Cent of Total |
	S	M	W	D	S	M	W	D		
Under 12	3	1	0	0	5	4	0	1	14	4.6
21-30	6	11	0	0	19	35	5	2	78	25.4
31-40	1	24	3	1	3	40	4	1	77	25.1
41-50	3	20	0	0	4	19	7	3	56	18.2
51-60	0	12	1	0	0	10	12	0	35	11.4
61-70	1	10	4	0	3	2	10	0	30	9.8
71 & Over	0	3	1	0	0	0	3	0	7	2.3
Age Not Given	0	1	0	0	1	8	0	0	10	3.2
Total	14	82	9	1	35	118	14	7	307	100.0

S — Single
M — Married
W — Widowed
D — Divorced

predominantly working people, with the unskilled group (35.8) comprising the largest percentage. Ranking second with regard to main street trading is the non-working group (31.9), the majority of whom are housewives. The very small size of the main street trader group which is unemployed, 10.2 of the non-workers, is not only symbolic of the middle class status of the community in which people are generally employed, but also of the character of the street. Although the street may perform many functions for a non-worker group, its "main stem" characteristics do not lend themselves to the imputed meaning that the "Bowery" has for the bum, or "Hobohemia" for the hobo, the real significance of which is taken up in the next chapter. Even though the non-trading group as a whole is small, it is interesting to note that the occupational group that does not trade on the street consists primarily of non-workers (57.1 percent), housewives again ranking first as non-traders and the unemployed second.

TABLE 12

Negro Main Street Traders and Non-Traders
By Occupational Group

Occupational Group	Number of Traders	Number of Non-traders	Total
Professional and Semi-prof.			
Barbers & beauticians	6	0	6
Dental technicians	1	0	1
Funeral directors	1	0	1
Lawyers	2	0	2
Musicians	1	0	1
Nurses and nurse aids	10	1	11
Physicians	2	0	2
Postmen and mail clerks	2	0	2
Preachers	2	0	2
Secretaries and clerks	6	0	6
Students	5	0	5
Teachers and principals	19	2	21
Skilled and Semi-skilled			
Auto mechanics	1	0	1
Bakers	3	0	3
Contractors	14	1	15
Gardeners	1	0	1
Launderers, cleaners, tailors	6	1	7
Managers of business	8	1	9
Railroad workmen	2	0	2
Taxi and draymen	5	0	5
Waiters	2	0	2
Unskilled			
Dishwashers	2	0	2
Domestic workers	73	9	82
Doormen and bellhops	3	0	3
Janitors and laborers	32	3	35
Non-workers			
Housewives	79	12	91
Retired persons	9	2	11
Unemployed	10	10	20
Occupation not given	0	1	1
Total	307	43	350

The percentage of Main Street traders whose work is of a professional or semi-professional nature (18.6) tends to be much smaller than the unskilled which makes up 35.8 of the traders and larger than the skilled and semi-skilled group (13.7). Exactly one-third of the professional group trading on the street consists singularly of teachers and principals, but it is this very group against which Negro businessmen direct their complaints about failure to secure representative patronage for their businesses. Exemplary of this complaint is the statement of a Main Street businessman who says:

. . . It (the Credit Union) hasn't done too well up to now. . . There's been no confidence in it on the part of the professional group because of their experience with the Co-op. We don't have but two groups here much, because there's no industry, and that's the teachers and common laborers. One group can buy stock but won't, and the other can't afford to buy. . . Look at the Gastonia Credit Union, it's one of the best Negroes have, started with $139.00 and now doing a million dollar business. WOY took out $5,000 worth of stock in it, just think what that would have meant to the Raleigh Credit Union. Raleigh people need to wake up.[6]

Interestingly enough, businesses listed by traders in the professional group as most often used on the Main Street are the drug store and bank. In only one instance is the motion picture theater listed as most often used. In no other occupational group are personal values and attitudes so immediately discernible. The large number of these persons encountered regularly in the bank and drug store attests to conscious efforts to patronize some types of Negro businesses and avoid others. Passing-by-but-never-entering the theater is just as obvious as the socialize-while-you-eat pattern at the drug store. Whatever the individual reasons for not patronizing the theater, the statement of a sign-painter as he worked suggests the nature of consumption of the group as conditioned by its values and attitudes:

I do this work for them (paint the signs) but don't go in often, see too many good pictures on TV. Sometimes I register for the jack-pot. Don't like to go there much, children are so noisy and popcorn all over the floor—that's what makes rats so bad; not as

6 Personal document.

many rats as used to be since they cleaned the place up. Seemingly they have no control over the decorum in there, let you do 'bout like you please; find more lower class people here, middle class go to the Ambassador, Mr. D has better control up there so you get less noise. Week-ends when country people come in and go to the movies they chew tobacco and dip snuff and spit right on the floor. So you see why I don't go.[7]

Negro Main Street consumption as it relates to occupational groups seems thus to be tied in with attitudes and ideologies, a fuller discussion of which will come in a later chapter.

Wide variation obtains in the monthly incomes of the 294 main street traders whose income categories are designated, ranging from $1.00 to $99 for some 14.3 percent of the traders to $600 and over for some 4.1 percent. The great majority of Negro Main Street traders, however, have neither such small nor such large monthly incomes but belong to the groups ranging from $100-199 for some 24.5 percent to $200-399 for some 42.9 percent, and $400-599 for some 13.6 percent. A median monthly income of $252.14 for Negro Main Street traders is no doubt reflected in the kinds of businesses and services offered or secured from the street, but while income may produce some effect thereon it is by no means a determinant of trading on the street.

According to 1950 census data the median school years completed for persons 25 years old and over in the total Raleigh community is 11.2, while that for the comparable non-white group is 7.6. Although no significant relationship is found to exist between educational attainment and trading on the Main Street, it is worthy of note that the median of 9.6 years of school completed by Negro Main Street traders is neither as high as that for the community as a whole, nor as low as that for non-whites as a whole. Nor is this contrary to expectations for a community with two colleges, a beauty school, barber college, and secretarial school for Negroes, aside from the public elementary and secondary schools. But, while differences in educational status exist, these are not especially manifest in Negro Main Street consumer patterns. Of the 296 traders giving years of school completed, not even the 63.9 percent having completed grades 8-12, nor the 10.8 percent of college and above, makes sufficient observable imprint

[7] Personal document.

on the street for the 34.1 percent of non-traders with 1-7th grade
education, or the 17.1 percent with no grade completed, to be
detected as absent from consumer groups.

Negro Main Street traders tend to be predominantly non-native
to the community, but their movement to the community is by no
means so recent as to reflect any revolutionary change in the nature of consumer behavior on the street. Of the 295 traders indicating length of residence in the city, 60.3 percent are non-
native as compared with 39.7 percent born there. Among the non-
native group 53.4 percent have lived in the community from one
to nineteen years, while 46.6 percent have lived there twenty
years or more. The median length of residence in the city of non-
natives is 16.4 years. When this factor is viewed against the fact
that those who moved into the city as much as 16-20 years ago
did so when the city was setting upon its rapid-growth period, it
would certainly seem to have implications for Negro Main Street
patronage. Whatever the effect produced upon the street by
migrants during the 1930 and 1940 decades, however, it made
no noticeable change in the nature of the street and its businesses.
Whether one migrated from a rural area or an urban one has
appeared to have little effect upon his trading on the Negro Main
Street, though the 55.5 percent of persons migrating from rural
areas is slightly higher than the 44.5 percent migrating from
urban areas. An apparent tie-in here may be a factor mentioned
earlier regarding patterns of trading on the Main Street, that of
preferential days for trading. One of the comments most often
heard in the community regarding Negro Main Street trading
pertains to avoidance of the street on Saturday because of the
prevalence of rural people there on that day. But since the actual
pattern of avoidance fails to coincide with the verbalized reasons
for desiring such, the original rural background of these now
urban residents might well be one of the factors related thereto.
Most noticeable regarding their relationship to the Main Street
is that the tendency to trade or not trade on the street is just as
prevalent among those native to the community as those non-
native. While 94.4 percent of those having lived in the community all their lives tend to trade on the street, 83.6 percent of
those who migrated there trade on the street. Among the non-
trading group 16.4 percent are migrant, while 5.6 percent are
native. The difference of 10.8 percent which obtains between
traders who are native-born and those who are migrant also ob-

tains between non-traders in the same migrant and native groups, thus showing an equal tendency among the groups of migrants and natives to use or not use the street.

Such characterizations as these pose a question as to the factors motivating Negro Main Street traders to patronize the business and service institutions located there. Since their consumer wants and needs seem to be similar to those of other Americans, and the items consumed through the Negro Main Street of a non-specialized type requiring no economic connoisseurs, explanation of the motivational forces must be sought in non-economic realms. Accepting the social psychologist's definition of motives as "habits built up in the individual through early and constant exposure to social and cultural values and expectancies," [8] and recalling that discrimination has been the principal social value conditioning development of Negro Main Street institutions, it can be readily assumed that discriminatory bans and or sanctions arising out of the culture matrix have given directional orientation to the motives for trading on the street. Thus, when 67.4 percent of those who trade on the street specify that they do so just to patronize Negroes, and an additional 20.5 percent feel it their duty to patronize the Negro businesses there, racial and moral considerations tend to form the motivational basis out of which Negro Main Street behavior is patterned. And since consumer lines of action, operating under culturally accepted values, help explain the meaning of the social definition "Negro Main Street," then consumer motives help impel the racial pattern of the community. The racial connotation of these motives becomes all the more important when giving a functional explanation of culture, as does Lynd, viewing the whole as "the patterned habits of behavior of individuals," [9] and realizing that "the pattern is what it is because of the rhythms, motivations, and processes of growth and learning of the dynamic individual creators and carriers of culture struggling fiercely to feel 'at home' with themselves and others in their world." [10] Desiring "to feel 'at home' with themselves and others in their world" is no doubt what prompts some 87.9 percent of the Negro Main Street traders to patronize busi-

[8] Hubert Bonner, *Social Psychology* (New York: American Book Co., 1953), p. 148.

[9] Robert S. Lynd, *Knowledge for What?* (Princeton: Princeton University Press, 1939), p. 37.

[10] *Ibid.*, p. 49.

nesses on the street just because they are Negro businesses and
to feel obligated to patronize them.

It must not be assumed, however, that these factors are equally
important to all Negroes. A composite list of reasons given as
first and second in importance to the person in his trading on the
main street can be noted in table 13. Despite the many devious
reasons given, the racial ones tend to remain dominant even in
the face of such factors as inconvenient location mentioned by
some, or the expensive, inferior, sameness of items mentioned by
others. And if the percentage of those trading on the Main Street
because of its racial identification is any index of the way Negroes
have internalized race relations in the business world, then few
can be categorized with the non-trader who said, "I don't use
nigger business none 'tall 'cause I ain't never been taught to use
'em." [11]

TABLE 13

Principal Reasons For Trading On the Main Street, By Rank in Importance, By Number of Persons

Reasons for Trading	Rank in Importance	Number of Persons	Rank in Importance	Number of Persons
To patronize Negroes	1	207	2	43
Feel it my duty to use them	1	63	2	139
Convenient location	1	7	2	24
Satisfactory service	1	6	2	11
Courteous operators	1	4	2	11
Easy to get credit	1	4	2	4
Open late	1	4	2	7
Friendly operators	1	3	2	13
Less expensive	1	3	2	7
Like trading with Negroes	1	2	2	13
Wide variety of goods	1	1	2	3
Absence of loiterers	1	1	2	1
They know me personally	1	1	2	0
Places not crowded	1	0	2	1
All reasons	1	1	2	0
Not given	1	43	2	73

[11] Personal document.

Only a small number of Negro Main Street traders indicates that the business personnel knows them personally. The majority describe their relationships with Main Street personnel as of a business nature only. This would tend to suggest that the same type of impersonality which obtains in business generally is characteristic of Negro business. To the extent that impersonal, business-like relationships are sustained between customers and business personnel, then it appears that maintaining personal identification through social relationships between shoppers and retail store personnel, as Stone proposed,[12] is certainly non-existent on the Main Street. But when the forms of trading relationships are seen in the light of social motivations and personal traits for which consumers look in those with whom they trade an apparent equilibrium is developed. A question arises as to whether or not these desired traits are presumed to exist in the Negroes with whom Main Streeters trade. Of the traits listed as desired in those with whom they trade, for example, some 84.6 percent of the traders designate being nice, kind, friendly, pleasing in personality, courteous, polite, respectful, fair, honest, reliable, dependable, business-like, efficient, appreciative, cooperative, and interested in the customer. At the same time, the majority of those indicating that they patronize Negro businesses in other parts of the city, as well as on the Main Street, name the following as things liked most about them: 1) Their being colored; 2) Services rendered; and 3) Treatment received. And again, "being colored" ranks first. Thus, Negro consumer behavior, in a culture where racial identity is continually re-emphasized, seems to constantly evoke a conscious awareness of an existing Negro business world that is functionally marginal to a larger social world in which discrimination serves as the directional orientation for Negro-white relationships. The nature of linkage between these two worlds is not only reflected in the dichotomized pattern of relationships embracing the Negro Main Street as a complementary one for consumers, but also in the social significance that derives from the use of the street from a spatial standpoint. How the Negro Main Street as a spatial area relates to the sociocultural requires consideration within the Negro business world context also, hence the occupation in the next chapter with the influence of spatiality upon the street.

[12] Gregory P. Stone, "City Shoppers and Urban Identification: Observations on the Social Psychology of City Life," *American Journal of Sociology* (July, 1954), Vol. LX, pp. 36-45.

Chapter 6

Negro Main Street and Usage In
Relation to Spatial Arrangements

HUMAN ecologists seem generally agreed that a city tends to develop a spatial pattern through which relationships exist between groups, institutions, and the areas in which they locate. Much of the emphasis on relationships between these, however, has been portrayed in terms of structural adaptations and adjustments forming under the impact of ecological processes. It is the contention of this chapter that the structural factors are of little import except for the social significance derived from the functional use thereof. The real clues to a city's spatial pattern seem to lie in the functional relationships issuing from the use of space, conditioned by social definitions arising out of the culture matrix. The selective use of a specific area by a particular group tends to make for homogeneity of attributes which characterize and give social meaning to those who do not use it, as well as those who do. Attributes of the Negro Main Street make it distinct as a spatial area, used primarily but not exclusively by one racial group, and particularly attractive to numerous intra-racial groups within the environs thereof.

Numerous ecological studies have shown rather conclusively how the spatial patterns of intra-urban areas develop. Any spatial pattern which grows out of the way man relates to his environment is admittedly of some import, but more socially significant perhaps are the factors that emanate from the functional and structural interrelationships that characterize the spatial pattern. It is not spatial patterning per se that ties the hobo to "Hobohemia," but the fact that this homeless-man area with its specialized institutions of cheap hotels, flop-houses, restaurants, and movies has become the exclusive province of transient patrons whose social relationships forbid delving into their private lives.[1] The residential area of Chicago whose characteristic institution is the rooming house would carry little distinct meaning except for the young men and women, usually white-collar employees, whose temporary patronage of the rooming houses is found

[1] Nels Anderson, *The Hobo* (Chicago: University of Chicago Press, 1923).

geared to anonymous and impersonal relationships.[2] The compact space in which high income groups live along the lake front in Chicago would hardly have become the "Gold Coast" except for its resident economic and social elites whose need for frequent and elaborate entertainment has made exclusive clubs and fashionable hotels the characteristic attributes of the area.[3] Nor would the 47th Street business nucleus of "Bronzeville", with its Negro-operated businesses, carry many of its minority group distinctions were it not for its closed-market appeal to Negroes' race pride for patronage.[4]

Each of these areas is, in a manner of speaking, a "main stem" within the metropolis, a spatial sub-area with its own socio-cultural attributes, each used by a special local group. All of the areas alluded to are located within one large metropolis. A smaller urban area with a less heterogeneous population and perhaps different types of social groups could be expected to not only have fewer main stems, but also less specialized, though distinctive, institutions, and to perform different functions for its main-stem groups. Such is the case in the Southern urban community where racial factors condition the chief attributes of its main stems, one of which is the Negro Main Street.

Any explanation of the location and use of the spatial area designated as the Negro Main Street must be necessarily related to the spatial distribution of the population. Although the group life of the Negro tends to be dispersed through several sub-areas, it tends also to become functionally centralized through its focus upon the separation existing between the Negro and white worlds. It is this factor of which the Negro Main Street is symbolic and which must be seen in relation to the use as well as location of the street.

If there is any one ecological theory which appears most applicable to the development of the Negro Main Street it is Quinn's hypothesis of median location. One of the basic assumptions upon which this hypothesis rests is that "the ecological unit which occupies a position in any areal order may be a) a single living organism, b) a group which produces or consumes as a unit, or

[2] Harvey Zorbaugh, *The Gold Coast and the Slum* (Chicago: University of Chicago Press, 1929).

[3] *Ibid.*

[4] St. Clair Drake and Horace R. Cayton, *Black Metropolis* (New York: Harcourt, Brace and Company, 1945).

c) any specialized function that occupies a spatial location of its own." [5] With this assumption posited, the hypothesis states that "within a free competitive system, social and aesthetic factors being equal, a mobile ecological unit tends to occupy a median location with respect to 1) the environmental resources it utilizes, 2) the other units on which it depends, and 3) the other units that it serves." [6] Measuring the tendency toward minimum ecological distance in terms of costs of movement from one location to another, the median is designated as that place within an area where one half of the spatially distributed units are on each side of it. Without using specific cost or distance techniques of measurement, the Negro Main Street can be assumed to be located at the median of the Negro world because of its centralization near the heart of the downtown area and the fact that equivalent distances have to be traversed by all to reach the street. Since Raleigh has neither census tracts nor official wards, and since Negroes live in many individual blocks scattered throughout the city, any attempt to specify the number of Negroes living on each side of the median would necessarily be inaccurate. However, a descriptive portrayal of the spatial distribution of the Negro population may help in visualizing the Main Street as being located at the median.

Frazier has pointed out that the locational patterns of Negro communities in large cities of the South are of two types, namely: 1) A widely scattered Negro population, with small Negro settlements composed mainly of servants having developed close to the whites whom the Negroes served; and 2) Several large concentrations of Negroes with the remainder of the Negro population scattered lightly over a large area. [7] The former pattern he mentions as being characteristic of the old cities of the South, and thus unaffected by the economic forces that have helped pattern the latter type communities of modern industrial and commercial cities. The first of these is referred to by many writers as the "back-yard pattern"; the second is representative of what Johnson alludes to as the "urban cluster" pattern, although he described the Southern city as having one large cluster of Negroes and

---

[5] James A. Quinn, "Hypothesis of Median Location," *American Sociological Review* (April, 1943), Vol VIII, p. 148.

[6] ————, *Human Ecology* (New York: Prentice Hall, Inc., 1950), p. 286.

[7] E. Franklin Frazier, *The Negro in the United States*, (rev. ed.; New York: Macmillan Co., 1957), p. 237.

several smaller ones.[8] The pattern of residential segregation in Raleigh is perhaps typically of the "urban cluster" type, but the clustering is not nearly so complete as that seen in many other cities of the South. Moving outward from Capitol Square, the center of the city, one finds the most concentrated cluster of Negroes in the southern part of the city, and the next largest cluster in the eastern part, with smaller clusters residing in the north and west of the city, as figure 5 will indicate. Outside of the highly clustered sections to the south and east there is not even complete segregation by blocks in many instances, for whites and Negroes are often not only block neighbors living on different sides of the street but on the same side. Nor is this a newly developed pattern. The more recent pattern is the solidly clustered Negro area containing no white residents, which is gradually becoming more and more obvious.

The origin of the two most highly concentrated Negro areas of the city, the south and east, like the Negro Main Street itself, was markedly influenced by one of the principal factors already mentioned as affecting the nature of race relations in the city, namely, its unique educational development. Some of the leading white families of the city lived originally in the southern section right beside Negroes. Erecting Shaw University in this area in 1870, and fronting it on South Street, just six blocks from the center of the city, was no doubt one influencing factor in making this a Negro area. Even more influential, however, is the fact that the American Missionary Society of New York "purchased a tract of land south of South Street and sold lots to the colored people of the town," and established there for Negroes in 1869 the Lincoln School from which the Washington School grew.[9] The second largest Negro section developed in the east around the Normal and Collegiate Institute which became St. Augustine's College, erected on the plantation originally owned by Willie Jones, one of the founding fathers of the city.[10] Just as the originally mixed areas of Negroes and whites have gradually been changed to all-Negro areas, so competition for space has

[8] Charles S. Johnson, *Patterns of Negro Segregation* (New York: Harper and Brothers, 1943), p. 10.

[9] Writers' Program of the WPA in North Carolina, *Raleigh, Capital of North Carolina,* Raleigh Sesquicentennial Commission, 1942, p. 58.

[10] Moses N. Amis, *Historical Raleigh* (Raleigh: Edwards and Broughton, 1902), p. 23.

forced the originally all-Negro area of the west, Oberlin, to gradually become mixed with whites. And the majority of these changes, like the Jim-Crow laws freezing the color line, are of

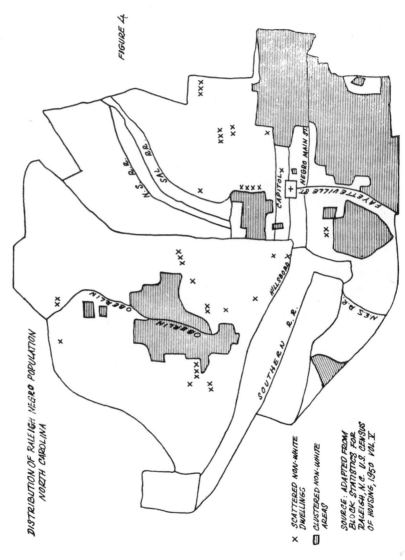

FIGURE 4

DISTRIBUTION OF RALEIGH NEGRO POPULATION
NORTH CAROLINA

× SCATTERED NON-WHITE
   DWELLINGS

▩ CLUSTERED NON-WHITE
   AREAS

SOURCE: ADAPTED FROM
BLOCK STATISTICS FOR
RALEIGH, N.C. U.S. CENSUS
OF HOUSING, 1950 VOL. II

twentieth century origin, validation for which is given thus by residents:

When it came to where people lived, Negroes and whites bought and lived in the same areas. Wherever they saw land they wanted and could pay for they got it. When our house was built here on West Street most of the other side was vacant and nothing but swamp land filled with trees. For miles away we could see nothing but trees. All this property has been built in here since we have been here, and all of our early neighbors were white. As late as 1899 whites were still living in here. This has become a thick Negro area in more recent years.[11]

We moved to Hungry Neck about 1879, that was the area where colored lived on the other side of Newbern going down the hill from the Capitol. After that we moved out to Oberlin. . . Oberlin used to be a colored community, just in recent years that the white folks have moved out there. There were whites around on the outskirts of it back then but they were poor whites. We had colored grocery dealers and everything right out there, and we lived fairly well. . .[12]

. . . We've always had a large group of Negroes living in the east and south of the city. Out here in Oberlin we had just a few scattered houses, stores, church, and a school. Everything out here was Negro and because of that nobody bothered about us, the city wouldn't even fix up the streets or give us lights or anything else. I tried to get Dr. P and several others to move out here a long time ago but they wouldn't, they said they didn't want to move out to the country. Now this is the most valuable property in town and if you don't already own you can't even buy out here. . .[13]

Negroes used to be able to buy or rent anywhere until whites rooted them out. The white folks tried to die when that property on Newbern Avenue was sold to Negroes, but the man who owned it said if Negroes wanted it he was going to sell to them. After all the Catholic church was right there and it was a good location. Negroes used to own a lot of property all over but many of them sold when whites offered them fancy prices for it. I remember when the property in Hayes-Barton-Glenwood section was $5.00 an acre. We were born and reared right out there on Tucker Street. My father was a Tucker and the first to buy and live there. He used to say that some day that would be the most

[11] Personal interview: Retired Negro female school teacher.
[12] Personal interview: Retired Negro chef.
[13] Personal interview: Negro orderly at Rex Hospital.

exclusive section in town and the richest, and sure enough he was right.[14]

. . . The old Fraps Building, Old Alfred Williams estate. Old Harris homestead (Colonel J. C. Harris), all had residences around the Fayetteville Street area. The Daniels homestead joined ours, some of the property I have now my father acquired from some of these old estates. This whole area used to be mixed, but more whites than colored lived here. The old Wilton estate, Milton Brown estate, Pepper place, old Bagley home, and all that property where Shaw's houses are—all these were whites. The poor whites lived back down Fayetteville Street. These old families had to send their children right along with the poor whites to the Centennial School there where the city auditorium is now. South St. from Blount to Person was practically all white too. And that hasn't been more than thirty-five or forty years ago. . .[15]

Negroes are living about as they have always lived, all over Raleigh. They have never been in Hayes-Barton or Longview Gardens but have otherwise lived anywhere they could buy. There has never been any objection it seems to their living anywhere they choose.[16]

The very nature of the spatial patterning of Negro residences in the city in relation to the location of the Negro Main Street offers sufficient reason for applying the theory of median location here. One might ask if this is likewise the median for all classes of Negroes, which makes it feasible to mention another locational factor. Here the situation reverses itself for Negroes from what it is for whites, and that is, no specifically differentiated class areas exist for Negroes. Thus, even the most upper class Negro may find himself living beside a lower class one, class in this instance being less contingent upon economic factors than upon educational, moral, and social values. Here again the authentic statements of a resident are most illuminating. Says he,

One thing Negroes in Raleigh don't have is any residential area where the upper crust lives. About twenty-five years ago a man came to me and said he was moving his business here and wanted a place to live. I told him then there were plenty places to live and a whole lot of living space to build if he wanted to, and he said, 'But I want to be with the better class of Negroes.' I told him

[14] Personal Interview: Negro female non-worker.
[15] Personal interview: Negro female non-worker.
[16] Personal interview: Retired Negro mail carrier.

then there was no area where nothing but the upper-crust lived. And the same thing holds today, though they are trying to make a better class area out in the Rochester Heights Development. The thing about Negroes is that the dirtiest, nastiest laborer can buy out the better folks. I had a man who was trying to make arrangements for some housing and he had to have $2,000. I tried to help him get it, he couldn't get it from the bank, and was talking to just a common ordinary working man who looked as though he had never seen a bathtub, and he told me to come to his house the next day and he'd let me have the money. I went, he lived in an old dilapidated shack but pulled out a paper bag from under the bed and counted out $2,000 and told me I could fix up the business angle about its being repaid. This type person sends his children off to school just like the better ones do, only thing is you seldom know how they live because they don't take their friends home with them.[17]

Although it seems to be the general consensus of Negroes that no residential area can be designated according to class, conceptions are often held regarding the spatial distribution of "certain types" of persons from an individual standpoint. As a carry-over from an earlier period when the city was divided into wards, many still distinguish between third and fourth-ward residents in terms of overt behavior differences, but the change of the former third ward from a residential to a sub-business area makes this distinction of little current value. Pointing up this change one resident remarked:

. . . If you were respectful at all you'd go to Hargett St. but never go through Third Ward to get there. Anything would happen to you in Third Ward. Now you have a different area in there, a small business area where there once was nothing but houses. . .[18]

This seems to suggest that only "the respectful" used the Main Street at one time and that the respectful lived in specific areas. Similar conceptions are still prevalent but more frequently connected with other areas, as can be gathered from the characterizations of such areas as Smoky Hollow and Joe Louis Park in one instance, Stony Hill and The Line in another, and Washington Terrace, Lincoln Park and Rochester Heights in still an-

[17] Personal interview: Negro Justice of the Peace and real-estate agent.
[18] Personal interview: Negro taxicab driver.

other. Even though the uses of these spatial areas give no evidence of the clustering of such groups as the professional or power leaders which Hunter located in "Regional City",[19] certain other clusterings are suggested. The names of the areas themselves imply specific types of residents, but to those who live within them their primary meaning reverts to being just a residential section for Negroes, though not without variations in material accommodations. Situated in different parts of the city, all of these sub-areas are relatively equidistant from the Negro Main Street when transportation is considered, and residents from all are included in the Main-Street-trader group.

The city of Raleigh is divided into seven classes of districts, namely: 1) Office and institution; 2) Business; 3) Neighborhood business; 4) Industrial; 5) Shopping center; 6) Buffer community; and 7) Residential.[20] Unlike similar streets of numerous other urban areas of the South, Raleigh's Negro Main Street is situated in the business district rather than a Negro residential area. If natural barriers, specifically "Moore's Square" or "Baptist Grove" (a city park), did not prevent its growth on the east it might eventually extend itself and obtain closer proximity to the community several blocks away which is being rapidly invaded by Negroes. But since this is not possible, it appears that the street can be expected to maintain its median location and remain a gateway or thoroughfare to, though not immediately adjoining, the two largest spatial clusterings of Negroes, the relationships of which were pointed out in figure 5. Since transportation routes make it equally as accessible to those residing to the north or west as to the south or east, retaining this locational position may be of signal value in its survival.

Among the values exemplified by the median location of the street is its proximity to the major business street and key institutions of the city as a whole. Adjoining and crosscutting the city's principal business street, the Negro Main Street is within a block of the state capitol, city market, and the largest local Negro church; at its functionally-terminal point on the northeast is a large chain grocery store, and on the southeast a city park; just off the street going south stands the public library for Negroes, and adjoining the street on the southwest is a street of resale and

[19] Floyd Hunter, *Community Power Structure* (Chapel Hill: University of North Carolina Press, 1953).

[20] *City Code*, Raleigh, North Carolina, Ordinance 419.

pawn shops, cheap clothing and household goods stores. Thus, the convenient location of the street and its easy access to the varied population groups appear to produce some effect upon its usage, but it is difficult to assess the amount of effect since the cultural force of discrimination has conditioned the nature of its composition, and consequently its usage. Although the majority of businesses located there tend to handle convenience and specialty items, rather than luxury or shopping ones, making special trips to the street to secure these is no doubt conditioned as much by cultural as spatial factors. In this respect the Negro Main Street, a commercial as well as socio-cultural area, is perhaps different from the commercial area described by Firey as consisting of banks, investment houses, commercial lawyers and other such social systems where accessibility and convenience to the population are unimportant.[21]

And only partially can it be classed with "string-street developments" which McKenzie says originate close to the central shopping district, attract those who pass along the street or are there for other purposes, and are only dependent upon the adjacent residential community to a minor extent.[22] The Negro Main Street does depend to some extent upon passers and those shopping nearby on the city's principal main street, but it thrives primarily upon the total Negro community which, though spatially distant, is brought in direct contact with it by racial forces that are of a cultural origin. This difference between the Negro Main Street and other such streets makes accessibility and convenience factors quite vital to the use of the street because of its basic dependence upon patronage of one racial group whose contradictory consumer values are suspended between racial factors on the one hand and democratic principles on the other.

That accessibility and convenience are primary conditioners of Negro Main Street usage is noticed in the considerations of trading and non-trading groups with their conceptions of the location of the street. Assuming that a Negro business street will exist somewhere in the community, the majority of Negroes tend to think it better to have one located where the street is at present rather than elsewhere. Of the 350 Main Street traders and non-

[21] Walter Firey, *Land Use in Central Boston* (Cambridge: Harvard University Press, 1947), p. 245.

[22] R. D. McKenzie, *The Metropolitan Community* (New York: McGraw-Hill Book Co., 1933), pp. 255-256.

traders, for example, only eight expressed no opinion about the location of the street, while 70.5 percent of the remaining 342 think its present location preferable to location in a residential area, as opposed to 29.5 percent who believe location in a residential area would be better. A larger percentage of the 342 (86.5) even thinks it more advantageous for the street to be located as it is, while only 13.5 percent considers its location a disadvantage, and the advantages given are practically identical with the reasons given for preferring the street's present location. And here again usage of the street seems contingent not only upon spatial location but also upon culturally-conditioned attitudes, yet the locational factor seems most important. More than one-half of these (56.4 percent) likes the fact that the street is centrally located, convenient, easy to find, and already established; 16.3 percent thinks it gets more white, as well as colored, customers and can better serve all people in its present location; 4.8 percent thinks its present location helps advance the race; 4.0 percent thinks Negroes need such a business area unmixed with residences; 2.6 percent thinks Negroes need, and the street gives, places to go when in town; another 2.6 percent thinks its present location better because it gives Negroes a center for congregating, while the remainder offer miscellaneous reasons for preferring the present location of the street.

It has already been shown that Negro Main Street patrons and frequenters are both male and female, urban and rural, workers and non-workers, Negro and white, but that variations in usage of the street exist among these groups. In the case of the white customers or users one might inquire about the nature of their relationship to the area. When it comes to spatial usage per se, observation and enumeration indicate that during early morning and late afternoon hours the street is a major thoroughfare for white pedestrians en route to and from a neighboring residential section. Numerical count on several consecutive days of the week, around the time that businesses are beginning to close, has often shown the number of Negro and white passers at specific locations on the street to be about equal, but while it proves to be a thoroughfare for whites it is more of a stopping place for Negroes. Not all of the white passers are non-patrons of the businesses there, however. Among the more striking patterns is the large number of whites among the clientele of the bank, the small number of whites who use the drug store, and the complete absence of whites in attendance at the motion picture theater. Reasons for such patterns cannot be fully validated, but their existence is verified by statements of business operators as well as patrons. As long lines of Negroes and whites formed at the loans, savings, and checking windows inside the bank on a Monday morning in late July, a male customer, striking up a conversation about the auditors who were busy verifying records at the windows, remarked:

Every ninety days they come and check and they never know exactly when they're coming. Wonder where the woman is that works at the third window? Reckon anything has happened that caused her to stay away today? Of course this is a pretty sound bank, only one that didn't close during the depression, and it was a small bank then, all these big banks shut down but this one didn't. That's why people have so much confidence in it, and they have as many white customers as colored, but you can see that from all these whites in here now.[23]

Over and above the ability of the bank to withstand economic pressures, whites' usage of the bank, like Negro usage of white banks, is often a means of averting primary controls. Whatever the reasons for such, the large number of white clients has continually increased and helped shape the nature of racial usage of the Negro Main Street. One person connected with the bank says:

. . . I'm a director of the bank and I happen to know that the only way we are able to function is through the money from the City of Raleigh, State Government, Carolina Power and Light, and the many white folks who use the bank. The Negroes who have money have it in Wachovia, First Citizens and the like. I guess it's a good thing that we do have so much white patronage. Of course many whites come to us for the same reason we go to the white bank, to keep the folks from knowing what we are doing. . .[24]

Usage of the Negro Main Street drug store is somewhat different from that of the bank, as attested to by the operator who says:

White doctors patronize the services of these pharmacists on a very small scale and, for the most part, only with Negro patients,

23 Personal document: Statement made casually to writer.
24 Personal interview: Negro undertaker.

while on the other hand Negro doctors give full support to the Negro pharmacists. . . . This is a good location for this type of business and those it serves. . . the people who come in here are nice. Most of them are Negroes, though we have a number of whites whose business surrounds us, and those living on Blount Street come in and do business with us. I find if you produce you sell.[25]

The theater presents still another picture, for whites' absence here is operator-enforced rather than customer-enforced, as the manager himself indicates. Says he:

. . . When I first came to Raleigh I only had men who came to this theater. There were no women, no boys, and no girls. Now we have men, women, boys, girls, professional, non-professional, common laborers, business-men—all types—coming here. We even have whites who would like to come here, but I wouldn't sell a white man a ticket for five dollars. I have even had white boys who tried to slip in this theater. Why not whites? There are other places they can go. This place is liked by those who come here, but it has a reputation among Negroes of being noisy and having many undesirable men around, so I am told, and I guess that's true. . . . The theater is presently owned by the Bijou Amusement Co. of Nashville, Tennessee. It is a chain theater. . . this is not a theater in the true sense, but I have reached the maximum in expansion. As I said before, I operate strictly for Negroes. All services performed are for Negroes and Negroes alone.[26]

Elaborating upon Simmel's contention that civilization is distinguished from tribal life by movement around fixed centers or focal points, Hughes notes that such inter-tribal centers as shrines and trade centers become socially established as symbols which dominate the sentiments of a people both spatially and temporally.[27] The Negro Main Street, though part of an urban civilization pattern, is not unlike the inter-tribal trade center in its symbolization of the sentiments of those who use it as a focal point for specific forms of economic and social life. The specific sentiments symbolized in the usage of the street are contingent upon the social values which its users attach to it, most of which can be

[25] Personal interview: Negro female drugstore owner.
[26] Personal interview: White manager of theater for Negroes.
[27] Everett C. Hughes, "The Ecological Aspect of Institutions," *American Sociological Review* (April, 1936), pp. 184-185.

inferred from the expressed attitudes of residents of the community. Thus, the principal values of which the street is symbolic include its usage as representative of that which claims profound social approval in the Negro world, and as active connective of Negro life and activity.

Striving to survive in a value-laden culture filled with contradictions, the Negro world seems not unaware of the many pervasive and perverse features of its own make-up. Hence, when making comparisons between businesses operated by Negroes on the Main Street and those in other parts of the Negro world, a rather general attitude toward these becomes apparent. Whatever else that general attitude may show, it can be said most assuredly that not only does the attitude toward main street businesses differ from that toward other businesses, but also that within the Negro world Main Street businesses represent the more socially approved enterprises. Social approval based on a conceptualized use of space in this instance tends to suggest that the Main Street is a clean, legitimate, respectable business street containing, in the terminology of mainstreeters, the big shot businesses and important offices. Summaries of this general attitude are given as follows:

East Hargett [the Main Street] has been a very desirable business street because it is close to everything. It used to be a very important street and a very popular street. It is not so popular now, but it's still the most popular one the colored have. All down in Third Ward there's colored business but it is not the same as East Hargett; they would go to Hargett St. if they could but there's no room up there.[28]

There has never been any illegitimate or non-respectable business on the street, no prostitution at any time. The main reason for this is that this has always been a street of business and people have not had residences there, thus a thing like prostitution had no place to thrive.[29]

Not only has there been no prostitution on Hargett St. but very little in Raleigh, among Negroes that is. . . there's never been a need for prostitution among Negroes here. In the first place most of the work is domestic, and you don't find it among that group.

[28] Personal interview: Retired Negro undertaker.
[29] Personal interview: Negro operator of funeral parlor.

In the next place many of the Negroes already had white fathers who simply took Negro women they wanted as their mistresses and put them in houses and took care of them, along with the children.[30]

There's never been any immorality on Hargett St. from the business standpoint. It's always been a clean business street. For one thing you have whites at both ends of it and colored all mixed in between.[31]

One thing you can say for Hargett St., it's never been a rough and rowdy street like in some other places. You never hear of any fights, shootings or killings there.[32]

One person who took a leading role in making the street one of Negro business, and who operated a business there himself for thirty years, says of the street and its reputation,

I don't ever remember any rowdyism on Hargett St. the whole time I stayed up there. There was one fellow I was afraid might cause disturbance though. His name was L; he was really a rough neck, he would cut you in a minute and I knew it; he made his money by selling liquor and would sell it anywhere to anybody who'd buy. When I built the Arcade I had in mind having a place where nice people could go and not be afraid of fights, etc. So what I did was go to L and say, look L, I want to keep this place nice and I rent it to any group that wants it, but I can't be here every time they have a dance, so I want you to help me keep order and I'll see that you get in free to all the dances; I'll tell whoever is having a dance that you are to help keep order and not to charge you to come in. He agreed to do this and we never had any kind of trouble. He was better than a policeman because all the rough necks knew him and would do anything he said, and since he was in plain clothes if anything started to happen he could get to the folks and stop it quicker than a policeman, cause they could see a policeman coming and run. . . Hargett St. has always been a reputable business street.[33]

Being a reputable business street, however, must not be considered as implying that the street has been completely lacking in all "undercover" business at all times. Individual businesses on

---

[30] Personal interview: Negro taxicab driver.
[31] Personal interview: Negro realtor and Justice of the Peace.
[32] Personal interview: Negro female school teacher.
[33] Personal interview: Retired Negro undertaker.

the street have been known to be characterized by some "under-cover" activities, but always within the framework of a legitimate, repectable business and always in addition to, rather than in lieu of, approved consumer items. This was especially true of the sale of alcoholic beverages after the period beginning in 1904 when saloons were replaced by dispensaries,[34] and during the days of Prohibition, as the following excerpts will indicate.

Dr. J took over M's drug store; all the drug stores but M's were fronts for their liquor business. I know because I used them all. Dr. J wouldn't sell you a drop of anything but L and H were noted for their liquor business. At one time you got it by prescription but in H's you didn't even need a prescription, all you had to do was ask for it and he'd wrap it up and give it to you.[35]

There were two drug stores that I know were fronts for the liquor business, both on Hargett. The law got them once; everybody was doing the same thing, but they slipped up that time and had to pay $500 each in fines. . . . H made his money on liquor, had runners out in the county and when they'd check in they'd have dishpans full of money. He didn't have much when he died due to poor business management.[36]

Using a legitimate business as a front for the liquor business, however, did not originate on, nor become the sole province of, the Negro Main Street. As early as 1893 retail liquor dealers of the city petitioned the city government to investigate grocers and druggists who they were informed were selling spirituous liquors without license. Asking that these grocers and druggists be made pay the same annual tax as others retailing liquor, the petition stated that two grocers were willing for this, for they said they didn't want to sell liquor but had to because others were doing it.[37] Thus was a city ordinance passed regarding the sale of spirituous liquors by druggists and all, with Sunday sale permitted to druggists only. Because of the diffusion of the liquor-front-business trait then, this cannot be said to be especially characteristic of the Negro Main Street but is a recognition of the fact that its existence did not alter the street's reputation as a clean, respectable business street. And the same might be said regarding the use of the street by hustlers or other such persons, as thus depicted:

[34] *News and Observer* (Raleigh), Tuesday, October 6, 1903.
[35] Personal interview: Negro mail carrier.
[36] Personal interview: Retired Negro school principal.
[37] *Minutes of Raleigh City Government,* July 7, 1893.

There've always been a lot of hustlers, people who sell hot goods, on both Wilmington and Hargett streets until recently. There's no place there now to hang out and hide hustling, so it has moved to the different neighborhoods. It used to be concentrated, now it's all over town.[38]

. . . You could buy anything hot you wanted (on Hargett), I've done it many a day from the best things all the way down. Of course the guys who were handling the stuff were stealing it from the places where they worked. It really belonged to them because the men they worked for were not paying them what they should, but technically it belonged to the white man. After they started closing up the gaps and cracking down on them it got so you couldn't get anything.[39]

Retaining respectability through the control of non-approved behavior has also been part of the patterned usage of the Negro main street. An example of the manner in which this has been done is given as follows:

About twenty-five years ago all the country folks and everybody else who came to Hargett St. went to the American Legion Club. We used to really do some business there and people enjoyed themselves there too. We kept them from bringing anything to drink there except what we sold legally in order to keep down anything that might cause things to get out of hand. . .[40]

To the twenty-eight Main Street business operators from whom information has been obtained regarding their attitudes toward having business located on this street, Negro Main Street respectability means paying relatively high rent, not desiring to move because the business was established there, liking the type of patronage received, and being centrally located. Some difference in emphasis on these factors does exist, however, between Negro and white operators of business. The nineteen operators whose monthly rents are designated are agreed that rent is relatively high on the main street, the monthly median being $90.53, but cheaper than many other places in town. White owner-operators seem agreed that because they are heirs to businesses originally established on the street they have not considered moving, while

[38] Personal interview: Negro mail carrier.
[39] Personal interview: Maintenance man at a Negro school.
[40] Personal interview: Negro printer.

white operators catering solely or primarily to Negroes consider this the best street for Negro patronage. Attitudes of the whites are summarized in their own statements thus:

. . . The business [furniture] was founded here, so we haven't thought of moving.[41]

. . . This is a good location but there are other streets that are better for my business [tailoring]. I like this street because the rent is not so high as some other places in town.[42]

. . . The business [shoe shop] was established on this street and I never thought of moving it. We get along well with our patrons. The persons coming from the rural areas on weekends keep our business going on Hargett St. [43]

. . . The business [shoe shop] was founded on Hargett St. and I never thought of moving off the street. Here I get the chance of coming in contact with more members of the Negro race that make nice and desirable clients.[44]

. . . When the business [café] was located on Wilmington St. it was known as the Star Cafe. It has always been an eating place for colored. The location on Hargett is the best for the customers we get, being in a Negro business area. It is much better than our previous location, and so are the clients, except for a few disturbances such as drunks. The customers are mostly laborers and farmers. Our best sales are on Saturdays.[45]

. . . I wouldn't move for this [theater] is in the heart of the Negro area and only a block and a half from the main street. . . my customers would object to moving the theater any place else. They love the location. They love it because it is in the heart of the Negro area and because of its closeness to the heart of town.[46]

While among the twenty-two Negro operators of business there tends to be unanimity of opinion regarding this street's being "the best street in town for Negro business," the reasons therefor are spatially-oriented. Conversely, reactions of the Main Street traders toward the street tend to be more operationally-oriented and

[41] Personal interview: White co-owner of furniture store.
[42] Personal interview: White business operator.
[43] Personal interview: White operator of shoe shop.
[44] Personal interview: White operator of shoe shop.
[45] Personal interview: White operator of café for Negroes.
[46] Personal interviews: White manager of theater for Negroes.

more variant. Of the 267 traders giving definite impressions of the street, 52.4 percent tend to be only partially satisfied with the street. They think it is all right but needs improvements and changes especially regarding appearance of buildings, personnel, variety of stock, standees and hangouters, places for rural people to go, seating space, and moving whites off the street. Some 19.3 percent of the 140 traders who think the street is all right but needs such designated changes want the change to revolve around moving whites out and giving the entire street to Negroes. Although this is only 8.8 percent of all main street traders, it is indicative of ever present racial sentiments among some segments of the Negro world. The expressions given below are not minutely detailed enough to embrace all the intensities of the sentiments held by the entire 19.3 percent trading group referred to above, but being uttered by traders themselves they are somewhat suggestive of the nature of these sentiments.

It's nice to have a street like Hargett with a lot of Negro businesses on it. I don't think the whites should be in there with the colored. I'm old timey and believe the whites ought to stay to theirselves and we stay to ours. My mother put that in me and I can't get it out. I always remember her advice. She had a lot of friends, 'bout as many white as colored, and people liked her a lot but she stayed in her place. She used to tell us, 'white's white and colored's colored and they ain't got no business mixing, you stay in your place and let them stay in theirs.' I'm old timey and I believe that's the way it ought to be, just can't get that out of me. . . People come round talking 'bout integration and asking what you think of it, and I tell you I don't think nothing of it. The whites ought to stay to theirselves and we ought to stay to ours, but I don't tell the white folks that. I say nothing when they ask, but I'll tell my own color what I think.[47]

They ought to put the whites out of the block, then Negroes could put up some more places there. We need to share in and make it nice for colored to have some place to go; if you don't go to Hargett St. colored got no place to go at all. One thing, the whites don't pay the colored like they should, so the colored don't have much money to do anything with.[48]

Some 35.6 percent of Main Street traders tend to be satisfied

[47] Personal interview: Negro female non-worker.
[48] Personal interview: Negro housewife.

with the street, considering it nice, fine, good, and convenient just as it is. Some 6.0 percent seem more impressed by the physical and social atmosphere of the street, laying special emphasis upon the street's being quiet, clean, pleasant, not crowded, and the people courteous, respectful, friendly, and making you feel welcome. An equivalent percentage of the traders (6.0) tends to be especially proud of the street because it is colored and represents the progress made by Negroes, progress being symbolic not only of a rising economic status but also of reverses in racial attitudes and sentiments. This is perhaps best portrayed by residents of the community who have said,

It's a definite advantage to have a large number of Negro businesses concentrated on Hargett St. Just seeing the businesses gives you personal and group pride; they offer job opportunities and make it convenient to satisfy your needs. Every time I go in the bank I can't help but think how nice it is, it's just as nice as any white bank in town and they have a lot of white customers. . . . It makes me feel happy to see our businesses expand. . . . White people should not be moved out of the block where Negro businesses are because no racial group should be excluded from an area. People are people and for that reason should have equal opportunities. . . . Negroes must compete in the midst of people of varying races and backgrounds. . . . Negro businesses give our children opportunities for some of the better jobs and help raise the appreciations of our people. [49]

. . . That café for colored on Hargett St. is the only place in town where Jews serve colored and they don't have to take the food through a window or back door. Whites go there too but they go in the back and eat, don't eat out front with the Negroes. If you're in there when any of them come in you notice that they keep straight to the back. At least that reverses the picture.[50]

Necessity for a culture medium through which to interrelate the varied activities and interests of a minority group is just as urgent in the Negro world as in any other. Lacking such institutions as "Sobranie" of "Russian Town" or the "Synagogue" of the "Ghetto" through which all life of the group is integrated, the Negro tends to manifest his life activities through other channels. The Main Street is one of the major channels through which Ne-

[49] Personal interview: Negro college professor.
[50] Personal interview: Negro carpenter.

gro life and activity are connected, and this space-use value of the street tends to be equally as conceptualized and emphasized as its representation of what is socially approved among Negroes. When the street was first developed, however, it tended to be a more complete connective of all major interests and activities in the Negro world than at present, for changes occurring in other parts of the community have been accompanied by changes in the space-use values of the street. Just as the Southern city has dominated its rural hinterland and brought city and country closer together, so Negro Main Street outlets for economic activities have served to minimize the distance between rural and urban groups, as evidenced in the excerpts which follow.

I had a lot of space behind the building (Lightner Building) when I first went in there and the country people used to come and park their wagons and stock back there for the day and then get out and do their buying and selling. They sold eggs, butter and the like all around the building. There were so many people up there on the street at that time that they could easily do this and not have to go any distance to sell what they had.[51]

Country people have always been seen on Hargett St. primarily because of the city market facing the Square right down in the next block. What happens is that they stop in the Square because it's across from the market where they bring their wares, and they drift on up to Hargett, especially on Saturday. Hargett St. is still a meeting place for many of the country people, for they can stop there and visit before and after shopping. They used to have rummage sales in the Square and that was a big attraction to the country people. After they stopped these a number of Jews opened second-hand clothing stores right on Hargett St. Then there are those second-hand furniture stores too, so these attract them.[52]

Many downtown business streets are often characterized as non-family areas. Although such a characterization fits the Negro Main Street at present, it has not always done so. With the lone Negro hotel located there, many family groups lived in it over long periods of time, thus making life on the Negro Main Street again different from that on many similar functioning streets. How the street served as connective between families or family

[51] Personal interview: Retired Negro undertaker.
[52] Personal interview: Negro female physician.

and non-family groups is again best described by a resident in this manner:

The hotel still functions as one of the best. It is not true that the hotel is going down, and if anyone should know I should because I have stayed there as much and long as anyone. At one time my whole family lived there and we stayed about five years. The better class of people still stay there when there's need to stay at a hotel. All the bands that come to town stay there. The place stays full, I've seen them have to turn people away because there was no space. Even this year that has been true, I stayed there this time until April when I moved into the present house. There used to be from six to eight families living in the hotel at one time, and all of them stayed there from five to six years straight. That gave status to the place because all of these were rather prominent families and had a lot of company always visiting. Now there are no regular tenants, just transients.[53]

The same factors that gave status to particular institutions on the Main Street likewise gave dignity and respectability to the street itself. A part of the status-giving pattern in the Negro world derives from knowing the VIPS (very important persons), or "bigwigs," among Negroes. Most often in the Negro world these have been such persons as college presidents, outstanding singers, name bands or any presumed "first-and-only" Negro to accomplish a special feat or gain singular recognition. In a world where a segment of the population places value upon knowing such persons, providing a means of knowing them has been of group concern. For a number of years the Negro Main Street performed this function by acting as a direct connecting link between persons of equal status or rank and an indirect one between those of unequal status or rank. The real significance of such a pattern is seen in the nature of contacts it provides, as portrayed by a resident in the ensuing excerpt.

. . . As long as the dining room (hotel) was on the front it was surrounded by glass and many people just came and stood outside and looked in; they could see all the important people in there, Mrs. Bethune, Bennie Mays, and any out-of-town bigwig, because they stayed there and ate there. I have even carried Guy J (a white bigwig) there for lunch, it was 'The' place to go.

[53] Personal interview. Former Negro college president.

That way Negroes always knew who was in town, what they looked like and all. Moving the dining room to the back was a big mistake and I have told the manager so.[54]

Reiteration of the factors discussed in this chapter as influencing the patterns of usage of the Negro Main Street area would merely result in presenting another portrait of the character of the street. Since that character has been so clearly shown by a local resident encountered late one August afternoon in the park adjoining Hargett Street, we might let her portrait suffice for summarizing and summarily presenting the character of the street in relation to its usage. Says she,

. . . oh yes, you certainly can tell this is a Negro street. The minute you see it you'd know. It's just like Harlem in New York—see Negroes standing around; and if you want to see anybody you know all you have to do is come and hang around long enough and they'll pass; and if you want to see anybody from the country all you got to do is come up here on Friday or Saturday. Used to be so you couldn't get through the street for country people and peanuts. They lined the street all the way from Love's drug store down on the corner of Davie and Blount up to and through Hargett. And you couldn't even get a seat here in the park, country folks had them all and were spread out all over the ground. Not so bad now because they all have cars and come and go like city folks. Can't even tell the country folks any more, they look like everybody else and have more than we do, and a whole lot more than I have . . .[55]

Such is the character of median-located Negro Main Street as influenced by numerous spatial factors, but fuller appreciation and understanding of these is contingent upon envisaging the street's characteristic style of life resulting from specific group usage thereof. The next chapter essays to help unveil the nature of this style of life.

[54] Personal Interview: Former Negro college president.

[55] Personal document: Conversation with woman waiting to meet husband after work.

Part IV

STYLES OF LIFE AND THEIR REFLECTIONS
IN GROUP FORMATION, ACTION AND THOUGHT

Chapter 7

PERSONS, PLACES, AND INTERESTS AS SYMBOLS OF MAIN STREET GROUP BEHAVIOR

The nature of groups formed on the Main Street might easily be analyzed as part of the functional use of space, but since the groups perform many broad social functions they merit special consideration. Not only do the Main Street groups serve as connecting links between spatially separate units of the Negro world, but they also unite those with similar interests, offer outlets for personal goals and aspirations, give evidence of types of activities on which the attention of the Negro world is focused, and aid the retention of the reputable characterizing traits of the Main Street itself. Motivated by personalities whose goals have been oriented toward maintaining the respectability of the Negro Main Street, attracted to legitimate places of business, and revolving around socially-approved interests, Main Street group behavior has tended to conform to expected values of the community. It must not be forgotten that this southern community is a middle-class, white-collar town, and that among the major forces shaping the Negro world have been its unique educational and economic alignments. Group behavior in the Negro world must necessarily reflect in some respect some of the features of these alignments.

In analyzing the components of human behavior social psychologists have observed that each person possesses an individual life style. The life style is defined as the manner in which one guides his actions toward a selected objective.[1] Inasmuch as one lives in and functions through groups, it seems plausible to assume that his life style is often projected through the group of which he is a part. Especially is this true where one plays a dominant role in the group and becomes the nuclear person around whom others radiate. And where groups of persons with similar life styles seek to obtain an objective in a specified manner, it would appear that a general life style could be expected to characterize the group. If, in turn, the objective sought is of in-

[1] Hubert Bonner, *Social Psychology* (New York: American Book Co., 1953), p. 91.

estimable social utility and linked with some tangibly externalized value, then it is also conceivable that a style of life may be imputed to the external factor itself. We may thus hypothesize that the Negro Main Street, as an externalized value in the Negro world, possesses a life style which has been imputed to it by the actions of groups which have been dominant on the street, the main features of this style of life stemming from special persons, particular places, and specific interests.

One of the things most immediately apparent about the Main Street's style of life is the continual change it has undergone under the impact of urbanizing forces accompanied by ecological shifts, new trends in the development of business, and alterations in race relations. Although the street has remained locationally fixed and its physical structure unaltered, except where catastrophic change has occurred, its social structure has been somewhat transformed. Most illustrative of the social structure transformation has been the decline in the nature and number of groups caught up in the web of Main Street relationships. Originating in a manner similar to a social movement, and acting toward a projected goal of supplementing or substituting certain institutions and practices involving discrimination against Negroes, the Main Street had become more or less institutionalized by the early 1920's. During this period the life style of the street was committed to both formal and informal group relationships, for this was the center of all activity for the Negro world. Only as urbanization influences began to decentralize business enterprises did group activities begin to shift from the Main Street to neighborhood sub-centers.

In a previous chapter mention was made of the fact that the current Main Streeter is predominantly in the older male category. This characteristic has resulted from the foregoing change just alluded to, for in the most formative years of the street's development young and older men alike maintained their group alliances, both formal and informal, through the Main Street. Through them the informal style of life of the street became one of congregating, conversing, news-gathering, and bull-sessioning right on the sidewalks, but with no specifically constituted membership. The real social significance of these informal groups of men allied with the Main Street resides perhaps in their unstable composition and lack of pre-formulated lines of action. From this standpoint they are no doubt different from the dissident groups of an ethnic community where culture conflict prevails. The very stable composition of "Cornerville" groups, for example, with their high rates of social interaction between members, tends to effect a high degree of organization in both the "corner boys" and "college boys" groups.[2] But no such organization obtains among the main street groups whose activities center around particular parts of the street. Nor is the status factor emphasized in the informal behavior of Main Street groups as it is in "Cornerville" groups where corner boys constitute the bottom level of society and the college boys a higher level, for one's mobility from one Main Street group to another may not only be high but frequent. Even though distinctions may be made between formal group memberships where certain rituals and admission qualifications obtain, one's participation in the informal assemblages on the Main Street tends to be more completely voluntary and spontaneous. More or less agreement between the nature of Cornerville and Main Street groups does exist, however, in the intimacy of relationships between members. Whereas in Cornerville groups a system of mutual obligations is effected, in the Main Street groups a system of mutual dependence based upon momentary interests tends to result. The nature of these group activities which have made Main Street behavior more characteristically informal than formal may be depicted thus:

There used to be a number of groups that were found on the street. You might say that this was the street of upper class bums, the lower class bums stuck to Third Ward. . . there were a number of informal groups on the street, but you could not name anyone particular as belonging to them because it was just a general congregating group. Anyone who wanted to pass the time away and just generally 'shoot the breeze' made his way to Hargett St. There was no YMCA then, no pool room that young boys could go in like they can now, the churches had no activities to interest young men, and the city had none. Thus Hargett St. became the meeting place. It was the only place Negroes could go for ice cream even. Everything Negroes had was there—cafés, beauty shops, barber shops and all—so you had to go there.[3]

[2] William Foote Whyte, *Street Corner Society* (Chicago: University of Chicago Press, 1943).
[3] Personal interview: Negro taxicab dispatcher.

In the days when I used to hang out up there one group hung out on the north side of the street and another group on the south side. The north side group was made up of professional men who had offices on the street and they would just stand around and talk. The younger group hung around on the south side of the street. If you were looking for fun, hilarity, talking about girls, whistling at girls, etc., then you joined the young group on the south side. School, girls, games, etc., made up the topics of the younger group. The news of the day made up the topics of the older men—it might be football when it was football season, or basketball, baseball, local politics, national politics etc.[4]

Hargett St. used to be Negro Heaven for the men. You'd see men and women there but the women didn't loiter. All types of men congregated there—one group in the morning, another in the afternoon, and another in the evening. Back in the early '20's between 12:30 and 1:45 the street was crowded with men. All the doctors would be out about that time too, and they'd all stand around and talk. Then about 5 o'clock you'd see them again, that was about the time the doctors were leaving their offices. Now the doctors aren't up there much.[5]

Occasionally a group would attempt through developing a specifically-constituted membership to draw attention to itself rather than become submerged in the anonymous groups of the street. Description of the following group is a case in point.

In the '20's there used to be an A C E club that hung out on Hargett St. This was called the Arcade Cake Eaters. They were teenagers who wore ties tied right tight with meat hanging out at the neck. One guy even ruined his appearance doing that so much. They wore peg-legged pants and little hats, didn't bother anybody but just enjoyed being different. . . There were never any really tough gangs to hang out on Hargett St. We used to have them, but they were in different parts of the city. You dared not go to Third Ward if you lived in Fourth Ward, or to East Raleigh, etc., without your gang and bodyguard because you'd get rocked to death. This stopped after 1924 when they got high schools in the city because the boys started going to school together and became friends instead of enemies.[6]

[4] Personal interview: Negro taxi driver.
[5] Personal interview: Negro mail carrier.
[6] Personal interview: Negro taxi driver.

Groups with memberships specifically constituted for other reasons, but still functioning along age and sex lines, were also a part of Main Street structure. Thus is it reported that,

There were two clubs of men that were the main formal groups for men. One I belonged to, but can't remember its name. Ours was the club for young men. The older men's club was the Cosmopolitan. Both existed in the '20's and held dances in the Yellow Rose Tea Room, which was the leading lunch room then because there was no lunch counter in the drug store and the hotel didn't have a lunch room.[7]

Any explanation offered for the formation of such groups on the Main Street rather than in some other spatial area must consider the fact that the frequency of contacts during the 1920 period was undoubtedly greatest at this point. Since all Negro business enterprises were located on the Main Street, and no other institutions attempted to meet the need for sociability among residents of the community, it is understandable how contacts between frequenters of the street led to such friendly social gatherings as developed there. Because the persons with the highest status level, the doctors, all kept office on the street and were regular participants in the informal groupings, prevailing intra- and inter-group relations there tended to be rather equalitarian. This no doubt enhanced the contact value of the street and at the same time gave it a status different from that of other streets. As the doctors began to set up office in residential areas, and organizations providing young men recreational outlets came into being, the informal male groups of the street began to subside.

Notwithstanding the fact that there has been a change in the number and constituency of male groups associated with the Main Street since the 1920 period, the congregating of men still remains a part of the street's style of life, but a less-conspicuous part than previously. However, Main Street behavior of such male groups tends to differ from that of similar groups in other areas. Women's alliances with the street have tended to remain somewhat the same through the decades but have varied from those of men, for congregating or loitering on the street has not been characteristic of their behavior there. Not only are these factors

[7] Personal interview: Negro funeral parlor operator.

borne out by participant observation but by mainstreeters themselves, being evidenced in the descriptive behavior of the 307
Main Street traders in the sample population studied. In the
words of main street traders themselves one notes the following:

Some of these men'll whistle at you and make passes anywhere
they see you, but I've never seen that kind of thing on Hargett
St. That street's just as nice as Fayetteville St., just not as much
business on it that's all. I never noticed many men hanging
around there much anyway, except maybe Saturday, and the
women who go there never seem to stop long. They go do their
business and go on back.[8]

Fewer men seem to hang around on the street now than did before. I have never seen women hang out on the street. I hate to
pass a group of men hanging around on the street because of
the way they yell and whistle at you, but I have not seen that
happen on Hargett St. Seems that everybody who goes there has
some business to transact.[9]

This obvious difference between male and female alliances with
the street seems to be most applicable, however, to the urban
Main Streeters. Inasmuch as rural persons tend to be mainly weekend and family-group frequenters of the street, more corporate
action of males and females tends to prevail among them. Both
patterns are of course in line with expected behavior of urban
and rural groups for, while differentiation is a more notable urban
trait, unity of action tends to be more characteristic of the rural
group. Such intra-group characterization, however, is not particularly conceptualized in the depictions which mainstreeters
give of Negro Main Street groups. What they see instead is a
difference between rural and urban usages of the street. To them
the street symbolizes a congested area where rural groups congregate, especially on Saturday, and become so absorbed in discussing their own interests that they become oblivious to other
Main Streeters. The characteristic features and changes in this
pattern are evidenced in the following citations:

I go there [Hargett St.] quite often and like to go there. Seems
like things there are well organized. Of course you get the im-

[8] Personal interview: Elderly Negro housewife.
[9] Personal interview: Young Negro housewife.

pression that there are more rural people than city people there, especially on Saturday, but there aren't nearly as many as used to be. Used to be you couldn't get through there on Saturday except by elbowing your way. I do know that the rural people go there. I guess they're patronizing the businesses, but the main thing they go for is to meet their friends, and talk and visit. That's the way they keep each other informed about who they saw at the different churches, and how many chickens they have, and who's doing what.[10]

Always it looks like nothing but folks from the country up there when I go on that street, but not as many now as used to be up there. You don't see many men hanging around until Saturday, and I ain't never noticed any women hanging around up there like the men do.[11]

. . . And it's Saturday that you see most of the country people there, but seem like there aren't as many country people nowadays as you used to see. Guess they've found other places to go.[12]

I go to Hargett St. any time I need to but I don't like to go on Saturday, especially Saturday afternoon. If I just have to go Saturday I try to go around 9:30 in the morning and do what I have to do and leave. You can hardly walk on the street on Saturday afternoon for the country people, and those who drink get all tanked up and knock you and if you say anything to them they want to fight. And it's the country people that do this, not the city people. Course ain't near as many country people up there now as used to be. Then too, the country people come to town a little later now from what they used to. I'm a country boy myself and I know when my parents used to come to town in an old wagon. We'd leave home about seven in the morning, didn't come every Saturday but those Saturdays we did come we'd leave early and stay in town until around two in the afternoon. Then we'd start back home so we'd get there before it got too dark. But now country people have the same kind of cars city people have, and they don't even start away from home until around noon, so they're there later in the afternoon than they used to be.[13]

It thus appears that during its most formative years of develop-

[10] Personal interview: Middle-aged Negro housewife.
[11] Personal interview: Negro housewife and day laborer.
[12] Personal interview: Negro housewife.
[13] Personal interview: Negro male maintenance worker.

ment the Negro Main Street, serving as a direct contact medium through which those with similar interests were able to interact, laid the foundation for the existent behavior form so characteristic of the street. Uniformity of behavior on the street has conformed to a pattern of congregating, loitering and talking on the one hand, and performing business transactions on the other. The absence of a riotous, rowdy, whistling-men pattern can probably be attributed in some degree to the influence of these informal groups on their participating members. One of the major findings of Festinger's study of small groups is that members of the same face-to-face group exhibit relative uniformity with respect to specified opinions and modes of behavior, and that the influence which the group exerts over its members is partially responsible for this uniformity.[14] Certainly this suggested influence appears evident in informal Main Street groups where behavior that is taboo on the Main Street seems rampant in other areas.

The assemblage of informal groups, whether stratified along lines of age, rural-urban distinction, or momentary interest, is only a part of the behavioral pattern in the Main Street style of life. Group activity also forms among those who congregate around special persons who are themselves Main Street attractions, persons whose roles have made them well-known Main Street figures; whose relations with certain groups of people have helped increase popular usage of the street; and whose absence from the street has effected a change in the nature of groups found there. Interestingly enough, all such Main Street figures who have been so recognized by the Negro world have been those performing services in areas in which the most marked discrimination against Negroes has existed. The main figures have been a doctor, an undertaker, and an operator of a place of entertainment. It may very well be, therefore, that they were not only personalities in their own rights but symbols of the changing status and attitudes of Negroes. The roles of these persons and their effect upon the Main Street are best understood through the portraits given of them by residents, and are so depicted below.

Lightner was the leading figure on Hargett St. when he was up there. He had a way of doing things to attract customers to his business. People came to his undertaking place to leave their

---

[14] Leon Festinger, Stanley Schachter and Kurt Back, *Social Pressures in Informal Groups* (New York: Harper and Brothers, 1950), p. 72.

packages while they shopped and to use the rest room he had provided for them, and they began to give him all their trade. Before he ran for mayor he was burying all the colored people. . . .[15] You could always tell when he was in trouble by the little whistle he uttered up and down the street, he never whistled when things were going smoothly. He really stuck his neck out when he built those two buildings so Negroes could have some place to do business.[16]

Comments by one resident indicating that when he operated a business on Hargett Street two of the leading drawing cards to the street were Dr. Plummer and Jimmy Taylor, Sr., both of whom attracted a lot of followers, are certainly in line with the following views:

. . . Dr. Plummer used to be quite a figure on the street when he was there. He was a great hand for giving away things, he'd sometimes buy 20 and 30 ice cream cones at a time and treat everybody around. So there was always a group hanging around him for his famous handouts. When he left the street many of those people who hung around him left too.[17]

Jimmy Taylor, Sr. was a country boy, went to Shaw but didn't finish. Started out in business with JC who drank a lot, later took in O, his brother-in-law, to work for him. . . Jimmy was quite popular, a regular fellow, liked to have fun, never allowed his wife in the business on Hargett, so she stayed out and let the son run it after he died. . .[18] Big Jimmy was well liked by everybody, made no difference between people and helped anyone he could, would just as soon take an old drunk from the street and carry him home and feed him at his table, white or colored. . . .[19] I used to shoot so much pool there every week that on Saturday I owed him so much he'd give me part of it back. If I owed $12 he could afford to take the $10 and tell me to keep the $2; that was good business and would keep you going back. . .[20] He was a personal friend of mine and I knew him well. He was one of the Hargett St. drawing cards. He was a high class racketeer, a good looking man, popular, excellent manners, knew how to carry himself. He

[15] Personal interview: Retired Negro school teacher.
[16] Personal interview: Negro realtor and Justice of the Peace.
[17] Personal interview: Negro employee in State Prisons Dept.
[18] Personal interview: Negro taxicab driver.
[19] Personal interview: Negro nurse and housewife.
[20] Personal interview: Negro barber.

ran his pool room there on Hargett for years and some gambling and bootlegging went on in it as in most, but he always managed somehow to keep it under control. He had a couple of close calls with the law but managed to get out of it without any trouble. It was primarily his name and what he had meant to the pool room that kept it alive under his son.[21]

After 1942, when neither of the three personalities described above remained on the street, the formation of groups around singular persons began to subside. Since they were loosely knit and often transitory, there was little reason for their re-formation. But there were other informal groups which had developed somewhat simultaneously around specific places, places that were not their exclusive province but where they predominated. Many of these outlasted those which had revolved around key persons. Though possessing no previously constituted membership, their designation as groups seems tenable because of the apparent regularity with which a community of interests brought them together at the same place to continually participate in the same activities. The changes that have taken place in this aspect of the Main Street's style of life are again suggested in the descriptive views of Main Streeters themselves as follows:

At first Malette's was the center of social activities for the country people, and Hamlin's was the center for the city folk. Of course later everybody got in both, but the country people would use this as their departing and returning point when their families came to shop.[22]

The intelligentsia came to the printing office and discussed matters of the day. Negro business was more unified then, everything that pertained to the life of Negroes was on Hargett Street. The church people used to go to Collins Walker's barber shop and sit and talk. Different groups had their various congregating places where on Saturday all met and talked. That doesn't exist any more because the businesses have spread out and not as many folks have to go there as before. The businesses started leaving Hargett Street during the depression and didn't come back after the depression. That was once the hub of everything for Negroes. . . .[23]

[21] Personal interview: Negro realtor and Justice of the Peace.
[22] Personal interview: Negro operator of funeral parlor.
[23] Personal interview: Negro printer.

You might say that East Hargett was the crosswalks of the city. You hadn't seen Raleigh until you had been to Hargett St. Everybody met here. The real place for hangout groups was the pool room, which is always the case when a group of men gather at such places. Fellows who had hot stuff to sell would show up at the pool room because that's where the folks were. Since the pool room has been off the street, got burned in '56, there's no place to hangout. Instead the informal groups have moved to other areas where pool rooms are and where new neighborhoods are opening up. . . . When the American Legion Club room was up over the Royal Theater that was another hangout place, but that moved off the street too.[24]

One of the most significant characteristics of Main Street structure manifest in gathering at particular places has been the group-place alliance by class position of individual patrons, a factor of which operators have been as aware as have the patrons. Two of the places in which the class alignments have been most evident embrace services where the most intimate relationships exist—eating and sleeping—and these have become symbolic of another form of Main Street behavior, one where groups are perceived through ascribed statuses of individuals. A partial view of this is given as follows:

When you hear anyone say there's nothing happening on Hargett Street any more, if they're upper class they are talking about the hotel dining room; if they're lower class they're talking about the pool room. The riff-raff and Saturday folks all hung around the pool room, it was a beer joint too. The main thing that took them there was Jimmie Taylor and Charlie Otey, who were real personalities. I was away most of the week then and would come to town on the weekend, and they'd wait for me on weekends to come in and tell them all the jokes. All classes went there but mainly the lower class and riff-raff . . . the hotel dining room used to be on the front and everybody ate in there. That was THE place to go to eat. You could go in and get a soft drink or coffee or the like and a piece of pie and sit and talk half the day if you wanted to. Many people did their visiting that way. When Lightner's funeral parlor was across the street all the workers from there ate lunch over in the dining room, and when the offices were all upstairs those workers ate down there. When these moved out that cut the number of eating-visitors in the dining

24 Personal interview: Negro taxicab driver.

room. And the moving of the funeral parlor took a large number
of out-of-towners off the street who used to eat there.[25]

Hall's restaurant in the Arcade definitely influenced the change
that has taken place in Hargett Street in recent years. Everybody
used to go there to eat, people from all over the state came there
to stay when in town and you saw everybody there, so you just
enjoyed going there.[26]

. . . it (the hotel) has too much class to it now. That very thing
has made it poor. When we had the Eastern Star meeting here I
carried large groups of them all over town to eating places. Took
a group to the hotel and the Mighty Miss LJ looked up and saw
who it was and wouldn't open the door. They didn't look like they
had any class to them. I've even heard her make remarks like
that. . . .[27]

My sister-in-law and I used to operate a business on East Hargett
Street. We stayed there for about sixteen years . . . the name of
the business was the Yellow Rose Tea Room. We served dinners,
prepared for and served parties there, and had a number of regular boarders . . . we served anybody who came in, so some of the
regular customers dropped, but we still didn't have the real rough
Negroes. Our place was under the bank, and most of the undesirable Negroes didn't frequent that block, they went down in
the next block. I often had people tell me that we would never
make much money because the kind of people we catered to
knew when they came in exactly how much money they were going to spend, whereas the other element of people would spend
and spend until all was gone.[28]

There never was much hanging out at the Yellow Rose Tea Room.
That was really a lunch room that catered to the better classes,
to school groups, etc. . . . The fraternities at Shaw used to have
many of their social affairs there in the evening after they were
closed for outside patronage.[29]

It was through such means as these that special groupings
gradually became identified with specific places of business on

[25] Personal interview: Former Negro college president.
[26] Personal interview: Negro mail carrier.
[27] Personal interview: Negro realtor.
[28] Personal interview: Negro housewife.
[29] Personal interview: Negro taxicab driver.

the Main Street. And it was through the groups themselves that much Main Street behavior became significantly reflected in a characteristic style of life. Through them the main street became the cross-roads and mecca of the Negro world, the point at which all types of persons and groups met. The nature and location of places of business on the street give some idea as to how and why group alliances made this the cross-roads of the Negro world. Many changes have taken place in the nature of groups meeting in this cross-roads area, for many of the former functions of such groups have been assumed by other groups. With the closing of the tea room, removal of the funeral parlor, print shop, pool room and one drug store, and a change in management of the barber shop and hotel, a decline in group alliances with specific places set in. And yet, the street remains a type of mecca for the Negro world with observable differences still existing between the behavior on the street of city and country people, upper class and lower class, men and women, but with fewer lines of cleavage within male groups. But there is still another way in which the Negro Main Street unites activities of the Negro world, and that is through its relationship to more formally structured groups.

A surprisingly large number of Negroes in the community tends not to participate in any formal group, 58.0 percent of the sample population not belonging to any group, while 42.0 percent belongs to at least one group. When they do participate, church-group participation tends to outrank other forms, with 37.7 percent of those specifying groups belonged to designating them as church groups, and with females comprising 80.0 percent of the church group participants. Lodges tend to rank second in proportional membership but far below church groups, with only 13.6 percent of the group members participating therein, and with their proportion of female participants (51.9) exceeding that of males by only 3.8 percent. Again female membership, though numerically small, exceeds that of males in both professional groups and social clubs, comprising 74.6 percent of the former and 88.9 percent of the latter. Equivalent numbers of persons tend to belong to business groups and civic groups, but in these male membership exceeds that of females, comprising 55.0 percent of the former and 63.1 percent of the latter. The number of those with memberships in specifically designated political, literary, and interracial groups is exceedingly negligible, there being only two memberships listed for each of these categories. Thus, within the Negro world it appears that belonging to formal groups is not of major concern, and that no one interest predominates among all to whom belonging is of concern. The major group characteristic, like that of the Main Street itself, stems from the difference in activities of males and females. What then does this imply with regard to the functioning and structure of the Negro Main Street?

Of primary significance is the fact that the street acts as liaison between the informal and formal group activities of the community. Just as the street was originally the center around which informal groups pivoted, so also was it the point at which the majority of formal groups, exclusive of church ones, had their inception. It held at one time the only available space for group meetings whether of business men, labor unions, lodges, fraternities, sororities, debutantes, professionals, the civic and political-minded, or any other, and thus cut across the entire social structure of the Negro world. And it still retains its position as permanent headquarters for three of the most distinctive types of groups in the society, namely, lodge, state-teachers association, and labor union. Though many other groups have no such permanent alliance with the street they maintain connections therewith through dinner meetings, parties, or other social gatherings held there.

If there is any one interest which claims the attention of men's groups in the community more than any other it is an economic one of taxation and spending as a form of social insurance. This seems evidenced in the philosophy and objectives of the group with the largest local membership, the Raleigh Safety Club, which started right on the Main Street among those that comprise the largest percentage of patrons there, the laborers. The role of this organization is perhaps the most re-emphasized of any group in the community when judged by the number of members, the frequency with which it is mentioned in regular conversations, and the numerous contacts made to gain new members. The significance attached to the organization, and its relation to the Main Street, are partially portrayed by two of its members as follows:

If Negroes would just cooperate some and stop fighting to get ahead of each other they'd be better off. About the most cooperative venture I know of right now is the Raleigh Safety Club to

which I belong. It has about 500 members and you have to pay
$12.00 a year and a dollar each time a member dies. So, if some-
one dies you've got $500 right then and there, and the auxiliary
(women's division) comes and brings and prepares all the food
the family needs, etc. It's not a social club but a business organization. Regardless of what it started out to be it is a business
now.[30]

The Raleigh Safety Club started right there on Hargett Street,
and for years met regularly upstairs in the Odd Fellows Building.
Since they have built their own building all meetings are held in
it. Though I am a member of that I am inactive for the moment,
for I'm behind with my dues. It costs too much to belong to that,
it's a dollar per member that you have to pay each time a member of the club dies. The first month that I was in the club it cost
me $8.00 because there were eight deaths that month. And that
doesn't include regular fees, etc. It's a good club for old people.
I am about to decide to get out of it because there are too many
old people in it. The members range in age from 21 to 65. You
might say that this is really not a social club but a business club,
for belonging to it is really a business and they do good business,
especially the old folks. Women belong to it too, but their division has another name.[31]

Even where men undertake the establishment of clubs intended
to be purely social, the tendency to have them related to the
Negro Main Street, though declining, is often retained. A case in
point is given in the following excerpt.

I am a member of one of the clubs that you might say is connected with East Hargett St. in that we sometimes gather there
just to socialize, but for regular meetings we hold those in the
different homes of members. This club is named the Downtown
Social Club. It is only about a year old. A group of us had been
talking about trying to form a club for some time, but we just
got it started. We had 23 members but are down now to 14. It is
composed primarily of young men. The women, most of them are
our wives, have a club called the Elite Nine.[32]

The relationship of women's organizations to the Main Street
has generally been somewhat more indirect than that of the

[30] Personal interview: Negro mail carrier.
[31] Personal interview: Negro dental technician.
[32] Personal interview: Negro dental technician.

men's. The indirection has sometimes come through the formation of groups that are counterparts of those in which males participate, such as the Raleigh Safety Club and Downtown Social Club already mentioned, the Quette and Alpha Wives counterparts of the Omega and Alpha fraternities, or the Eastern Star which functions under the Masons. But even where no organizational connection exists an indirect participant relation obtains. Since there are no highly exclusive social groups in which membership is denied to certain classes, except for some few where educational and professional qualifications are required, the women's groups, like the men's, tend to contain cross sections of the population, the majority of whom are Negro Main Street traders. Herein lies further indirect relationship, although a more direct line exists between the two when their groups, again like the men's, often hold dinner parties or other social affairs on the street. A most vivid description of women's formal groups has been given thus by one resident of the community:

. . . Seems that the major contribution of women to the life of the city has been in the promotion of social affairs, for they do more of that than the men do. They give parties, dances, etc., and invite the men. The women have and belong to more clubs than the men do, for one thing you only have two groups of women here—teachers and domestics—no inbetweens. And you don't see much class consciousness in the groups. I belong to five of the groups myself: a sorority, the Gay Matrons, Jack and Jill, Queen of Hearts, and Quettes, and none of these has the same group of folks in them. You get some professionals and some otherwise. They are fairly selective but can't be but so selective for Raleigh has no basis for class distinctions—can't do it on the basis of homes; has no family heritage like some places; a few persons like the O's tried to hold themselves aloof for a while but all they had to fall back on was the fact that their father had been a barber for white people, and what's that? And there's no culture that has made it distinct. These half-white folks like DS, the O's and L's who may have tried to hold on to their mixed breed heritage couldn't get far with that because their children were so different. And most of their children have turned out to be nothing, wouldn't half go to school and aren't educated, so that keeps them out of many top groups like sororities and fraternities.[33]

[33] Personal interview: Negro female school teacher.

While formalized social groups developed around economic interests for the men, for the women they have tended to form around entertainment, that is in extra-church groups. Both male and female groups have tended to allocate space for civic projects within their schematic frameworks. One who lives in the community and is a part of the reading public of the local Negro newspaper, for example, cannot help but be struck by the stress placed upon arm-chair aid to civic groups, although direct participation in civic groups is most often lacking, as attested to in the 9.5 percent persons in the population who list membership in civic groups. While fewer women than men are among this 9.5 percent civic members, one of the most substantial and extensive projects has been formalized by a woman's group. In active participation the group reaches only a small percentage of the female population, but the permanency of its objectified efforts through the establishment of a social settlement house gives it a significance unmatched by many other civic groups. Commenting on the nature of women's activities, one of the well-known women of the community says,

Women in Raleigh have usually been domestic workers, teachers, or just housewives. That has kept them from many involvements in business. . . . As for the social activities of women, there have been several clubs but not much you could say about them. I am a member of the Women's Club, originally called the Woman's Reading Club. It was for married women, and while possible members were discussed, no invitation was necessary to join it. In late years it started taking in unmarried women too, for we felt that both should belong. The Mary Talbert Home grew out of this club.[34]

The origin, development, and functioning of the Mary Talbert Home are especially representative of the implied indirection which has obtained in relationships of women's formal groups to the Negro Main Street. The ensuing statements bear this out.

I organized the Mary Talbert Home for working girls. Started it on Shaw's campus in the old pharmaceutical building. My husband was teaching there and Dr. Peacock (president) gave me permission to use the building. Not sure of the date of origin, but it was around 1923, for I can judge from my son's age. When the government started demanding that you put in certain fixtures

[34] Personal interview: Negro female non-worker.

and fix up the buildings according to their specifications, it cost too much to do this to that old building. The women decided they didn't want to do that, so we bought Dr. Wortham's old home there across the street from the YWCA, number 317 East Davie.[35]

We hired a woman to stay there as matron and made it a housing project for working girls. It was a neighborhood affair and girls stayed there for $1.50 a week. When Shaw got ready to tear down the building and put up a new structure we had to move, so we got this place where we are now. At one time we belonged to the Community Chest and got funds from that. A few years ago they asked us to let the YWCA share the building with us, but we didn't feel that we could do that and have enough space for our purposes. Without even telling us that we were being dropped from the Community Chest, we were suddenly cut off and the only way we knew it was from reading the papers. Of course we felt that the reason had been our refusal to join with the YWCA. Since then we have had to work harder to keep the place going but were determined not to be outdone, so we usually take in women in the club who are interested in civic affairs and don't mind working, for it (the home) is really a job for workers.[36]

Thus does it appear that as the Negro Main Street has become an integral part of the structure of the urban community, it has tended to functionally integrate the associational life of one of its major sub-culture components, the Negro world. In so doing the street has reflected, either directly or indirectly, the major interests upon which the attention of the Negro world has been focused, resulting in a characteristic style of life for the Main Street itself. The informal alliances pervading this style of life have been symbolized in congregating around key persons, places, and interests, with lines of demarcation existing between the alliances formed by men and women, rural and urban groups, upper class and lower class individuals. The more formal alliances forming part of this style of life have evidenced fewer distinct cleavages and been more indirectly related to the Main Street. Constant changes in the nature and number of these group alliances has effected some alteration in the social structure of the Main Street, but has not appreciably altered its function as inte-

[35] Personal interview: Negro housewife and civic leader.
[36] Personal interview: Negro female non-worker.

grator of Negro life from the associational standpoint. Its functional utility has thereby made the street a culture medium through which to relate the varied intra-racial groups which have developed under the impact of certain interracial attitudes. The resulting effect of this upon the Negro world will be the next point for consideration.

Chapter 8

SOLIDARITY AND RACE-CONSCIOUSNESS WITHIN THE MAIN STREET COMPLEX

The externalized culture medium known as the Negro Main Street has been a means of so sustaining social relations through the psychological bond of race that the street has actually helped promote solidarity in the Negro world. This solidarity, however, is one of tenuous unity in social action accompanied by a high degree of race-consciousness. Explaining the nature of social solidarity Durkheim states that it is "a completely moral phenomenon which, taken by itself, does not lend itself to exact observation nor indeed to measurement. To proceed to this classification and this comparison, we must substitute for this internal fact which escapes us an external index which symbolizes it and study the former in the light of the latter." [1] Moreover, Durkheim indicates that social solidarity receives its character from the group whose unity it assures and that what exists and really lives is the particular forms of solidarity.[2] In the light of this the Negro Main Street appears to be an acceptable index of the nature of solidarity in the Negro world, and a vital medium through which to study the same. For Durkheim law became a visible symbol of social solidarity. For viewing solidarity among Negroes, the Main Street is not only a visible symbol but a sentimental symbol of the common conceptions, meanings, and experiences of a people. This makes the street, using the terminology of Durkheim, a collective representation, which is "not merely a convenient process for clarifying the sentiment society has of itself; it also serves to create this sentiment; it is one of its constituent elements." [3] But over and above this, the symbolic function of the Main Street seems even more synonymous with the purpose given of collective representations for, says Durkheim, "without symbols, social sentiments could have only a precarious existence . . . social life is made possible only by a vast symbolism." [4]

[1] Emile Durkheim, *The Division of Labor in Society*, trans. George Simpson (Glencoe, Illinois: Free Press, 1947), p. 64.
[2] *Ibid.*, p. 66.
[3] Emile Durkheim, *The Elementary Forms of Religious Life*, trans. Joseph Ward Swain (Glencoe, Illinois: Free Press, 1947), p. 230.
[4] *Ibid.*, p. 231.

The Negro Main Street—a visible, sentimental symbol born out of the interracial experiences of Negroes—does not exemplify profound social solidarity characterized by complete cooperation and unity of social action. No incident comparable to the Montgomery situation evoking the city-bus boycott has arisen in the Raleigh community to bring the potential unity of the Negro world into focus. Two of the contemporary social action programs which give evidence of a lack of complete unity among the Negroes are the Holt Case and the movement to elect a Negro to the City Council. The Holt Case itself, one in which a Negro boy has sought entrance to an all-white high school for three consecutive years, is being processed through litigation. However, the nature and degree of unity among Negroes relative to the case is shown in the partial support given the boy's father who lost his job because of the case. For a number of years Negroes have tried to get elected to the City Council, there being usually only one Negro at a time seeking to be one of the seven members so elected by the voters, but in the last election two Negroes sought seats on the Council. So far none has been elected, while in several smaller cities of the state Negroes have been elected to their respective city councils, though often by "single-shot" voting. In the Raleigh community there has been little evidence or encouragement of single-shot voting among Negroes. Here then is evidence of the lack of complete unity in social action, and hence the tenuous solidarity within the community. But there is one area in which a high degree of unity and solidarity is apparent, namely, in the goals for status. Nowhere are these goals made more evident than in the race-conscious reactions of Negroes which manifest themselves in attitudes toward Negroes, as well as toward whites.

If minority and majority attitudes are complements of the same profile, as Locke and Stern have said,[5] then similar reactions of large numbers of individual Negroes toward themselves and whites might easily be variations on the same racial theme. Viewed thus, race-consciousness can be said to develop within the descriptive framework set by Locke and Stern thus: "Minority group consciousness, although it may have originated in culture distinctiveness, becomes increasingly a product of enforced relations to a majority treatment and policy. A minority group, ir-

[5] Alain Locke and Bernhard J. Stern, *When Peoples Meet* (New York: Progressive Education Association, 1942), p. 466.

respective of size or constituency, is thus best characterized as a social group whose solidarity is primarily determined by external pressure, which forces it to live in terms of opposition and ostracism." [6] Race-consciousness, an attitudinal part of the Negro's internalization of his minority status and treatment, thus becomes characteristic of the solidarity of a social group striving to become equal with other social groups in the culture. Since race-consciousness is marked by "the tendency towards sentimental and ideological identification with a racial group," and causes the race to become a collective representation for the individual,[7] it goes without saying that insofar as the Main Street symbolizes the Negro's struggle for status it becomes to individual Negroes a collective representation of racial behavior. Through Main Street behavior we are thus able to point out the lines of cohesiveness along which race-consciousness has developed.

One of the indices of the type of solidarity found in the Negro world is the consensus regarding business patronage. Within the

sample population of 350, 93.4 percent of Main Street traders and non-traders tend to think that all Negroes should patronize Negro business, although the percentage of Main Street patrons is slightly less (87.7 percent). Males are even more in agreement on this than females, 96.6 percent of the males thinking all Negroes should patronize Negro business, and 91.8 percent of the females. Not only does this belief prevail but, as was pointed out in an earlier chapter, the majority of those who actually patronize Negro businesses give as the chief reason the fact that they are Negro. Thus, consciousness of kind tends to be a major factor promoting the existent solidarity of the community. The consciousness-of-kind factor takes on added significance when recognition is taken of the large proportions of Negroes who indicate things they "would do" in Negro businesses in comparison with the smaller proportions who would do the same things in white businesses. The following table gives some indication of the nature of behavior thought to involve this consciousness-of-kind factor.

[6] *Ibid.*, p. 465.
[7] W. O. Brown, "The Nature of Race Consciousness," *Social Forces* (October, 1931), Vol. X, p. 90.

TABLE 14

Things Main Streeters Would and Would Not Do,
by Number of Persons Making Such Designations

The Behavior	Would Do This		Would Not Do This	
	Number	Per Cent	Number	Per Cent
1) Eat in a Negro café	310	89.3	20	5.8
2) Eat in white café with special provisions for Negroes	56	16.1	124	35.7
3) Attend an all-Negro theater	277	79.8	33	9.5
4) Attend white theater with section set aside for Negroes	91	26.2	77	22.2
5) Bank with Negro-owned bank	304	87.6	17	4.9
6) Bank with white-owned bank	115	33.1	68	19.6
7) Use rest rooms marked "colored" in white places of business	95	27.4	82	23.6
8) Go to Negro places of business to use rest rooms	269	77.5	24	6.9
9) Use professional services of Negroes	316	91.1	9	2.6
10) Use professional services of whites	121	34.9	57	16.4

Data from the preceding table indicate that of the 347 persons making some designation of things they would or would not do, the greater proportions would definitely use professional services of Negroes (91.1 per cent), eat in an all-Negro café (89.3 per cent), bank with a Negro-owned bank (87.6 per cent), attend an all-Negro theater (79.8 per cent), and go to Negro places of business to use rest rooms (77.5 per cent). Although some Negroes would likewise secure the same services from whites, the value placed upon such can be inferred from the smaller, but sizeable, percentages of persons who would eat in a white café which makes special provisions for Negroes (16.1 per cent), attend a white theater with section set aside for Negroes (26.2 per cent), bank with a white-owned bank (33.1 per cent), use rest rooms marked "colored" in white places of business (27.4 per cent), and use professional services of whites (34.9 per cent). Even if one reacts similarly to both white and Negro places of business, the most striking thing noted among those things they would not do is eat in a white café which has special provisions for Negroes, the percentage being 35.7. Not only does this begin to show the self-conceptions which Negroes hold of themselves, but the fact that 77.2 per cent of those mentioned above would make a special effort to go to the Negro Main Street to carry out the aforementioned actions shows also conceptions of the street sustained by ideological identification therewith.

Another index of the nature of solidarity existing among Negroes is the collective opinion which considers individual achievements as group advancement, and business failure as racial failure. One is invariably reminded of the individuals in the community who formerly owned a great deal of property; of those who ventured into businesses where some amassed fortunes while others speculated and lost; those who made financial provisions for their families and gave them the status of a leisure class; and those who entered professional and business areas which gave opportunities to other Negroes. In each of these instances the same group of individuals is repeatedly mentioned, and in only a few cases are the individuals themselves still living, the current status of their survivors being used to illustrate their accomplishments. Whether related privately or publicly, the accomplishments of these individuals are always made synonymous with achievements of the Negro race. Among Negroes emphasis on personal achievement is important, for it is used to express the potential possibilities of the Negro for gaining increased recognition and status. Descriptive views of the achievements of three leading persons, one deceased and two living, will suffice to illustrate the point as reiterated by local residents. Regarding the deceased person it is reported that,

When Berry O'Kelley negotiated for the bank site he was not free at first to abandon his relations with other banking institutions of the city. All sought his support and made overtures to him to represent them in various transactions in and out of the city. He was known as the town's leading trader because of his ability to bargain. Later he changed to our bank. . . . When I first came to Raleigh in 1895 the late Berry O'Kelley was the biggest merchant in these parts. He was the only commission merchant here, serving the entire city and other points nearby from his warehouse in Method. He supplied nearly all the schools and colleges with merchandise and foodstuffs. . . . He bought the property on Hargett Street from Wilmington St. up to the bank from a white woman and the State Department leased it from him for a long time. . . . One day I asked T. F. McGuire of the Wachovia bank what he thought Berry O'Kelley was worth. 'Professor,' said he, 'I have just checked up on Berry and I find that he is worth about a quarter of a million dollars.' Of course he did so much for others and lost so in 1929 that he didn't have too much when he died. There were ten of us who formed a company to buy the old *News and Observer* property on Fayetteville Street. We all sold out to Berry and he made a hotel out of it. He was urged to sell the property for $80,000 but he kept holding out for $100,000, and when the depression came he couldn't hold it. Taxes, insurance and interest began to make inroads upon his capital outlay and sapped his investments.[8]

One of the best Negro businesses was Berry O'Kelley's wholesale and retail business. He was a commission merchant, along with other things. He . . . got a commission on the goods (groceries, etc.) that came into Raleigh regardless of who did the buying. He owned a lot of real estate in business spots in Raleigh. He was postmaster and freight agent in Method, handled the goods right from the freight car because it went right by his place. He was a great politician but never got into politics himself, he just manipulated politics. The men uptown had him work with Negroes to get their votes. Of course there weren't many people then, but even a few votes counted.[9]

Negroes used to be pretty well off. Berry O'Kelley was easily worth a quarter of a million. . . . He was uneducated but a good business man. His word went as far as any man's. He had a lot of influence. When they were about to run that hard-surface road through Method he asked that the city pave in front of his store. Nobody thought the city would do it, but they turned out of the way and put a mile of hard surface right along in front of his store. He was also postmaster at Method, and they still have a nigger postmaster out there. Whites have to get their mail there too, but there's always been a nigger postmaster there. If he hadn't made so many bad bargains borrowing, trading, and trafficking with so little training he wouldn't have lost so much of what he had originally.[10]

The person next mentioned is most often held up in the community not as a financial tycoon, but as a symbol of the Negro's faith in his own potentialities for gaining status. A deaf mute who does much of his communicating by writing, he states that he was graduated from Shaw University with the LL.B. degree in 1907, from Yale University with the LL.B. degree in 1912, practised law

[8] Charles R. Frazer, Sr., *The Uses of Adversity* (unpublished autobiography).

[9] Personal interview: Retired Negro undertaker.

[10] Personal interview: Retired Negro school teacher.

in Salisbury, North Carolina from 1914 to 1919 and in Raleigh since 1921.[11] Featuring him as personality of the week the local Negro newspaper said of him:

Perhaps the greatest tribute that could possibly have been paid to this week's *Carolinian* personality of the week was that of Lucy Sewell writing in the March, 1927, issue of "The Silent Worker" (pp. 169-74) in which Attorney Roger Demosthenes O'Kelley . . . is described as the only Negro deaf-mute lawyer in the United States. . . . He renders excellent service on questions of domestic relations, conducts real estate transactions, organizes corporations, and performs countless other legal duties, and lists white firms among his clients.[12]

The third individual mentioned often receives more criticism than commendation for his efforts, but whichever is given it is usually a racial, as well as personal, implication for showing possibilities for advancement. Among the collective opinions of him are these:

DH is one man who has really done well in business, and he has tried to give all his relatives a break. He has offered some of them work who wouldn't take it, and where some others have worked but he found he couldn't trust them he let them go. If his boys had the personalities those L boys have they'd do much more business. At one time they were burying practically all the bodies because L had gone down, but his son came in and took over the business and really made it boom. . . .[13]

D has easily about $100,000 tied up in that property on the corner (filling station, etc.) and he doesn't have the records he ought to have. D's funeral parlor is, piece for piece, brick for brick, one of the best in the state, not just in Raleigh, and he never has a meeting with his employees. He'll pull one aside and tell him what he wants him to do but never a meeting to define jobs and the like.[14]

The general consensus that all Negroes should trade with Negroes, and that achievements or failures of any one Negro repre-

[11] Personal document: Written communication with writer.
[12] *The Carolinian* (Raleigh, North Carolina), May 3, 1952.
[13] Personal interview: Negro mail carrier.
[14] Personal interview: Negro taxicab dispatcher and funeral parlor operator.

sent the entire race, has tended to make the Negro quite race-conscious. Stemming from techniques of discrimination, race-consciousness has created in the Negro co-existent attitudes of equality-seeking, loyalty-retention, racial resentment, and keen censure. The Main Street, a reciprocal of both discrimination and race-consciousness, has been one of the principal media through which the Negro has been able to express his ambivalence toward both Negroes and whites. Thus, the nature of interpersonal relations between businessmen and customers, Negroes and whites, Main Street traders and non-traders gives insights into the race-conscious attitudes which have been effected through discrimination for, to use the words of Drake and Cayton, "race consciousness is not the work of agitators or subversive influences—it is forced upon Negroes by the very fact of their separate-subordinate status in American life." [15]

One of the lines along which race-consciousness has developed is that of equality-seeking. Conscious efforts to attain a status equal with that of whites have tended to make the Negro sensitive to the application of democratic principles in human relations, though these are not always applied to his own personal actions. Among those who contend for the application of democratic principles Negro business that caters strictly to a Negro clientele is decried, refusal to use or accept discrimination is desired, and both parallel and integrated equality-situations are approved. Illustrative of this attitude are the following:

1) Non-discrimination Against Whites

. . . sometimes you have to use both colored and white. You can't break down discrimination if you use Negroes only. We got to let the white man know he can't get along without us and we can't get along without him. We have to try to get the man who's going to do us the most good regardless of his race, must use both white and colored. If we don't do that we're going to get left behind. Got to stop fighting segregation if we going to cater to Negroes only. To get equality we got to use both. Take this house I was building not long ago down on the corner there, some things I could use Negroes to do and some things I had to use whites to do. It takes a whole lot of folks to build a house and no one man has all the know-how in doing it. [16]

[15] St. Clair Drake and Horace R. Cayton, *Black Metropolis* (New York: Harcourt, Brace and Co., 1945), p. 390.

[16] Personal interview: Negro employee of a railroad company.

On the whole . . . Negro businesses operated on East Hargett Street are operated as well as any of similar type in the city operated by any other ethnic group . . . the white stores on Hargett Street in the colored area should hire colored help . . . the theater in the heart of the Negro business area should have a colored manager . . . the segregated café operated by whites for colored should be open for everybody. I don't think white people should be discriminated against in any business managed by Negroes, or one operated in a colored business district.[17]

An attitudinal axis that claims even more attention of the race-conscious is that of loyalty-retention. In order to help the race advance many Negroes insist that Negroes just have to patronize Negro business, and there seem to be three major ways in which this loyalty expresses itself, namely, in the need for business developments; in the patronage of Negro business despite its deficiencies or unpleasant experiences encountered; and in keeping embarrassing behavior within the race. Underlying these is a mutual-aid philosophy of sticking together and helping each other. A variety of specific attitudes showing how this general philosophy with regard to remaining loyal to the race is portrayed in the excerpts which follow.

1) *Need For Business Developments*
There are a lot of businesses colored ought to go into and help the race. Seems like all a Negro can think of opening when he starts in business is a café, or funeral parlor, or juke joint. Why can't they do some of the same things that the white man does? They don't think of enough things to do. If they'd get together and develop more businesses they'd soon find that the colored are behind them. The businesses on Hargett Street are all right, they just need to develop more of a variety of businesses.[18]

2) *Patronage of Negro Business*
I use everything colored, don't use no more than I have to if it's white. Some things the whites are in charge of you have to use, but where I can make a choice I always use the colored. And I try to encourage others to do the same thing. Sometimes folks come here to call a cab and every time I call one for them I call a colored one. I know about all the Negroes in business personally

---

[17] Personal interview: Negro college teacher.
[18] Personal interview: Young Negro housewife.

and I think I ought to use them as much as possible, you know the white man ain't going to help them but so much, so if we don't patronize them they can't make it. . . . What Negroes need to do most is stick together and they could buy up nice places and have really fine businesses. White folks don't care what they do to colored folks. Look at that state building out on Tarboro Road and filling station right there at St. Aug. When they rezoned that for business Negroes could have prevented it if they hadn't waited so long before petitioning. Then when they did they didn't stick together. . . .[19]

I just enjoy going to Hargett Street and I'm always up there, don't mind passing through the crowds even 'cause there aren't too many people up there any day but Saturday . . . and most of the folks there are going on minding their own business just like I am. As long as there's any colored business I'm going to use them. I want to help my race all I can 'cause they [whites] always want to keep us down.[20]

I go to colored to do all my work for me. My fore-parents weren't like that. They were slaves and believed more in trading with the white man. There's no way for the Negro to come up unless they patronize each other, whites are not going to exalt us. Only thing I'm afraid of is the Negro business might fall apart by Negroes not having confidence in each other.[21]

I had a very unpleasant experience once with a Negro business on Hargett Street, took an iron to an electrical appliance store for repair in 1954 and never received the iron. A year later I was given another iron to use until mine could be repaired, and it was old and lasted about a month. However, I still feel it my duty to patronize Negro business. I find Negroes treat me equally as nice as whites.[22]

The colored ain't got but one real business street and that's Hargett. Negroes ought to use that street and patronize what's there. Whites try to keep the colored down, so we got to depend on our own color if we're going to get anywhere. Colored don't have much money anyway and they need to spend what they can with the colored man. Out there at State College where I was working

[19] Personal interview: Retired Negro railroad worker.
[20] Personal interview: Negro housewife.
[21] Personal interview: Elderly Negro female non-worker.
[22] Personal interview: Young Negro public school teacher.

me and a white man was working side by side and doing the same work. At least we was supposed to be doing the same work, I could never stop working, but half the time he was off sitting under a tree resting or smoking while I worked. I was getting $75 every two weeks and he was getting $96 every two weeks. One day he asked me how much I made and I told him; then he told me what he was getting, and I raised a fog 'cause I had been there a long time before he even came there to work and I taught him the work. When I went to the boss man and asked for more money he wanted to know why I wanted more, and I told him what the other man was making. He asked me how I knew and I told him he told me so hisself; and you know what he said? It takes more for a white man to live on 'cause his wife has to pay a maid and all that. Seem like he wa'n't thinking about my wife at all. But that's why I say the colored got to try to help theirselves.[23]

We just don't patronize each other enough. I'm guilty myself, but not because I don't like to trade with the Negro, I just go to the most convenient place. Take this store up here on the corner, now a white man runs that and that's where I go most of the time. I can run up there and not even lock my front door because I can see all the way to my door. Back down here under the hill is a Negro grocery store and it's just as nice, and I really think a lot more of the person who runs it. He's a personal friend of mine, but I don't go there as often as I should because it's a little further away . . . we just have to learn that to be a race we must stick together and patronize each other and stop being jealous of one another. That's all we got anyway is our own people. The old po' whites, and that's who it is 'cause the better class of white people are more for you, the po' whites don't want to be with you and they're always trying to keep the Negro down. I feel like I'm better than them. The low class Negro is just as bad, he talks about and kicks the Negro in business just as much as these old whites. It's the upper class Negro that tries to help you get somewhere. I feel ashame, of not using colored business more than I do, but I do use most of those on Hargett Street because it's convenient and near town. Then too, I go there to pay my insurances and to lodge meeting.[24]

3) *Keeping Embarrassing Behavior Within the Race*

As to what inspired me to go into the funeral business, I remember as well as if it happened yesterday. I was working on the

[23] Personal interview: Negro maintenance man at N. C. State College.
[24] Personal interview: Negro housewife.

house that is now occupied by Rev. S, which was at that time property of Shaw University . . . there was a boy who lived down the street a few houses from the site of Tupper Hall. The boy died. Some man came up where I was working on the house and asked me to come down to serve as pallbearer. I gladly consented. This was in October of 1908. The funeral was held in the little rock church now called Fayetteville Street Baptist. A white undertaker had the body of this boy. In eulogizing the deceased the minister used this text, 'Oh, how often would I have hovered you under my wings as a brood would her chicks but you wouldn't let me.' Further on he said, 'Yes, Jones is no longer wanted by the hen here on earth, he is gone to rest with the hen above, he is hovered safely.' At that time an old lady jumped up and said, 'Oh, you done it now'. The house shook with laughter, just like a theater crowd. The white undertaker laughed out too. This disturbed me greatly. I then thought that if my people were to be so ignorant I wanted to keep it within the race. I went home and began to think about the funeral business. I thought of every possible man who might be in a position to establish a funeral home. Meanwhile I found myself making excuses for every one I thought of. Suddenly the thought came, why couldn't I do it. . . this made the decision for me. Meanwhile I enrolled in embalmer's school.[25]

. . . I rather deal with my color, they don't cheat you any more than whites do, but when you go in some of these stores colored make you shame. They blab, and grin, and twist, and the whites make fun of them and they don't know it. . . Just last week I was in Dianne Shop and there was a colored woman in there trying on a sack dress. She looked awful in it, but those old white clerks kept telling her how nice she looked, and she kept saying, 'At last I've found me a sack I can wear.' She really made a fool of herself there and the clerks snickered and laughed to each other but kept on telling her how nice she looked. I just stood there and looked. Colored will let whites put anything off on them.[26]

. . . and a Negro'll embarrass you too. Seem like they wait 'til there's a white person around to see how loud they can get and show off and they'll show off on you right in front of them. Just let one try to say something to you and you ignore him when there's a white man around and they'll really embarrass you then. That's one reason I think colored people ought to have their

---

[25] Personal interview: Retired Negro undertaker.
[26] Personal interview: Young Negro housewife.

places separate from the whites, then when they show off whites don't see it.[27]

Believing that they can change their subordinate status to one of equality with whites through loyalty and assistance to each other, Negroes tend to resent any intra-racial differences and inequalities made by Negroes themselves. Thus, a race-conscious attitude of resentment has resulted in hatred, fear, distrust, and suspicion of Negroes who act toward other Negroes in such manner as to give whites stereotyped impressions of the race. This resentment is specifically manifest in complaints about the aloofness of businessmen, inadequate service rendered by business personnel, and failure to help and respect each other. Even though these are all viewed through the Main Street and its business institutions, their significance to Negroes reaches beyond purely economic realms into areas of racial interdependence and cohesiveness based on interpersonal relationships. It is impossible to show the many intense ramifications of this as portrayed by residents of the community, but a few illustrative attitudes can be indicated.

1) *Aloofness of Businessmen*
. . . Negroes won't let you help them but so much anyway. Those who are in business feel above you and so independent that most times they're not nice to you. Cause you don't have as much as they have seem like they look down their nose at you, so I don't bother with them.[28]

I think you ought to use colored business when you can, but some time you just can't. For one thing the colored feels independent. Seem like they hate to do for each other, and the low class are not recognized by those higher up. Those in business act like they don't care whether the low class man trades with him or not, so if you stay away you don't have to get your feelings hurt.[29]

Negroes could be a little more courteous. They're too independent to be in business, act like they don't even want your money, and if I'm going to spend my money I at least want to do it where people are nice to me. I said that to a friend of mine the

[27] Personal interview: Young Negro janitress.
[28] Personal interview: Negro male laborer.
[29] Personal interview: Negro female domestic worker.

other day and she said, what difference does it make, you aren't in the store that long, all you do is go in and get what you want and come right out. I said, yes, but in that short time I want to spend with nice people, not hateful ones who snap at you.[30]

A Negro'll shove you aside quicker than a white man will. Seem like there's something mighty in us makes us feel big when we get in business. You walk in a store of a Negro and almost get a cold shoulder. They act like they feel above you.[31]

Negroes are just getting so now that they'll patronize one another . . . some used to say the Negroes were uppish, that they'd try to make a fool out of you. They'd go in the dry goods store (H's) and ask for some nice material to make a dress, and the Negroes would ask what kind of material they wanted. They didn't know quality of material, so they went more by sight; they'd say show me what you have and I can tell you what I want, but the Negroes didn't want to do that. . . .[32]

2) *Inadequate Service of Business Personnel*
I would like very much to patronize Negroes because I know they need all the colored patronage they can get, but you can't patronize them like you should . . . my pet peeve is the colored cab. I used to take a colored cab to work, would call them every morning. They would never get here on time, and if they came on time they'd come too early and expect to get paid for all the time they waited. . . . I went to a colored lawyer once, won't call his name, just to ask him something. He didn't answer my question but told me how I could get it answered, and when I asked what he charged he said $5. Every time I see that man now I think of that thing. I ain't never paid him because I went straight to a white lawyer and he told me what I wanted to know and didn't charge a penny. . . . One time I had a bad leg and Dr. C was treating it, and he had to go away when his father died. He left his patients in care of Dr. T. I went to Dr. T to get my leg dressed and he never did let me sit or get up on the table, he had me stand while he changed the bandage. As soon as I walked out of the door the bandage broke and the girl with me told me to buy some bandages and she would fix it herself when I got home, so that's what I did but I had to pay him. I had such terrible experiences trying to patronize Negro business. . . . I still use a

[30] Personal interview: Negro housewife.
[31] Personal interview: Negro janitor.
[32] Personal interview: Elderly Negro female bakery employee.

colored doctor and buy groceries sometimes from Williams'. My
biggest complaints are the cabs and lawyers . . . you just get
better service from whites than colored. Can't hardly depend on a
Negro, their businesses are all right but their personalities are
so bad. They need to improve theirselves, can't say much about
their businesses 'cause they got a right to be in business . . . but I
do know they'll hurt your feelings every time and your feelings
are all you got.[33]

I've had some raw deals from colored business. I used to take my
car to Shell Service Station when JL was there because he was a
personal friend of mine and I wanted to help him all I could. One
time I took the car there for one thing and they did something
else to it, and I was on my way to Chapel Hill and a fellow came
up behind me and told me to pull over, and I did and discovered
all my oil was leaking out. They had taken the filter out of the car
and hadn't put it back right and I didn't know it. . . . I carried the
car back to them and asked them to fix it right and thought they
did, but even that time they messed it up and I had to carry it to
a white filling station to get it straight. You can't depend on
colored folks, they just won't do right, but you have to help them
all you can.[34]

I don't use a colored doctor 'cause I get better service from the
white. Of course you have to pay, but colored keep you lingering
on while whites serve you and let you go. A white doctor he'll
tell you 'I can't do you no good' and let you go, or he'll do all he
can for you and dismiss you, but a colored doctor won't tell you
and keeps you hanging on and still expects his pay.[35]

Right now the colored business I use most is the drug store and
taxi cab. Used to use colored doctors and tried this last time I
needed one to get a colored one, but you can't get colored doctors
to get out and come to you at night. I tried to cooperate with
them but you can't get them when you need them. Here a few
weeks ago my wife called Dr. H to come to me and he said he'd
be here. Two or three hours later she called back to see if he still
intended to come and he said he was busy but would get here
some time that day. So she called Dr. G, a white doctor, 'cause I
needed relief then and he was here in a half hour. About five
o'clock Dr. H came driving up and she had called him that

---

[33] Personal interview: Negro female domestic worker.
[34] Personal interview: Negro male construction worker.
[35] Personal interview: Negro maintenance worker.

morning about nine, so she told him she had to get another doctor. Before that I tried to get Dr. T to come out to see me and he said he'd treat me if I came to the office but couldn't come out to the house. Since home visits cost so much I'd have gone to the office in the first place if I'd been able. You just can't get these colored doctors when you need them. Now I go to a white doctor and he sends me to a white hospital. I tried to get him to send me to St. Agnes, primarily because that would be closer for my wife to visit, but he said he was going to send me where he knew what kind of treatment I'd get. Naturally I couldn't say nothing 'cause I know what the colored'll do for you.[36]

The bank may have money but I don't see how they can, the personnel is so awful. Mr. S gives you the runaround every time. I financed my house on Person Street through them. Two years after paying for it I went to get them to finance some repairs I wanted to make on the house, didn't want but a few hundred dollars. For three weeks S gave me the runaround and said he'd let me know. Finally I got tired of waiting and went to First Citizens to get the money. They came and looked at the house and told me I could get more than I applied for even. Later that day when I went to get the money they said they couldn't release the money until the mortgage was cleared; now the house had been paid for twenty-six months and they hadn't cleared it; only one who could do it was H, and the man at First Citizens told me if I didn't clear it right away and anything happened to H his heirs would get the property and I'd be out. I had to run S down to get this done. Finally one day I went up to the bank, and I was going to whip him that day, I raised plenty sand in that place . . . raised so much stink that S called my uncle and told him to come up there and talk to me. He came and went to Durham and got the thing straight that day. Even after that I was going to deal with them, just felt I should throw as much their way as possible. Went to get them to finance the present house in Rochester Heights but they were too slow . . . had to go to First Citizens again. I should have learned my lesson with them but went on a note this summer, wasn't but fifty dollars, for a fellow . . . the fellow didn't pay a cent on the note so I had to pay it off. I paid it down to $21, then went up there and told the girl I wasn't going to pay any more unless I just had to, but if he didn't pay to deduct it from my reserve. She said all right. Two weeks after that, just a few

[36] Personal interview: Negro maintenance worker at N. C. State College, temporarily unemployed due to illness.

weeks ago, I got home from summer school and there was a summons there for me. I went to see about it, and S had done it because I hadn't paid the balance on that guy's note . . . I asked him how much my balance was and how much I owed. He said $21 plus $10 for the summons and $2 for late payment. They showed me my card and I wrote them a check for the money due them and another to myself for the balance. The girl asked me if this meant I was closing my account and I said yes, it's two years overdue.[37]

The bank itself is good and makes an excellent appearance, but the personnel is so difficult. I really think anything bad anyone says about the bank has to be traced back to the manager. Since we are in business ourselves and are a Negro business we feel obligated to use the colored bank some, but we had so much trouble trying to get loans or financing for some particular purpose that we had to go where we could get ready cash when we need it. So we do our minor business with them and our really big business with white banks where it is not difficult to get money in a hurry when you need it.[38]

Negro business would go much better here if the colored bank had another manager, or different system, or something. I use a white bank now, but tried to use the colored bank; had a little money in there when I got ready to build this house we live in, and had the house part of the way up when I found I needed some more money. So I went to the colored bank and tried to borrow it but they wouldn't let me have it. Some people they just won't lend it. I'd like to deal with them if the manager gave me justice. After I couldn't get the money from them I went to a white bank . . . and in three hours' time I had the money in my hands. You get hitched when you try to deal with the colored. Seems like the colored don't want to help you.[39]

. . . any substantial citizen working every day for the government like I am and can't get a loan from a bank without S giving you the runaround for two or three weeks just ought not bother with them any more, but I still do. If Negroes don't patronize Negro business how are they going to make it? [40]

[37] Personal interview: Young Negro electric appliance dealer.
[38] Personal interview: Negro female co-operator of business.
[39] Personal interview: Negro employee of a railroad company.
[40] Personal interview: Negro mail carrier.

3) *Failure to Help and Respect Each Other*

. . . colored people scared they might do you a favor, and don't ask none for credit do you sho' fall out. If colored people would trust you a little more they might have more trade, after all they got to depend on their own race.[41]

. . . the colored'll be courteous and nice as pie to the white man, but not courteous to their own color.[42]

The main trouble with Negroes when they get in business is they try to make money too fast. They been down so long that they try overnight to reach the white man, and you just can't move that fast in business and expect to stay open . . . one thing that holds the Negro back in Raleigh is the Negro bank, they won't lend to Negroes like they ought to. Negroes don't try to help each other. Those few who get to the top try to take advantage of the rest. You take Mr. S up at the bank, he won't even help those who need money the worst to get a loan, but the people who don't need it he'll lend to in a second. Dr. P told me he went up there and in a few minutes' time borrowed $2,000. He said he didn't really need it but got it to help the bank. People like that can get it with ease, but a person like me can't even get a loan without signing over everything you've got to them. D told me the other day about a woman who tried to borrow money from the bank and really needed the money, but when the board met S gave them every reason why the woman shouldn't be granted the loan. He said he knew she needed it, so he took a chance and lent it to her himself . . . that's why colored people can't get anywhere here . . . then too, if the Negro didn't have such high prices he might do a little better. This building JD is moving from, they charge $75 a month rent for that. And what happens is a person will go rent and stay as long as he can and when things start getting tight he moves out and the place stays idle a long time. Now it would be much better to charge cheaper rent and keep the place occupied, but that's the way Negroes try to get rich quick.[43]

Integration is going to change all this. It's going to drop us back where the Jews were when they had nothing and couldn't go a number of places, but the Jews stuck together and got some place . . . we have to learn to stick together and buy places and

[41] Personal interview: Negro housewife.
[42] Personal interview: Negro male laborer.
[43] Personal interview: Negro beautician.

make them so that people will like to come to them. We have to
do just like the Jew, but to do it we have to drink less wine and
save more money.[44]

The three preceding interrelated race-conscious attitudes of
equality-seeking, loyalty-retention, and racial-resentment are directly linked with a fourth, that of keen censure. Using the Main
Street as a medium through which to view these attitudes, one
becomes immediately aware of the Negro's critical opinions of
himself. As he accounts for his failure to secure equality of status
with whites, by-products of which are his attitudes of loyalty and
resentment, he assesses the blame therefor upon the Negro himself rather than upon whites. Thus, in trying to change statuses
the Negro becomes his own enemy and obstacle, and through his
jealousy, envy and non-cooperation, covert relations with whites,
and lack of leadership hinders the unity necessary for elevating
the status of the race as a whole. The excerpts which follow offer
clues as to how keenly Negroes censure themselves along these
lines.

1) *Jealousy, Envy and Non-cooperation*

The thing that hurts Negro business most is jealousy. We just
hate to see another one do more than we can do, or get ahead of
us in any way. There's no reason in the world why that Co-op
shouldn't still be operating on the corner there, but you can't run
a business with each man in it trying to dictate the policies,
running to the cash register to check on the other fellow, and taking out goods as you please. On the other hand, as soon as some
of us make a little headway we get so independent and throw
our heads so high you can't hand us a red apple.[45]

There seems to be a tinge of enviousness among Negroes. Wherever you see a Negro business man doing well you can trace and
find that he's an alien, not a Raleighite. They'll even ask where
you're from, etc., and you lose their trade if they find out you belong here because you seem to be doing a little better than they
are. . .[46]

. . . I don't know what is wrong with us but it seems that the

---

[44] Personal interview: Negro realtor and Justice of the Peace.
[45] Personal interview: Negro male business operator.
[46] Personal interview: Negro female co-operator of business.

worst acting we are and the more things we stoop to the more
we think of you. Just let us be clean and try to live aboveboard
and we kick. Take my firm here—we try to have a business that's
run like the very best funeral establishments; because Negroes
don't see my name in the paper for giving bogus checks like
these other folks, never hear of us not meeting our payroll and
on time, never see us running after bodies and the like, they
swear I'm rich and don't need any bodies to bury. Out at St.
Agnes is a regular race track running after bodies, and they give
them to the highest bidder. I have never given anyone a pint of
liquor to call me about a body, never gone out to the hospital
asking for one or anything of the kind, for that's against my
philosophy. I never intend to do that type of thing and it disturbs
me a little to know that's what is going on among other funeral
parlors. Just last night I was in a group where they said, don't
bother to call DH if anyone dies because he doesn't need the
money. My boys are disturbed about it too, sometimes they ask
me why I can't do these things since the others are doing them,
but I tell them we'll never stoop to that.[47]

Negroes ought to trade with each other and help each other all
they can, but they treat each other so bad. I believe one is jealous
of the other and hates to see another get ahead. I wish somebody
could do something to help the po' Negro, though I guess I don't
do all I could. . . . If the colored people would just cooperate and
stick together a little more we'd have finer businesses than we
have. You can't even help one but so much because the minute
you mention one somebody's got something to tell you about
it to keep you from using it. When I bought this house thirteen
years ago I did it through Mechanics and Farmers Bank, but I
declare Negroes 'bout scared me to death at the time talking
'bout how dirty Mr. S is, but I went ahead and tried him and
didn't have any trouble. . . . He got my daughter her job at St.
Agnes Hospital, told the folks there that he knew her father and
he was a fine man and she came from a good family. So he's been
mighty nice to us but he sure is talked about and hated by the
Negroes.[48]

. . . you have to trade with Negroes some because they're colored,
but you have to choose the white man for some things because
you can't trust a colored man . . . seems like a Negro wants to pull
you down all the time. Any time he sees another Negro making

[47] Personal interview: Negro undertaker.
[48] Personal interview: Elderly Negro housewife.

any progress he tries to do something to trick him, catch him, or lower him in some way. . . .[49]

The colored businesses in Raleigh all need to be together and to cooperate. They should all be up there on Hargett Street. Should move the whites out and let more colored move in because they need to be together. And they could get this done if the right people set to work to do it. If they went to the city council . . . the council would help them get it. But the folks who'd have to do it are the lawyers, doctors, undertakers, and folks who can talk and have something to stand on, not us little fellows who own no property. After all, they pay taxes just like the white folks do . . . most cities have their Negro business streets in the area where Negroes live. That seems to be the general pattern I have noticed in traveling around. It's nice for us to have a street right in the heart of town, but it would be better if all the businesses were there so there'd be more cooperation. Negroes in these other cities cooperate more than those in Raleigh, though I don't know why.[50]

After slavery Negroes were all in all . . . Negroes patronized each other more then than now in comparison, they were just out of slavery and found it necessary to stick together. . . . In early days there was no such thing as jealousy between colored who owned property, or went into business, or any such thing. They stuck together closer then. When I was a boy I didn't think Negroes would ever lose power. I used to think education would bring them closer together, but I don't think so now because of jealousy. I think education drives them further apart.[51]

2) Covert Relations With Whites

There should be separate places for white and colored such as cafés, theaters, and all. Negroes won't do right nohow, so they need to be separate. Take that fellow that raped that white woman up at the Occidental Building a couple of weeks ago, that kind of stuff is what holds us back. Seems like we are, as an old woman put it the other day, 'promoted to white folks cause their faces are different from ours.' A Negro man just has to try a white woman out it seems. That's why the white folks don't want integration, they think all Negro men are that type.[52]

[49] Personal interview: Negro construction worker.
[50] Personal interview: Negro construction worker.
[51] Personal interview: Elderly Negro male non-worker.
[52] Personal interview: Negro laborer.

I declare this race situation make you mighty mad sometimes, and still our men fool around with these white women and get in trouble over it when the women just as much to blame as the men. I know two white girls right now who come down here on this street to see colored boys, or men rather 'cause one is 21 and the other 23. They don't let the men come in the white neighborhood, they come down here instead and get the fellows and go off with them. And I know another case where I spoke to the boy and his mother about how he was carrying on with a white girl. He said he was going to stop but he didn't, and his mother is trying right now to send him away from here before he gets in trouble . . . all colored places ought to be completely separate, that's the only way to keep Negroes and whites apart and help build up the race.[53]

. . . I don't like these places where the whites are on one side and the colored on the other. Take that old café up on Wilmington Street where the colored are on the right side and the whites on the left. I go in it but don't like it. Those old white men sit across on their side and wink their eyes at the colored women. Of course I don't have much use for white people anyway. I got an old salesman who comes to my house and always wants to come in the house, but I stop him at the door. I told him one day that his wife wouldn't let my husband come in her front door if he was selling something or collecting and he wan't going to come in mine. He said, I didn't mean no harm, and I said, I don't mean none either. . . . Negroes ought to have everything separate if they could, cause you can never trust what the white man will do. Whites work you for nothing and the men always want to go with the colored girls that work for them. . . . I worked for an old white woman who asked me didn't I think white men were giving these Negro women all the fine cars they ride around in. I told her she ought to know more about what her men did than I did . . . of course, some of our men need to learn how to act and stop fooling around with these white women. And we need to learn how to treat each other, but we're a whole lot better than we used to be.[54]

3) *Lack of Leadership*

A major obstacle to solidarity, and one severely criticized by Negroes is the lack of current leadership. As one moves around among varied groups he continually hears statements to the effect

[53] Personal interview: Negro female domestic worker.
[54] Personal interview: Negro female domestic worker.

that Negroes have no leader. The two principal persons recognized as leaders in past years have both had social monuments
erected to their memories, one in the application of his name to
an American Legion Post and the other in naming the recently-
established junior-senior high school for him. The lack of a recognized leadership at the present is perhaps the most significant
factor underlying the tenuous solidarity existent in the community. It must be hastily added, however, that both of the leaders mentioned here were informal leaders who received recognition as leaders by virtue of the esteem with which they were held
by the community, their dynamic and integrative functions, their
being symbols of accepted values of the culture, and their ability
to get things done in the interest of their followers, to which the
following excerpts will attest.

One thing wrong with the Negro in Raleigh is we don't have a
leader, and haven't had one since Colonel Young died. We got a
lot of would-be leaders but they're all afraid to stick their necks
out and too independent to be bothered with trying to build up
the race. . . .[55]

Politically the strongest man in Raleigh was Colonel James Young.
He was once a legislator, was also a great lodge man . . . he was
the main political leader of the town and state. My personal opinion is he wasn't worthy of all that, but my personal opinion
doesn't matter because he was so recognized.[56]

In 1894 when Populists and Republicans merged . . . Wake
County's James H. Young, the outstanding Negro in the General
Assembly, at once became the target of the daily press. But in
spite of the widespread journalistic criticism, James Young's high
position in the party was recognized by Speaker Zebulon Vance
Walker of the House of Representatives . . . 'Young's position on
such committees as election law, county government, finance, and
judiciary was noteworthy because around the results of these four
committees hangs the crux of Fusion Politics' . . . Political
enemies could hardly call Young ignorant because the persuasive
manner in which he accomplished things was testimony of his in-
tellectual competence. . . . The *House Journal*, 1897, reported that
a political enemy paid Young this tribute . . . 'Outside of Butler,
Pritchard and Holton, hardly any man had so much influence as

[55] Personal interview: Negro carpenter.
[56] Personal interview: Retired Negro undertaker.

Jim Young' . . . one of his first political offices was an appointment
to the office of internal revenue for the Fourth District in Raleigh.
As revenue officer, Young handled a million dollars annually until
President Grover Cleveland removed him. From 1887-89 he
served as register of deeds in Wake County.[57]

The next recognized leader had no such political career to his
credit, but was a social engineer in dealing with social problems.
To Negroes he, even more than Young, symbolized acceptable
and desirable values by possessing little evidence of racial mix-
ture, having the tenacity to "talk up to white folks" in behalf of
the Negro, and making decisions about necessary community actions. Showing how he came to be recognized as leader residents
note:

. . . anything the whites did was all right with these older men,
they looked like white too, so you didn't find them speaking up to
whites or boosting the Negro; they just lived quietly . . . the man
that really started talking up for the Negro was J. W. Ligon,
principal of the school. He was not good to look at but had a
whole lot of sense, just a little country boy from over near here
and never had too much opportunity but had it upstairs. Most of
the others stayed close, didn't push for the Negro, and were not
outspoken.[58]

. . . Back over here where Crosby-Garfield is was nothing but a
slum before they put that project in there. That used to be a red
light district for the whites. The first Negro to move in there was
Mr. Ligon and he was severely criticized. People thought it was a
shame for him to take his children in there to live, but he had the
idea that if he moved there he could help clean up the place, and
sure enough as Negroes started moving into the area whites
moved out.[59]

Not enough is known of the roles of these leaders to compare
them with the contemporary conservatives and radicals who serve
as representatives of their respective social worlds in the neighboring community of Durham.[60] However, there is ample evidence to show how the clamor for status among Negroes brought

[57] *The Carolinian* (Raleigh, North Carolina), April 5, 1958.
[58] Personal interview: Negro orderly at Rex Hospital.
[59] Personal interview: Negro mail carrier.
[60] Harry J. Walker, "Changes in Race Accommodation in a Southern
Community" (Unpublished Ph.D. dissertation, University of Chicago, 1945).

them to focus upon these leaders as symbols. We might well adopt here the views of Turner and Killian who have said: "The symbol that a leader represents is partly a product of his own personal characteristics, partly a creation of the promoters of the movement, and largely a projection of the followers. . . . Some apparent success, recognition, or personal strength is a necessary condition for such large-scale projection to take place." [61]

Preceding statements about the nature of the most recently recognized leadership in the community suggest a number of requisite leadership qualifications, and help account for the community's projection of certain values upon its leaders. To become a leader among Negroes one must not only be a property owner, businessman, and spokesman for the race. He must also be able to get the support of whites, get things done in the interest of the race, but at the same time represent "the new Negro," that is, stoop to no uncle-tomming, not guilty of verb-splitting when conversing, and be well groomed. There have thus been several qualified, momentary, one-purpose leaders recently but none has been able to gain sufficient support to effect a leadership role. Their primary aim as one-purpose leaders has been to participate in local government. Included among the group have been two undertakers, a woman physician, a lawyer, and two college professors.

Speaking of the dynamics of status-group structure LaPierre says that leadership is by persons rather than by office, that the powers of those who exercise leadership in a power structure stem from the personal respect in which they are held by the group members, that the personal respect upon which rest the powers of those who exercise leadership through a power structure are earned, and that the personal qualities that characterize those who earn such respect are initiative, selfless regard for the best interests of the group, understanding of and consideration for the idiosyncrasies of the various individual members of the group.[62] In the Negro world business leadership has been a pertinent part of the status-group structure. Occupational alignments and accomplishments have been the chief bases for individuals earning the personal respect entitling them to be recognized as leaders.

[61] Ralph H. Turner and Lewis M. Killian, *Collective Behavior* (Englewood Cliffs, New Jersey: Prentice Hall, Inc., 1957), p. 472.

[62] Richard T. LaPierre, *A Theory of Social Control* (New York: McGraw-Hill Book Co., 1954), pp. 177-179.

Practically all leaders have thus been proclaimed successful businessmen first. The current lack of leadership is not due to a lack of successful businessmen, but seems dependent upon the fact that the business leadership, with all of its personal initiative, exhibits little "selfless regard for the best interests of the group." This shows especially in the most critized business institution of the community, the bank. The controlling functionaries of the bank are among the most business-minded, property-owner, educated, highly respected men of the community. They thus possess the designated qualifications for leadership among Negroes. It is difficult to assess the extent of a current lack of selfless regard for the best interests of Negroes among businessmen, but community residents tend to attribute its existence to the fact that individual businessmen have been so involved in securing personal fortunes that they have been disinterested in helping others. Whether the failure to recognize a current leader stems from this accusation or from another that the businessmen have been frightened into conservatism, the nature of business leadership is held responsible for the community's lack of a leader. One business person has summarized the situation thus:

. . . not only is there a lack of business leadership, but the leadership tends to be conservative. All this goes back to the things people are reluctant to discuss now, namely, the bank hold-up . . . the timid man now in charge at the bank is afraid to lend money because of the situation he inherited at the bank; and the conservative men on the bank committee who have all they want and aren't interested in helping others, and are afraid of large loans. . . . This conservative bank committee consists of the same men who have all this property in Acme Real Estate, the men who have the largest businesses already. These guys have money and are not venturesome themselves.[63]

It thus appears that the very attitudes which have made the Negro so race-conscious have likewise influenced the tenuous solidarity of the community. Indices of the nature of community race-consciousness and solidarity are readily found in expressed consumer attitudes and practices. Growing out of the localized nature of intra- and inter-racial experiences, these consumer attitudes and practices have been so manifest as to help sustain the

[63] Personal interview: Negro physician.

style of life which characterizes the Negro world, and of which the Main Street is a part. Reinforcement for such sustention comes from the common beliefs justifying the expressed attitudes, beliefs which have formed a Main Street ideology. Understanding this ideology is thus of immediate concern.

Chapter 9

RACIAL IDEOLOGIES EVIDENCED THROUGH THE NEGRO MAIN STREET

STYLES of life of the Negro Main Street, characteristic of the outer-world of the Negro, are not only sustained by an inner-world of race-conscious attitudes, but also by an inner-world of common viewpoints or beliefs. The common viewpoints and beliefs relevant to Negro Main Street alliances, usages, and practices have given support to a Main Street ideology. An ideology may be defined as "a number of interrelated beliefs about some matter of major concern to the members of the society," the beliefs tending to be supported by a superstructure of ritual as a means of preserving or securing some value.[1] The ideology of Negro Main Street is based upon four major interrelated beliefs, namely these: 1) Negro business is different from other types of business; 2) Negroes have little confidence in the Negro business man; 3) The contemporary Negro businessman differs from the early Negro businessman; 4) Training in personal-service occupations is a compensatory means of raising one's status. Such an ideology has as its chief value the justification of varying consumer patterns of behavior, and it involves rituals covering preferential patronage, credit and cash payments, and techniques of business operation.

The belief that Negro business is different from other types of business has special significance within the framework of this study, for it appears as a contributory factor in the patterns of Negro Main Street consumption and usage. That the majority of Negroes tend to believe that numerous differences exist between Negro and white businesses is substantiated by the fact that 55.3 percent of the sample population of this study made such a designation. The principal difference designated revolves around treatment of customers or clients, attitudes of businessmen, the operation of business, and the nature of business operated. Among those who consider Negro and white businesses as being different, the majority (56.2 percent) envisage the differences as residing in

[1] Richard T. LaPierre, *A Theory of Social Control* (New York: McGraw-Hill Book Co., 1954), p. 270.

213

the nature of businesses operated by Negroes and whites and re-volving around the quality and variety of stock; size of the busi-ness; type of ownership; irregularity of prices; and the main-tenance of physical structures. Specifically they state that whites have better stock and more of a variety of stock and businesses; that Negroes have irregular and higher prices, little to work with, and small, independently-owned, ill-kept businesses; and that Negroes cater to Negroes though they serve all people.

The second largest proportion of those believing that Negro and white businesses differ (17.6) think that the difference is in the way Negroes treat Negroes, with the majority indicating that Negroes are nicer, kinder, friendlier, and more courteous, while whites ignore Negroes, make them wait, and are unfriendly. Although a smaller percentage envisages this as the major differ-ence between Negro and white business, the extent to which this is believed is seen in the fact that only 1.6 percent of all those specifying differences and similarities between Negro and white businesses believe the difference to be that whites are nicer and more courteous to Negroes than Negroes are to Negroes.

A third major difference emphasized with regard to Negro and white businesses is noted by those indicating that Negro attitudes differ from whites. In this instance 13.1 percent of those pointing out differences between Negro and white businesses say that Negroes act too independent, uppish, selfish, uncooperative, and distrustful when they operate business. Most of these factors were mentioned in the preceding chapter when discussing race-con-scious attitudes of Negroes and need not be elaborated upon here. Suffice it to say that, comparing this view with the one immediately preceding offers further validation for the tenuous solidarity found characterizing the Negro world and, while it questions the contention that the Negro has been moving away from a low morale to a high morale, it re-affirms the idea that ideological differences block group morale or solidarity.[2]

Another 13.1 percent of those specifying differences between Negro and white businesses believe the difference to rest upon the way the businesses are operated. They point out that whites are more business-like, more prompt, and give better service, and that Negroes don't know how to run business. The lack of possess-ing a business know-how has been one of the most vocalized con-

[2] Arnold M. Rose, *The Negro's Morale* (Minneapolis University of Min-nesota Press, 1949), pp. 3-5; 57-95.

tentions among residents of the community and worthy of consideration at this point. An important aspect of business know-how which Negroes tend to lack is business ideas and training, including on-the-job training. Residents have succinctly reviewed the situation thus:

One of the things wrong with Negro business is too many people trying to run it without knowing anything about business. Take the Co-op store. There's no reason why that shouldn't have prospered but they didn't have the right folks to run it. When they were looking for a manager I recommended two fellows, U and W, both of whom have built up nice grocery stores of their own. No, they wanted a college man to run it. These men weren't college men but had experience in business, and I thought they could put one of them in there along with any college man they might get. No, they didn't want that, they wanted a class business. Now they're closed and these men are still in business. Of course U's place wasn't so nice at the time as it is now. His dad had the place before him and it was little more than a good place for folks to sit around and chew the fat, but the young man has built it into a fine place. Negroes try to carry this class business too far. You can't make money that way. The same few men try to start a number of businesses, they have the ideas but no money; and the men with the money don't have the ideas, that's why we've lost so much money in business . . .[3]

One thing a Negro doesn't do is train employees for the job. He'll give you hell for not doing something the way he wants it, but he doesn't train for what he wants. He expects you to read his mind. I was in K's place the other day and he had a new girl there. I asked him, 'K, what kind of training have you given the girl?' He said, 'I ain't give her none, what you think I am'? A few minutes later someone ordered something that the girl didn't know how to charge for. She asked him and he said, 'Hell, I don't know, this is the first time that has been called for, charge what you think it is worth.' . . . How Negroes think you can work in a business continually and not learn anything about it is another thing that beats me. You work there and stay there day in and day out and the minute they find you know something about the business or make suggestions about it they curse you out. They try to slip and transact the business so you won't know what's going on. That's Negro business.[4]

Another element of business know-how which Negroes lack is how to control credit, which factor has not only brought criticism

[3] Personal interview: Negro Justice of the Peace.
[4] Personal interview; Negro operator of funeral parlor.

against Negro business but also caused much business failure. More and more, however, Negro businessmen are mastering credit-giving techniques and thus minimizing the differences between Negro business and white business. This is especially noted in the views of businessmen themselves, as indicated below.

Some folks are always arguing that you can't get credit from colored stores, but that isn't true. You can get credit for anyone if you have a good credit record. Where Negro businesses fail with their business is that they don't ask for credit references. They ought to get the same credit information as the whites do. If you try for credit in a white store they check all the places you ever dealt with before they grant the credit. But Negroes can't get the same information. Take my printing business, when a man comes in there to get a job done we ought to be able to ask for the same information from him as a white firm would do. We do the printing for a number of white firms and have done ever since we've been in the business. These firms are some of our staunch supporters, but if we started asking for any credit information we'd lose the jobs, and when you ask Negroes for any they get mad and knock you. So the Negro business just has to take a chance. But if you have security you can get credit, and that security isn't always tangible either, sometimes it just means showing evidence of character, initiative, and stability.[5]

I learned another lesson last summer. Never again will I sell anybody anything without a contract. Last summer Mr. S and his family had just gotten back from vacation and it was hot and they called me to bring them an air-conditioner out. When I asked what type they said, use your own judgment, just make it about one ton. I carried it out . . . after I got it installed and left, the next day she sent for me to come take it out, said it was too cold, her husband had a chill because of it. I couldn't talk to her any kind of way about the thing, just had to take it out. I had to pay for that one myself.[6]

. . . not only am I a member of the North Carolina Credit Control Board, but I'm also a member of the Raleigh Credit Bureau, as you can see from this plaque. The North Carolina one doesn't mean much but this one does. Any Negro business that wants to can belong, but you know what they charge you? It costs $40 a

[5] Personal interview: Negro co-owner of printing business.
[6] Personal interview: Young Negro electric appliance dealer.

year for membership and 50¢ a call. I was getting as many as ten and twelve calls a day and not getting anything for them, but every time I called I got billed for 50¢. I continued to get so many calls that finally I told them I would have to collect for all these calls, and I still get some but not as many. These white firms don't fail to call and check on folks when they ask for credit with them. Every month the Bureau sends you a list of all the folks who have gotten loans and how much the loan is for, all those who owe any money, their credit rating, etc. And at the end of the year you get a list of all those who haven't paid bills and who won't pay, and there are thousands of them. So each time one comes to you for credit all you have to do is check this list and see if his name is there, and if it is you don't let him have anything. Negroes lose because they don't push this type of thing. Then too, you got to have them sign something or you can't collect. I make them all sign this contract and I follow that through after so long a time. Most times Negroes think 'cause you're colored you won't do anything to make them pay and that's why they cheat and beat the Negro. They're scared of the white man because they know he'll make them pay, but they're not scared of the Negro. I had a fellow who owed me for some merchandise and I tried and tried to collect my money but couldn't. I finally took out a warrant and made him go to court about it. They let him out on $300 bond and $14 court costs, and he still didn't pay. I waited and tried again and again to collect, but he still wouldn't pay; so he had to go back a second time, and that time they put him under another $300 bond and made him pay another $14 court costs. He still wouldn't pay, so the third time the judge asked me what I wanted to have done with him, and I told him to send him on up, I was tired of fooling with him. That time he paid me, but that's just how determined he was not to pay me my money. I collect my money and don't worry about their knocking me because if a fellow doesn't pay you don't want him again anyway as a customer, and if you have to take him to court or turn them over to the credit folks they aren't going to tell that they owed you.[7]

Negro business know-how lacks further the record-keeping requisite to organization and efficiency. This too is a realization of businessmen themselves, as the following statements will show.

One of the things that makes it so hard for Negro business to make it is that they won't keep records. These big firms aren't going to lend you money unless they can see your books and

[7] Personal interview: Negro operator of jewelry store.

check on the kind of business you do. Negroes don't have any books for them to see so they can't get large loans, not even to improve the business.[8]

. . . I got $10 in my pocket right now that a man just gave me a few minutes ago on the street for keeping his records, only I ain't had no records to keep. I'm supposed to keep them, but he hasn't had any for me to keep, so he paid me for what I am supposed to do. 'I ain't done nuttin' for this money.' He said he just hadn't had time to get the records together, so he is paying me for what I promised to do because not doing the work was his fault, not mine.[9]

Another important element in business know-how which Negroes seem to fail to utilize to the satisfaction of many is a business etiquette. The nature of the business etiquette that often characterizes Negro business involves imprompt service, discourtesy, and unbusiness-like relationships. These are illustrated in the excerpts which follow.

Negroes have no business courtesy. They'll sit down and watch you enter and never get up from where they are sitting. They'll yell 'What you want?' instead of jumping to their feet and saying 'May I help you?' I know one man who used to sit and read Funny Books and not even get up to help wait on customers. One day I saw the girl in the place trying to wait on about six people at the same time, and he still sat and read his Funny Books. He never did get up to help. Another man I know had a business on a street where the only good parking place was right in front of the door. One day I went there and his car was parked in the only good space there was. I asked why he didn't have the street fixed up so people could park. You know what he said? 'I got parking space for my car.' I said 'Yeah, but what about your customers?' 'That's their business,' he said, 'they don't have to come here.' Of course he's closed up now but that's the kind of attitude you find in Negro business. And another thing, Negro business places aren't clean. The minute you walk into a place you can tell if it's a Negro business. I'll tell you something else, Negro men have to learn that night-kissing, money-handling by girl friends, and business don't go together. Right . . . in B's Soda Shop his wife and girl friend both work there. When the wife leaves work she has to walk home, when the girl friend leaves

[8] Personal interview: Retired Negro mail carrier.
[9] Personal interview: Negro operator of a funeral parlor.

she drives the Cadillac. . . . If I had my way I'd keep all Negro women from working in business places. They haven't learned the business smile. I can walk into a Negro business and practically tell what kind of relations she has at home. Negro women carry their home problems on the job. Maybe this isn't a Negro problem, I wouldn't know. Maybe white women do the same thing, I wouldn't know, but I do know Negro women do.[10]

. . . if I go to a Negro place of business you have to wait too long to get waited on. I just left a Negro café where I had to wait thirty-five minutes before they even asked me what I wanted. If that had been a Jew or some other white person he'd jumped to see what I wanted the minute I walked in.[11]

. . . the most discourteous of all Negro business men is the druggist. The thing that peeves the druggist is that Negroes come asking for credit, and when they do the druggist gets real ugly about it. They figure that the Negro runs to the chain drug stores when he has cash and comes to them when he doesn't. Of course they do doctors the same way and get mad if we don't credit them. Then the Negro becomes 'a bad person to trade with' so far as they are concerned. The young men in business are much more courteous than the older ones, and those who have stock in the business are more courteous than the hired help. Once a Negro spends his money for the initial capital outlay of business he does not want to put any more into it for improvements, and that's another shortcoming of Negro business.[12]

One of the main tenets of Negro Main Street ideology then is the belief that Negro business is different from white and that the difference is due to lack of business ideas and training, credit control, record keeping, and business etiquette. This in turn tends to make the Negro consumer personality different from the white, the difference being reflected in the nature of Negro-white relationships. In the industrialized neighbor community of Durham Walker finds a tendency to move away from a structure of race relations in which each individual Negro depends on an individual white person toward more impersonal and symbiotic relationships.[13] The non-industrialized capital-city community of

10 Personal interview: Negro funeral parlor operator.
11 Personal interview: Negro dental technician.
12 Personal interview: Negro female physician.
13 Harry J. Walker, "Changes in Race Accommodation in a Southern Community" (Unpublished Ph.D. dissertation, University of Chicago, 1945).

Raleigh deviates somewhat from this pattern where relationships in the business world are concerned, for here exists a racial ideology that shows Negroes to be not only dependent upon whites but also to have more confidence in whites as businessmen. The culture heritage of the community, embracing such amicable relations that early Negroes were often set up in business by whites, is perhaps one major reason for this prevailing ideology. Its existence has been a part of the historical development of race relations as analyzed by Park, who noted that "racial ideology and the point of view from which people in the South and in the North look at race relations seem to have changed but little, if at all, and the conflict going on in the South seems to be the expression of determined efforts of Southern whites of all classes to maintain at any cost the traditional racial etiquette and traditional symbols which reflect the traditional racial structure of Southern society." [14] The ideology of Negro dependence upon whites has no doubt been perpetuated by traditional practices of whites, but it stems also from race-conscious attitudes of Negro resentment toward other Negroes, and has resulted in patterns of deferential patronage of whites and concessionary patronage of Negroes.

Deferential patronage of whites, though presumed to rest upon economic factors of cost, is conditioned by specific racial attitudes as well. The Negro businessman has been as sensitive to this as has the Negro consumer. The nature of such deferential patronage and the Negro's sensitivity to it are both evidenced in the following accounts.

Seems to me that Negroes would rather trade with whites. I think they are envious of each other, have prejudice against Negroes. White business has the advantage over colored. They have lots of money to put together and buy at low prices and discounts, Negroes can't, so the whites sell at cheaper rates. Sometimes the Negro problem isn't in race so much, it's just the matter of a cheaper store. Of course that's not the only reason because a slap on the back from a white man will carry as far as money will.[15]

... I had hoped to sell a number of appliances to the folks mov-

[14] Robert E. Park, "Racial Ideologies", *American Society in Wartime*, ed. William Fielding Ogburn (Chicago: University of Chicago Press, 1943), p. 175.
[15] Personal interview: Retired Negro undertaker.

ing into Rochester Heights. Every time I see someone building or moving in out there I go see if I can sell them a stove, air-conditioner, or refrigerator, or something. I get a number of promises but when I look out the next thing I see is some white backing his truck up to the door. Then, when I say, 'I thought you were going to let me sell you that', their excuse is, we already had an account with them; or, they knocked off ten percent; or, we didn't have to pay cash; or, something like that. A man told me the other day the refrigerator he bought from Belk's he got cheaper because they knocked off $10 and allowed $5 for their old one. Actually they had even then paid ten dollars more than the list price, and I showed it to them. I was going to allow them $50, which would have meant no down payment unless they wanted to pay one. Negroes just like the white man, even the Rochester Heights bigwigs. These are the same type experiences we had in the business on Hargett Street. There isn't too much difference in the way Negroes deal with Negroes, don't care where the business is.[16]

I saw Dr. P give a man a prescription and he took it to a drug store and got it filled and started taking the medicine but declared it made him sick. I followed him to see what he would do next. Well, he went to a white doctor and got another prescription. He carried the other bottle of medicine back and left it at the drug store. The white doctor gave him a prescription to the same drug store. I was curious and asked the druggist, knew him pretty well, what was the difference in the prescriptions. He said they were exactly the same, all he did was wash out the same bottle the man had returned and put another label on it and give it back. That man swore he got well from that medicine the white doctor gave him.[17]

The concessionary aspect of the ideology of dependence upon the white man is the counterpart of deferential patronage. Not only does the Negro make his patronage of Negro business contingent upon non-exaction of payment, but he expects the Negro businessman to make special concessions to him and thus tends to substitute personal relationships for business ones, for one of the principles by which the Negro lives is that the bond of color makes all Negroes equal. Deferred payments, non-payments, accepting whatever one can afford to pay, lending money on a personal basis, and rendering service after closing hours—these

[16] Personal interview: Negro electric appliance dealer.
[17] Personal interview: Negro realtor and Justice of Peace.

are among the most frequent concessions which Negro business-men are expected to make to gain customers. Specific application of such concessionary techniques can be gleaned from the views given below.

About ninety-five percent of our business is credit accounts. With the white man business can be all business, but with the Negro business has to be tinged with emotion. Negroes won't let it be any other way. They make a distinction between business and Negro business. Considering the ability to pay, when we look at those who owe us, the teachers are much poorer payers than the common laborer. Some have owed us for a long time and seem to think nothing about paying. If that had been a white firm they would have called the school superintendent and garnisheed their salaries, but J has his first time yet to report one to the superintendent. He says if we do that then that person will go around and tell others, guess what ole J did to me, and that will hurt with other trade. Now they won't tell when the white man does it, and they wouldn't tell how long they had been owing us, but they'll try to get others not to trade with you. Negro business just has to carry emotions along. . . A Negro expects more from a Negro and thinks you are supposed to do him special favors. Take this for example, the other day a fellow came in for a beer and when J told him it was 36¢ he said, 'I ain't got but 35¢.' J said 'No, beer is 36¢, you don't go in a white man's store and tell him you lack a penny; if you don't have the money you don't buy; come back when you get 36¢'. That same Negro went up the street a few paces and came back in a few minutes and said, 'I found another penny.' So he got his beer. When he left J said 'These folks try to beat you all the time, I knew he had the other penny, that's why I wouldn't let him have the beer.' Don't care what a thing costs they'll try every time to see if you'll let them have it a few cents cheaper. Something else Negroes won't do, they don't accept hours from a Negro. They expect you to give them service any time they ask for it, any hour of the night, any holiday, etc. They know, for example, that Belks closes at 5:30 and they don't dare call that man and ask him to go in his store and get something for them after hours. But they'll ask a Negro and if you refuse, when they start telling it they say, 'That's why you can't deal with a nigger,' but they won't tell that they asked you to get out of your bed at some ungodly hour to do them a favor.[18]

You know, a Negro'll pay a white man much quicker than he'll

[18] Personal interview: Negro female co-operator of business.

pay a Negro. The bank has to get heavy mortgages on houses to be sure of getting their money back. Of course most of the time the people lose the houses and the bank gets them. That's the way they have built up so much real estate at Acme. You know Acme Real Estate belongs to the bank. If they didn't do that there wouldn't be any bank because Negroes just won't pay their own race. . . L and I went on a note for a man twenty years ago, a man who is in business and we considered a substantial citizen. He didn't pay, so we had to pay the note off, and he's still in business. I've gotten about $40 of my money back but L died without getting a cent of his. I've gotten that back in dribbles, had to corner him for $5 or $10 when I could. . . . Don't know what kind of psychology Negroes have, but they sure won't pay their own race.[19]

. . . Negroes here still depend on the white man too much—that old master-servant idea. They still like to borrow from the white man, and will pay him. . . I had a teacher I went on a note for $250, and she wouldn't pay. The bank got after me and I had to pay. I paid $170 of it and still couldn't get a cent out of her, so I finally called her principal and she paid me and the bank balance too and did it in a hurry.[20]

I changed my place where I get my gasoline because Negroes don't want to do you any favors, where the white man will. If you trade with the white man and you get in tough and need money you can go to him and say I need $25 or $30, and he'll let you have it without asking a lot of questions. If you ask a Negro for that he wants you to pawn something or pay about 20% interest. I stopped trading with them for this reason. Negroes lose money that way.[21]

Deferential patronage of whites and concessionary patronage of Negroes not only involves individual dependence of Negroes upon whites, but also group reliance upon whites for philanthropic support. One might posit varied explanations for the existence of such a pattern, but in the conceptions of residents of the community the cultural tradition of paternalism seems the most likely or tenable explanation. Illustrative of this paternalistic ideology are the views contained in the excerpt cited below.

One thing wrong with us is that our organizations don't mean

[19] Personal interview: Negro carpenter.
[20] Personal interview: Negro operator of jewelry store.
[21] Personal interview: Negro dental technician.

anything. We have no objectives in our organizations like the Lions, Kiwanis, and Rotarians have. We used to have an organization called the Citizens Association, and when the Lions decided to prepare food for the colored blind like they were doing for the white you could hardly get us to take our cars and transport the blind to be fed. First thing they started saying was, I believe I can get Mr. So and So to give so much to transport them to the place. We're so used to begging and having Mr. So and So do for us that we think or care very little about each other. We treasure the idea the white man put in us, don't trust a Negro, so we don't trust each other. I used to handle real estate, and still do handle some, and almost every time it comes to selling property the Negro will go ask the white man what he thinks before he'll let you know whether he'll really buy or not. And what sells the property is what the white man says and who the property belongs to, for the first thing he asks the Negro is who is selling it. . . All we do is dance and have feasts and don't care a thing about civic work. I've got them right in my own family that same way, some teaching school too, but they never have money to give to a civic cause. I have a son who'll pay $25 for his fraternity dance but doesn't want to give a thing to Oxford Orphanage. We buy what we want and beg for what we need. Take the situation at Shaw some time before they got rid of all the white teachers. Well, they fired one white teacher and she went to New York and was in on a meeting when the Shaw folks were up there begging money for the school. The board was about to decide to give it when this teacher rose up and said, I think you ought to go down there on Founder's Day and see what the Negroes do for themselves before you decide to give this money. They came down and found the Shaw teachers all riding around in fine cars and not giving to the school themselves, yet begging others for help for the school. And the adults put that same stuff in the children. That's the kind of thing we must get away from if we are ever to make any progress in business or otherwise. We need to be thrown out on our own so we'll have to do for ourselves.[22]

The belief that the contemporary Negro businessman differs from the early Negro businessman forms another part of Main Street ideology. Differences between contemporary and early business men have been most evident in personality traits, attitudes towards business, and attitudes towards whites. Being

[22] Personal interview: Negro Justice of the Peace.

younger, and more venturesome, the contemporary Negro businessman has not only begun to operate such businesses as laundromats, TV repair and electric appliance places but has also become
salesman for many white firms. Having fewer kinship ties with
whites, his reactions to whites have tended to change. Although
his business is operated primarily for Negroes, he tends more
and more to solicit white patronage in areas where conflicting
culture patterns do not prohibit it. While he recognizes the fact
that the attitudes and practices of business operators and patrons
make Negro business different from white, he essays more and
more to minimize the differences that characterize Negro business. His economic interests in business as a means of livelihood
may be equally as keen as those of early businessmen, but his
individual interests embrace more race-conscious attitudes. Even
though he still clamors for status in the business world, his status-
seeking through business location extends beyond the main
street. Many of the implications of this ideology are pointed out
by the residents quoted below.

The Jews dominated Back Street. H had a business there, but he
was old and went out of business soon after I went into business.
You couldn't tell H from white, so it didn't make much difference
anyway as to where he had business. The Os, Ls, and H'n were
all in the same category—looked like white. The family that
white people held up and talked about most was the Os. O and
his family looked like white. He had a lot of children, took good
care of them, never saw the wife and children just roaming the
street. He himself was quiet, never said much, was the submissive
type and that's what the whites liked. . . . Most of these older
Negro men were barbers and this was helping the whites and
doing what they wanted them to do, so naturally the whites
praised them. H'n looked like white but didn't like whites one
bit. He was one who'd get them told in a second. He was quite a
liquor man and the whites accused his business of being a front
for the liquor business, so he was always getting them told because he figured they were always after him.[23]

Negroes have gone out of the clothing business but have gotten
in new fields, such as laundromats and the appliance place that
H and J had. They did a flourishing business and only went out of
business because one partner went back into the Service. One of
the results of their business has been a number of young men

[23] Personal interview: Negro who formerly operated a shoe store.

going into business for themselves, for some of them started working there. One of these was N, who now has his own appliance repair place. . . When Negroes stopped catering exclusively to Negroes and whites put on colored salesmen, and as whites let Negroes try on clothes in stores and to give credit and the like, there was less need for some of the businesses Negroes were operating. . . where the young guys have gone into business it doesn't matter much where they locate, they don't have to be on Hargett Street and they service anybody. The depression broke down what was the Negro market, people were so hard pressed, and whites started bidding for Negro trade more. Some businesses would never have moved off Hargett Street if it hadn't been for the depression or some such factor. . . Negroes have missed the opportunity to get more businesses because they didn't encourage the men who could have profited from the GI Bill.[24]

Another important element in Main Street ideology is the belief that training in personal-service occupations is a compensatory means of raising one's status. Within the Negro world emphasis upon education has continually increased since the Civil War. Because a college education has been considered the chief means by which to achieve economic and social mobility, says Frazier, it has become the task of Negro higher education to educate the black bourgeoisie, the new middle-class, white-collar Negro.[25] Present education of the Negro, like that of an earlier period, has been shaped by bourgeoisie ideals, but the ideals have shifted from industry, thrift and piety to money and conspicuous consumption.[26] The significance of money and conspicuous consumption as a means of achieving economic and social mobility is constantly re-emphasized in the business world where educational substitutes are offered to those unable to go to college. The business areas in which educational substitutes have made tremendous appeal include barbering, hair-dressing, secretarial work, dressmaking, and cafeteria management. In these areas striving toward professionalization has meant patterning as much as possible after colleges, even to the point of imitating social life by organizing into fraternities and sororities. So conscious of such status factors has the Negro community of

[24] Personal interview: Negro female physician.
[25] E. Franklin Frazier, *Black Bourgeoisie* (Glencoe, Illinois: The Free Press. 1957), Ch. 3.
[26] *Ibid.*

Raleigh been that there was established here in 1930 the first permanent and state-approved barber school for Negroes; in 1935 the first school of beauty culture approved by the State Board of Cosmetic Examiners;[27] and more recently a business school and a trade school. So important has the beauty culture business become to both the business world and the woman vying for social acceptance by being well groomed that, in 1954, 33.0 percent of the 2,800 beauty shops in North Carolina were operated by Negroes; over 54.0 percent of these were located in fourteen cities; Raleigh alone had 71 such shops, as compared with Durham's 88 and Winston-Salem's 102.[28] The import of this emphasis on beauty culture becomes immediately discernible when it is recalled, as shown in table 4, that the Negro population of Raleigh is far smaller than that of the industrialized communities of Durham and Winston-Salem. The emphasis upon barber school training as a means to a rising status is best gleaned from an advertisement about the school in which the following facts are given.

Harris Barber College of Raleigh. Organized 1930 by the late Samuel Harris to provide opportunities for useful careers for young men and women unable to go to college. Mrs. Brown President and owner. J. I. Stredwick, Manager. Eight months required for course. Have employment bureau. Train men and women. The largest and most progressive school in the South for barber training.[29]

Though some emphasis is placed upon business and trade school training, the number of resultant businesses established in this connection is far less than the number established by those with training in barbering and beauty culture. It is quite likely that barbering and beauty culture receive additional emphasis in the culture because of their value in helping change the appearance of the race, for the most severely criticized and ridiculed persons in the culture are those who dare let their hair look like that of the African Negro. This has not only been important as a means of gaining individual social approval, but the philosophy behind the maintenance of an acceptable personal appearance

[27] John R. Larkins, "The Negro Population of North Carolina, 1945-1955," pp. 15-16.
[28] *Ibid.*
[29] *Negro Progress in North Carolina,* ed. R. Irving Boone (Wilmington, North Carolina), Vol. V, 1952, p. 3.

has broadened the occupational horizon and aided the establishment of businesses through which Negroes believe a rising
status can be effected for the race as a whole.

When this factor is viewed in relationship to the common views
of Negroes regarding the characteristic features of Negro business and business men, then Negro Main Street styles of life are
made more understandable. In general, Main Street ideology,
embracing beliefs in differences between Negro and white businesses and businessmen, has its basis in the socio-historical nature of race relations in the community. Reverting to the social
history of the community it may be recalled that relations between Negroes and whites have involved strong kinship ties;
whites setting Negroes up in business; Negroes serving as fronts
for white business firms; Negroes operating personal service enterprises for white clients; Negroes seeking Negro votes for
whites; and large numbers of Negroes employed in the personal
service of whites. But the pattern of race relations also shows
that Negroes have operated businesses right along beside whites,
have owned business property wherever they could afford to buy,
and have occupied residences in numerous sections of the city.
Moreover, race relations have been of such nature as to provide
aid for raising the educational status of the Negro; to give the
Main Street businesman an ascribed status different from other
Negro business men; and to divide the Negro world into two
major status groups. Thus, while a survival pattern of Negro
dependence on whites exists, some semblance of equality of
status between Negro and white business men is suggested. But
the sharp distinction between those with more formal education
and training and those with very little or none, between professional or business and common labor groups, has so heightened
the personal struggle for status as to augment Negroes' conceptions of differences between themselves and other Negroes; between Negroes in business and other Negroes; and between Negroes and whites. Beyond this, the interrelated beliefs held about
the business world, of which the Main Street is symbolic, help
explain the persistence of the street with its special types of institutions and consumer behavior patterns. Full understanding of a
social phenomenon, however, rests not alone upon knowing what
brought it into existence, or what causes it to persist in a particular form, but also what changes it has undergone, and it is
the latter which is next portrayed.

Chapter 10

Main Street Changes as Reflectors of Social Change

STREETS are significant symbols of the life of a city, for their structure, function, and change reflect both community attitudes and cultural practices. Just as the early political history of North Carolina is summarized in the names, location, and structure of the central streets of the Raleigh community, so the economic history of the Negro is summarized in changes occurring in his principal business street. Since the street has developed under the impact of socio-cultural forces in the community, its history and growth are inseparably bound with the many changes that have taken place in the community. And since its history and growth have been influenced by numerous racial factors, any long-range perspective on racial group behavior must necessarily take into consideration the effect of the group's special trade-area characterization thereon. The Negro Main Street trade-area is not only important because of its effect upon the Negro but also because of the implications it carries for the study of other racial groups and trade areas.

Once East Hargett became characterized as a place for the operation of Negro business, an increasing number of Negro businesses continued to locate there. Although the number of businesses located there tended to fluctuate some from 1925 on, the fluctuation has been slight. The number of Negro businesses in the community as a whole has continually increased, but there has been little change in the number located on the Main Street. Relative stability of the street in this regard can be attributed to the availability of space. Except for total renovation of one building, partial remodeling of a few others, and replacement of two structures by parking lots, the physical appearance of the street remains relatively unchanged also. But there are some areas in which changes in the street have not only been evident but also far-reaching in their influence. These have been interrelated with general twentieth-century community changes and help explain current social trends. One such factor in this category pertains to the nature of Negro-operated business.

At the beginning of the twentieth century Negro Main Street

229

business was of the personal service, craftsman, eating and drinking, food store and fuel dealer variety, complete listing being
given in the Appendix. During this period, however, Negro Main
Street business was no different from Negro business on other
streets, for Negro business at that time consisted of barbering,
restauranting, blacksmithing, boot and shoe making, grocerying
and the like. But this was likewise the period when numerous
changes began to occur in the nature of business operated by
Negroes. Insurance and investment companies, drugstores, doctors, lawyers and publishers' offices, lodge halls and funeral parlors began to be included among Negro businesses. Thus, at the
end of the first decade of the twentieth century Negro Main
Street business had not only increased in volume but changed in
type. Such change was impelled not by economic motives alone
but by many social changes which the community was undergoing.

Significant among the many community changes affecting
Negro business in the 1900-1910 period were these: growth of
the population from 13,643 in 1900 to 19,218 in 1910, which meant
more potential customers for Negro as well as white businesses;
the onset of a new era in education with the inauguration of
Aycock as governor in 1900, which brought new opportunities for
Negroes though within a separate society for which Aycock proposed aid; the growth of Jim Crow legislation, which forced the
development of a closed Negro market; the renewed fight for
prohibition resulting in the closing of saloons, which influenced
Negro saloon keepers' going into other types of businesses; the
steady but slow growth of white barbers, butchers and hucksters,
which introduced the element of competition that began to force
Negroes out of occupations over which they had previously held
a monopoly; and the increased number of benevolent societies,
the large Negro memberships of which led to the establishment
of subsidiary, complementary, and related business institutions.

At the onset of the second decade of the twentieth century the
pattern of Negro Main Street business had a slightly new form,
which was altered by the advent of new businesses and a predominance of certain types of business. Offices of Negro doctors,
lawyers, dentists, insurance companies, real estate agents, employment agents, funeral directors, and drug stores began to
dominate the street and to make it one of white collar business.
Doctors, lawyers, and druggists have been continuously abundant

in the community. Prior to and during World War I the Negro business world's high visibility was partly attributable to the large number of doctors' offices and drug stores. In 1913-14 seven of the major Negro businesses were drug stores and eleven doctors' offices, two of the former and the majority of the latter remaining on the Main Street until the 1950 period. It was during this war period that hair-dressing parlors, cleaning and pressing clubs, and printing offices became firmly established on the street, and immediately after the war an auto repair shop began to operate there. These changes in Negro Main Street business accompanied general economic prosperity, a building boom, an increase in white collar occupations, and the extended use of automobiles in the community. Especially relevant to Negro Main Street development was the business opportunity resulting from the building boom. Before 1911 there were but two office buildings for whites in the city,[1] and there were only two that provided limited office space for Negroes. With the construction of the Lightner building in 1915, however, the Negro Main Street began to attract many Negro professionals in search of office space, thus contributing to the high concentration of professional offices on the street.

The building boom continued after the war period and, while many new structures were erected in the city at large, the Negro Main Street continued to share in the results of this building boom. Thus, by 1926 erection of the Lightner Arcade, Mechanics and Farmers Bank, and Delany Building, and the purchase of two other buildings increased the number of Negro-owned Main Street structures to seven. But growth and expansion of business and business property in the period 1920-30 also felt the blow of the national depression, unemployment, and business failure. While Negroes did not lose their Main Street property, building was arrested and some few businesses began to leave the street either through attempted relocation or through failure. However, the very nature of basic Main Street business—embracing a bank, funeral parlor, insurance companies, drug stores, hotel, printing office, pool room, barber shops, beauty parlors, cafés, real estate agency, and offices of doctors, lawyers and dentists—kept the street intact even during the depth of the depression years. Nor

[1] Writers' Program of the Work Projects Administration, *Raleigh Capital of North Carolina* (Raleigh Sesquicentennial Commission, 1942), p. 45.

did Main Street business remain completely stationary during the depression period. In 1932, for example, the number of Main Street physicians increased, as did the number of associations and societies, most of which were benevolent; in 1933 the number of Main Street lawyers and insurance companies increased; and in 1934 the number of cafés increased.

After 1935, when economic recovery had set in, the Main Street added such new businesses as a burial association, ambulance service, and public library. Beauty parlors increased, dress-makers returned, and beer parlors began, but otherwise Main Street business changed very little in the 1930-40 decade.

Some of the most profound changes in the nature of Main Street business came after 1940 when a new trend in business location set in. By this time congestion, lack of ample parking space, and the shift of many consumer items from luxury to convenience categories began to institute a redefinition of Main Street business values. As a result physicians began to leave the street and establish offices in or near their residences. Undertakers began to seek more spacious areas also. Thus, two of the principal Main Street offices have tended recently to become neighborhood institutions. But new businesses moved into the street and additional possibilities in business became of interest as taxicab, radio repair, and electric appliance places developed. More barber and beauty shop operators made their advent too, but the constant and rapid rise of these in the community has made them more neighborhood than Main Street businesses. To accommodate many of the new businesses Negro Main Street made use of its newest structure, the Taylor Building, which was erected in 1948. The most singularly different businesses undertaken during the 1950 period perhaps have been the operation of a private parking lot, using space left by the destruction of an amusement place, and the revival of instruction in trades through a trade school, from which the "new Negro" has sought to escape.

Such Main Street changes as these reflect a number of broader community trends. They reflect trends in a constantly expanding local market, one in which building permits increased from 270 in 1940 with a total valuation of $1,900,419.00 to 1,550 in 1957 with a total valuation of $13,083,287.00; they point toward the increase in retail establishments from 635 in 1947 to 875 in 1957; they suggest existence of an effective buying income with average weekly wages increasing from $51.00 in 1953 to $60.87 in 1957 and per capita incomes from $1,557.00 in 1952 to $1,871.00 in 1956.[2]

Another major change that has taken place in Negro Main Street business has been a growing tendency toward more diverse ownership of business. When the street first began to assume its character as one of Negro business one-man ownership prevailed. One man constructed and owned two of the largest buildings on the street. They housed numerous businesses, but each business was individually owned and operated, and this pattern in main street business persisted for several decades. Corporate businesses have not been non-existent, but except for the Odd Fellows Building, insurance companies, and the bank few survived prior to the 1930's. Since then, however, partnership and corporate forms of business have tended to supplant many individual ones. Not only have groups become owners of all buildings previously owned by single individuals, but most Main Street businesses are likewise owned and operated by partners or large professional groups. Some of the most highly individualistic businesses, in terms of past operation, have now formed partnerships, including a drug store, law firm, and beauty parlor. A few individually-owned and operated businesses remain, but when both buildings and businesses are considered these are in the minority. There is even one co-operative business, a credit union, operating on the street—another variation from the pattern of individual business ownership. Moreover, the shift from individual to group owner-ship has meant a change from family to non-family ownership.

Again the Main Street has changed from being the only center of Negro business to the major center for such. During the 1920 period practically all Negro business, except grocery stores, was Main Street business. After 1923 Negro-operated grocery stores ceased to exist on the Main Street and became strictly neighbor-hood business, but they did not become the nuclei of business sub-centers. The first significant business to locate outside the main street was a filling station, set in operation in the early 1930 period. This initiated a new trend in the location of business and sub-centers began to develop. These, however, did not seriously affect Main Street business for they failed to attract the major enterprises that thrive on downtown patronage. They included such service institutions as barber, hair-dressing, and shoe repair

[2] J. R. Drummy, "Industrial Survey of Raleigh, North Carolina," Indus-trial Department, Raleigh Chamber of Commerce, 1953 and 1958 editions.

shops, cafés, soda shops, pool rooms, and dance pavilions. Where new buildings provided office space the sub-centers did attract an occasional doctor or dentist. Two of the largest of these sub-centers have developed in the areas where the Negro colleges are located. Increased student populations, expanded college communities, heavier concentration of Negroes in specific areas, increased competition with whites instituting chain business enterprises and with Negroes offering duplicate services, and undertaking business not previously engaged in—all these produced some effect upon the development of the sub-centers of business. They thus affected the status of East Hargett as the only center of Negro business but did not appreciably alter its status as the dominant center, for it remains the Main Street with its characteristic financial, professional, and technical business enterprises. Except for a theater operated by whites for Negroes, the street's most complete losses of business enterprises currently engaged in by Negroes have been grocery and entertainment places. Impersonal, secondary business functions are gradually taking precedence over the personal, primary ones previously dominant on the street. Although it has not reached the stage of complete specialization, the street is gradually losing its generalized, diffused character of being "all things to all Negroes."

Another major change in the Negro Main Street has been effected through the decreased attachment of informal groups therewith. Although institutions tend to follow people, as in the case of sub-center business developments, people also follow institutions. As long as all Negro business was concentrated on the Main Street informal gatherings were centralized there, and the street was especially characterized by its congregating groups. Males tended to congregate on specific sides of the street, rural people around special places, and special-interest groups within certain businesses. With the development of business sub-centers socializing assemblages of males began to follow barber shops and pool rooms to their neighborhood locations. With the building of an all-inclusive super-market on the outskirts of the city, reduction of local city market functions to the sale of vegetables, fruit and flowers, the extension of market functioning of neighborhood grocery stores, and increased mobility through the use of automobiles, congregating rural groups began to disperse. With the departure of certain nuclear business personalities from the street, and the increasing development of groups around interests rather than persons, special-interest groups began to decentralize also. Nor can one disregard the effect of removing the "picture window" dining room of the hotel with its glass front attractions for standees and hangouters. With the glass front of the hotel removed and the dining room shifted to the rear, passers-by have little reason for stopping and socializing there as before. Hence, one of the most immediately observable changes in the street, and equally as significant as the aforementioned ones, is the decline in congregating groups. The impact of this upon personal relationships is evidenced in the growing tendency of Negroes to know few other Negroes—the reverse of the pattern which apparently prompted whites to assume that all Negroes know all other Negroes and hence to readily ask any one Negro about another. Just as past Main Street tends helped intensify personal relationships, current trends are helping increase impersonal ones.

Accompanying these specific changes have been certain interrelated culture changes which appear to be contributing to current trends in Negro Main Street development. Readjustments in the occupational structure have wrought changes in work and employment patterns. Thus, whites now employ Negroes as automobile and electric appliance salesmen; Negro women still hold a monopoly as elevator operators in downtown stores; and the professionalization of barbering has increased the popularity of the barber. In addition, the mores have had a relaxing effect upon segregation practices, making it less necessary for the Negro to go to the Main Street to use restrooms and telephones, leave packages, rest while shopping, or secure credit. Since provisions for these are now made by the larger downtown stores, those in which clients are less likely to number heavily among the elite, it is no longer culturally mandatory that Negroes use Negro places of business for such. No longer are all Negroes forced to seek office space on the main street, for new trends are suggested by the Prison Department's placing its Negro personnel directors right in the office with whites. Nor is the Negro forced to use solely such facilities as public libraries made available for Negro use, for the state libraries have deleted the separate reading rooms for Negroes.

Although these are portrayed as local changes, they seem to suggest what's transpiring on all similarly situated main streets of Negro business worlds. They are but miniature forms of the many broad changes occurring at the national level, and represent above all current trends in race relations. They reflect both deliberate and non-deliberate efforts to implement action taken by the Interstate Commerce Commission in 1946 forbidding segregation on interstate buses; Supreme Court action in 1955 forbidding segregation on interstate trains, at public parks and bathing beaches; and the 1954 Supreme Court decision declaring racial segregation in public schools a violation of the Federal Constitution. They are indicative of attempts of industrial unions to break down occupational racial barriers. They portray occupational gains made by the Negro during World War II, and the increase in white collar workers among Negroes. And all of these point ultimately toward one of the most profound changes of all, namely, that the door of the white world is beginning to open far enough to admit Negroes as equals. Negro laborers have always had access to the white world, but via the back door. Such a group may always have a place in Southern society, but the constant increase in white collar workers is making deliberate readjustment in race relations more and more necessary.

Deliberate efforts to facilitate desegregation and thus participate directly in the racial readjustment processes have been going on among interracial groups in the Raleigh community for some time. They have included an institute on religion under sponsorship of the United Church, which brings together outstanding speakers with varying racial backgrounds; an interracial Bible school and day camp by the same church; a youth movement in which Negro and white youth interrelate through leadership, training, and discussion processes; attendance of Negroes at the Catholic high school; organization of a book club in which Negro and white, men and women, seek to exchange ideas through reviewing and discussing current best-seller books; a committee on integration, composed of Negroes and whites interested in informal discussions of local race situations; and the State College chapter of Alpha Kappa Delta (sociological honor society) taking in members from the Negro, as well as white, undergraduate colleges in the community.

It must not be assumed, however, that the tendency to admit Negroes to the white world through the front door is all formal. One familiar with the white collar strata of the Negro world has but to look around and see Negroes inviting their white friends to dinner at their homes; whites likewise inviting their Negro friends to dinner; an increasing few attending the Governor's Ball; exchange social activities and meetings among the college groups; and the reciprocal, though infrequent, holding of meetings of interracial groups in the private homes of whites and Negroes. It thus appears that the previously closed white world is beginning to offer to the Negro what the Negro has never been able to deny whites—access through the front door, but temporarily available to the white collar strata only.

This poses a series of questions as to whether or not the Negro Main Street can withstand the impact of these changes and changing forces. Will it survive as a Negro street or lose its racial characterization and become just another business street? Will its basic enterprises remain of the same type or become different? Will the street remain a downtown business street or migrate to a business sub-center? Will its patrons continue to be predominantly Negro or will race cease to be an influencing factor in patronage?

There is no validating evidence which can be used to substantiate answers to the foregoing questions. Nevertheless, using current characteristic features and trends as a basis for projection, the writer would like to propose the following with regard to the Negro Main Street.

1. It cannot continue to survive as a Negro street catering to a Negro clientele. Assuming that desegregation trends will continue, the Negro businessman will lose more and more of his Negro clients. Devices like the Pearsall Plan, which permits the yearly reassignment of North Carolina's student population to public schools, may retain a demand for Negro teachers. The need for doctors and lawyers will no doubt persist, for until the mores effect a change in social values Negro doctors and lawyers will be forced to depend upon their Negro clients. Assuming, however, that Negro teachers will remain in Negro schools, that doctors will continue the trend of establishing offices in residential areas, and that Negro businessmen must continue to compete with whites for Negro patronage, the Main Street business man will be the heavier loser.

Since the street has always contained some white-operated businesses, any further invasion of the street by businesses which duplicate those Negroes operate there will so increase competition as to push racial factors in the background. The precedent for this has already been established in such businesses as a tailoring, cleaning and pressing establishment owned by a white person but operated jointly by a Negro and a white, and situated diagonally across from a Negro tailor, cleaner and presser whose business is much older. Meeting the forces of desegregation, decentralization, and competition with businesses possessed with trained and courteous personnel, efficient records, superior service, and other business know-how, the street may survive but as just another business street. It cannot long continue to survive under the implied connotations of the current label of Negro business, for with increased availability of goods and services to customers irrespective of race the Negro businessman can no longer expect to receive patronage from Negroes just because he too is Negro.

2. Persistence of the Negro Main Street, or Negro business in general, is going to be contingent upon the nature of business in which Negroes continue to engage. If the Negro is to survive as a businessman he may have to reactivate many businesses which he undertook earlier but which subsequently failed, such as clothing, department, shoe, and large grocery stores. This will mean doing business on a large scale, amassing large amounts of capital for investment therein, and making the business comparable to that operated by whites. It will even entail expansion and new methods for such businesses as cafés, hotels, and beauty parlors.

Although the folkways and mores relative to customer treatment of Negroes have changed appreciably, whites still resist accepting Negroes in cafés and hotels. The need for these may therefore persist for some time to come, but small, dingy, unclean, uninviting cafés and hotels must now be made passé. Motels and drive-in eating places on the outskirts of the city are too convenient to those who are constant users of such, for in the Southern culture, where life tends to be especially centered around the home, sleeping and eating-out folkways are not widely diffused, and the number of hotel and café patrons is thus comparatively small. The highly-prized art of hair-dressing may keep beauty parlors operative for some time to come, but unless the Southern beautician keeps abreast with new methods she too may lose, for competition with do-it-yourself products is becoming keener. The Negro has remained constantly an operator of grocery stores, but these have been small, independent stores and they can no longer compete with the large chain grocery stores. To survive as a groceryman even is going to mean developing chain grocery stores capable of holding their own in the competitive struggle with whites.

As desegregation increases and customer discrimination decreases, the Negro businessman will be forced to cease competing with other Negroes but compete with whites for both Negro and white customers. Corporate ownership of business must thus replace one-man ownership, the basis for which will have been set with relationships between Negroes and whites becoming more nearly equal and cooperative forms of interaction superseding the conflicting ones of envy, jealousy and hate.

3. Since Negroes own the greater portion of Negro Main Street property and can thus determine whether the occupants be Negro or white, the centralized downtown location of the street may be maintained. But just as building ordinances have already required adherence to certain specifications, any new regulations made a part of increased city planning may so affect existing structures as to lessen the possibilities of some businesses remaining on the street. When a recent fire destroyed one of the Main Street structures, for example, the owner found specifications for erection of new buildings requiring too much capital outlay to warrant rebuilding, thus forcing relocation of the business in a neighborhood area. Impact of numerous social forces may thus cause Negro Main Street business to decentralize. It is quite possible that decentralization may effect more sub-centers and that downtown Main Street may become more specialized with corporate businesses in financial position to expand becoming dominant. It is most unlikely that any large sub-center shopping area patterned after the non-congested Cameron Village location will develop, the reason therefor being twofold. On the one hand, the Negro population formerly concentrated at the periphery of the city is being replaced by whites and gradually becoming a central-city population. On the other hand, one can expect more dispersion of Negro business in the downtown area. Such a trend is already in process, for within the past two years four Negro businesses have been established in the midst of white-operated businesses a block away from the Negro Main Street. In one Negro-owned downtown building whites have operated a business on the ground floor and Negroes had offices upstairs since the 1930's. Prior to the development of the Main Street as one with a high concentration of Negro business Negroes operated businesses on several downtown streets. The present trend represents a return to the pattern

of dispersed Negro business. If the trend continues dissolution of the Negro Main Street may accompany the dispersion of Negro business.

4. Assuming that a number of impinging social forces may operate to perpetuate the Main Street as one of Negro-operated business, its characterization as a street of predominantly Negro customers can be expected to change. While involuntary segregation is disappearing and discrimination being made less apparent, the possibility remains that discrimination may become more subtle and produce voluntary segregation sufficient to influence the continued existence of the street. But, even in the face of waning segregation and more subtle customer discrimination, one can hardly expect an increase in the number of Negro patrons of Negro-operated business. Any increase that may occur in the number of Negroes patronizing other Negroes will result from changes in the nature of business and services rendered, and not from racial ties, for in the daily life of the urban Negro race is becoming less important as a factor of intra-group control.

Continued development of such businesses as electric appliance, hardware, jewelry, and TV repair, businesses that are without a history rooted in sentiment and tradition, will make the race of customers of decreasing concern. With segregation outlawed in intra-urban modes of transportation, and the need minimized for using private transportation to escape embarrassments and insults on public conveyances, such businesses as taxicabs may have to secure customers wherever available. Thus, while the number of Negro patrons of Negro business may decrease, an accompanying increase in the number of white patrons may help keep the Negro in business, provided the changes in the nature of business operated continue along newly developed lines, rather than the predominant personal service lines of many current Negro businessmen.

The future character and development of Negro Main Street will be influenced by changes in the nature of race relations, just as its formation and persistence to the present have been products of past trends in race relations. The Main Street may feel the impact of changing relationships between Negroes and whites even more than many other urban phenomena, for it has been and is perhaps one of the most profound sources and effects of contradictory and uncertain behavior in the Southern city. The major contradictions and uncertainties have arisen from culture permis-

sives and implications, custom and tradition, more than legal pro-
scriptions. Legal codes have specified that separation of the races
must exist in certain institutions, but they have not said that Negroes and whites cannot use the same banks, rent property from
each other, patronize the same doctors, dentists, drug stores, or
other such businesses. Custom has separated Negroes and whites
in many personal service and professional institutions, but it has
not prevented whites from trading with Negroes or holding interracial meetings in Negro Main Street buildings. Thus, while some
relationships between Negroes and whites have received their social definitions through both law and custom, many less defined
ones have produced areas of contradictory and uncertain behavior.

Contradictions in expected behavior patterns are more prevalent at the present than they have ever been before, and Negro
Main Street behavior as varied as Southern patterns of race relations themselves. Negroes taking their white friends to dinner in
the Main Street hotel dining room has become an accepted pattern. Negroes and whites sitting beside each other as they eat
snacks in the Main Street Peanut Shop in no longer a novelty; and
whites entering and securing food at the Main Street "Café for
Colored" whenever desired is not unusual. Thus, while a culture
ban has been placed on the intimate relationships involved in Negroes and whites publicly eating together, it has not been effective on the Negro Main Street. Its real effect has been the barring
of Negroes from white eating places rather than the reverse.

Contradictions and uncertainties outside the Main Street area
are even more prevalent than inside. The uncertainty of social expectations surrounding them tends to further unsettle the Negro's
attitude toward the Main Street and to threaten the continued
existence of the street. In the past the extended use of signs reading "colored" over doors or seating areas outside the Negro world
kept the defined status of the Negro forever before him. But this
previously "well-defined" status is now ill-defined, contradictory
and uncertain. It now confronts the Negro with the removal of
signs saying "colored"; the frequent substituting of labels "men"
and "women" over public facilities intended for Negroes, and
"ladies" and "gentlemen" over those intended for whites; the placing of the term "colored intra-state passengers" over one railway
station waiting room and omission of any designation over others;
and leaving the signs "white" and "colored" over bus station wait-

ing rooms but accommodating and serving any Negro who enters the one marked "white." The result has been the production of a confused Negro personality which, in its quest for certainty about its status, finds changing racial folkways and mores more unsettling than ever before. Part of the confusion is evidenced in such behavior as Negroes standing over seats vacant beside whites on buses rather than sit and have the whites move, as is sometimes the case; in groups of Negroes taking seats in the basement of a large department store assuming, as those who sit there often say, that the basement benches are for Negroes and those in front of the store for whites, although no display of signs indicates such; in Negroes standing and staring rather than entering a rest room in another downtown store where the only label thereon is "ladies"; and in some Negroes loudly ridiculing others whose actions they consider as "integrating" (with whites) rather than "associating" (with Negroes).

These are the kinds of paterns that one sees in today's Southern city. They are not as immediately apparent nor readily substantiated by statistics as the forces of industrialization and occupational shifts so often discussed by sociologists as impacts on race relations. But to the Southern Negro they are nonetheless realistic and meaningful, for in the community under analysis here increases in the number of industrial establishments have not markedly changed the occupational patterns of the Negro. Where industry has been established employment of the Negro, except in unskilled capacities, is still nil. Although there has been some change in the occupational structure, the pattern of Negroes being predominantly laborers, domestics, and white collar workers is still maintained. Increased employment of white women continues to curtail the hiring of Negro males for numerous jobs, for the taboo against contact between Negroes and whites still prevails in many occupational spheres. Changes wrought through legal battles and increased desegregation have not abolished attendant cultural conflict of psychological uncertainties confronting those who must readjust their behavior accordingly. And all of this forms a facet in the constantly changing status of the Negro as a minority group.

Adjusting to his changing status as a minority group has not only produced an impact upon the social world of the Negro, but has been symbolic of the nature of adjustments involving other minority groups. It led to the development of a separate Negro economy after the Civil War. It affected the internal development of the Negro world, and helped produce a Main Street characterized by businesses and services from which Negroes were excluded, both overtly and covertly, in the white world. It was interrelated with Jews' development of "back street" businesses in which Negro patronage was solicited. It has evoked comparisons with the forms of accommodation made by the Chinese in their urban concentration in Chinatowns, which tend to dissolve as the Chinese disperse and the Americanized Chinese youth cease to be restrained by Chinese custom; with Japanese Americans whose urban settlements and minority occupational status, influenced by forces of relocation and migration, have found outlets in new communities and occupations; with Puerto Rican migrants from small cities to the mainland, whose distribution in metropolitan centers is adding to the problems of central-city slum congestion and location; with Hawaiians, recently proclaimed members of the fiftieth state of the United States, whose cultural background is one of racial diversity and integration; and with minority peoples throughout the world who, in rejecting the inferior status imputed to them by dominant peoples, are seeking to raise their status through the sharing of resources and opportunities. It follows therefore that, whether viewed in retrospect or prospect, the changes and trends in Negro Main Street development are but facets in the comprehensive arena of human relations involving racial and ethnic minorities locally, nationally, and internationally.

Chapter 11

Summary and Conclusions

Urbanization brings together in cities concentrations of different racial and ethnic groups whose modes of adjustment tend to result in the formation of separate social worlds. Separation between the social worlds does not consist of physical isolation or economic self-sufficiency but of social distance between groups. The social distance is lengthened or shortened by the systems of social values and culture norms which grow out of the nature of relationships existing between the majority and minority groups residing within the city. Roles, statuses, and social expectations relative to such groups are socially defined, and urban living in terms of these results in differentiated patterns of group relationships. Constructing cultural media through which to adjust to the socially defined behavior is one of the ways in which intergroup relationships express themselves.

The materials of this study show how a culture medium is constructed and used by a racial group as a means of adjusting to socially defined behavior. The data have been organized around the problem of determining the nature of functions of the culture construct "Negro Main Street" relative to dominant social values in urban society. They have been analyzed so as to give a meaningful perspective of factors which condition the formation, usage, persistence, and change in the principal business street of the Negro world. Three general factors of sociological interest are evidenced. One is that the Negro Main Street has not developed as an isolated cultural phenomenon but as a functional part of a set of interrelated social forces. A second is that the street has its functional existence in the attitudes and ideologies of those for whom it has social meaning. The third is that the immediate society maintains its equilibrium between continuity and change by redefining social situations in the light of social changes occurring at varying levels, thus making changes in the Negro Main Street part of a total pattern of a broad scope. Following the sequential presentation made here we may thus summarize the findings of the study under three major categories.

1. Interrelated Forces

Generically speaking each chapter of this study gives an analysis of some specific function of the Negro Main Street. But since the materials presented in chapters two, three, and four resolve themselves into the major forces conditioning Main Street formation, a better perspective of the street's development can be achieved by viewing the forces operative in this connection.

Urbanization. One of the major forces whose impact makes the Negro Main Street an intricate part of contemporary community growth is urbanization. Increased urbanization of the South, though developed later than in other parts of the nation, has produced a region of many small cities and few large ones. It has brought distinct forms of metropolitanization in which central cities dominate agricultural hinterlands and in which functional uniformity obtains. It has effected changes in the occupational structure which, in turn, have affected the economic and social status of potential consumers, numbered among whom are many Negroes.

The Southern state, and the urban community within the Southern state reflect such trends in varied ways. Population composition and distribution, occupational specifications, unique local characteristics, and accompanying marketing potentialities are among the many community features which reflect both regional and state patterns of urban development. The economic and social life of racial groups living within urban communities of the South is necessarily affected by such factors. Since the Negro is caught up in the web of southern city living his social world reflects the same patterns, though the specific form and content thereof may differ.

Ecological and Cultural Forces. In the context of social living ecological forces do not operate independently but are interrelated with social and cultural ones. Their influence upon urban communities in which Negro Main Streets arise is rather selective, for they not only influence the location of streets under given sociocultural circumstances, but also their functions and usage. Location and functional usage of the Negro Main Street are most illustrative of this factor.

The manner in which a community originates and grows is one of the means by which ecological forces translate themselves into overt culture phenomena. Thus, the purposeful origin of the city as a state capital, the structured layout of its streets, erection of its governmental institutions at the center, and the patterned arrangement of its people and business enterprises around governmental institutions were major factors influencing the growth and location of Negro business. And with Negro business occupying first a downtown location, shifting from a pattern of dispersion over several streets to concentration on one, then migrating to another street and becoming firmly established there, the ecological processes thereby contributed to the latter's transformation into a street of business enterprises operated by and for Negroes.

Further, ecological processes, accompanied by cultural forces and social values, have operated to help fix the location of businesses according to type. Consequently, variations exist in the location of enterprises according to race of operator and race of customer or client serviced. This has contributed to the differences between "front street" businesses and "back street" ones and between basement, ground floor, and upstairs enterprises. Where the enterprises are operated by Negroes numerous sociocultural factors, arising out of the nature of Negro-white relationships, have influenced their growth and distribution. Included among these are occupational displacement through competition for jobs; occupational opportunities provided through education and kinship bonds between Negroes and whites; and the permissive use of space enabling one to rent, purchase, inherit, or receive as a gift any property in the community regardless of its location.

Socio-cultural Forces. Social values vary from one culture to another and from one community to another. The significance of a particular social value to a community is denoted by its run of attention. The Southern community's run of attention on discrimination, the most overt form of which is segregation, suggests that discrimination plays a major role in the shaping of patterns by which people live. Economic and social patterns affecting both Negroes and whites are in many instances by-products of the nature of discriminatory usages. Since these discriminatory usages and patterns are directed at the maintenance of a subordinate status for the Negro, they tend to produce a profound effect upon the social world in which the Negro lives and the social life in which he participates.

One of the principal effects of discrimination upon the life of the Negro has been the production of a rationalized value system whose major business enterprises are prototypes of those in which discrimination by whites is directed against the Negro. The Negro

Main Street, with its special business enterprises and services catering specifically to Negroes, tends thus to encompass a rationalized value system which counteracts against discrimination. The nature of its identifying businesses and services results not only from direct usage of discriminatory policies but also from indirect usage of such. Custom, gentlemen's agreement, institutional arrangements, private bequest designations, legal and political devices comprise the techniques through which discrimination operates. Such discriminatory techniques, operating in conjunction with numerous status-fixing codes of behavior, have helped implement a number of culture norms by which certain patterned relationships between Negroes and whites in the community are sustained.

2. Functions, Attitudes and Ideologies

The persistence of social structures in particular forms is contingent upon the functions they perform for the social group upon whom their survival is dependent. The manner in which the groups are disposed to behave toward the structures forms a significant element in their survival. Where group dispositions and orientations toward a particular structure involve a color line both the attitudes and ideologies of the group are important to an interpretation and understanding of the structure's functions. Negro Main Street is such a structure.

Functions. Since the Negro Main Street is one of business enterprises whose definition implies a market, one of its functions is that of serving as an index of characteristic patterns of consumer behavior. Social characteristics of the consumers, items available for consumption as well as those actually consumed, dominant consumer patterns, and the socio-cultural conditioners of consumption comprise the primary media through which the functions of the street are discernible. With his consumer behavior oriented toward the Main Street through cultural trade marks of custom, law, occupational availability, and racial selection, the Negro becomes a Main Street trader not by choice or preference only but also by cultural compulsion. His patronage and usage of the businesses and services located there become patterned into a Main Street style of life in which weekly visits, young women, older men, married persons, unskilled and non-worker groups are predominant. Consumer patterns tend to manifest themselves in variations in the patronage of the street and its institutions. Thus, preferential consumption and specific consumer-group patterns of consumption tend to impute to the street its quality of serving as an index of consumer behavior.

Another function performed by the street is evidenced in its pointing up an existent relationship between the location and use of space. Though characterized economically as a market area and ecologically as a spatial area, it is the uses made of the street in both instances that make it a significant socio-cultural area. Medianly located in the downtown business area of an urban community, and equally accessible to the spatially distributed population upon whose patronage it is dependent, the street becomes a mecca and a cross-roads juncture for varying types of persons. Used differently by male and female, rural and urban, worker and non-worker, Negro and white persons, its usage and downtown location become interdependent. Accepted as a socially approved and reputable business street by business operators and patrons alike, the differential usage of the street becomes another means of expressing functional relationships between the location and usage of spatial sub-areas.

The function of integrating formal and informal group activities indicates how the Negro Main Street becomes expressive of the nature of personal relations in the urban community. Acquiring a part of its life style from the types of groups identified therewith, the street tends to show how group values derived from social interaction, cultural conditioning, and community participation find expression in explicit behavior patterns. The assemblage of special-interest groups, informal groups of men, rural and urban individuals, and class-designated persons around specific Main Street personalities or places is but an expression of the nature of relationships among Negroes in the Southern community where the culture sets limitations upon their relationships with others in the community. The rather indirect relationship of women's formal groups to the street, and the tendency of all groups to sever relationships with the street in time, accompanied by changes in group values and community participation, are but further indications of the effect of socio-cultural forces in the community upon group behavior, whether racial or any other.

Attitudes. The style of life assumed by the Negro Main Street is further conditioned by the social attitudes of those for whom its functioning has meaning. Acting as a medium through which group life is integrated, the street tends to promote an intra-group solidarity whose foundation rests upon race-conscious attitudes. Collective opinion regarding Negro Main Street patronage and racial advancement through individual achievement forms the index of solidarity, but the divisive lines along which the race-consciousness develops render the solidarity rather tenuous when concerted action is involved. Seeking to attain equality of status with whites and remain loyal to the Negro race, but at the same time resenting and keenly censoring attitudes and actions that establish intra-group inequalities, these race-conscious attitudes are the same divisive forces that make for the tenuous nature of intra-group solidarity. When these are connected with Main Street patronage and coupled with a recognized lack of current leadership, nuclear leaders having usually been Main Street business-men, a reciprocal function of the street becomes apparent in its role as both promoter and deterrent of solitary group action.

Ideologies. Functional significance of the Negro Main Street is extended into the realm of thought through the street's serving as a focal point around which racial ideologies are expressed. Basic Main Street ideology expresses the belief that specific forms of customer treatment, business types, operation and attitudes make Negro business different from other business; that Negroes have little confidence in Negro business, as seen in the deferential patronage of whites and concessionary patronage of Negroes; that the contemporary Negro businessman differs from the earlier one in personality make-up and in racial and business attitudes; and that occupational training, even as a substitute for formal higher education, offers the Negro an avenue through which to raise his status.

3. Social Change

Society, considered concretely as a complex of organized habits, sentiments, and social attitudes[1] is affected more by change today perhaps than ever before. Its varied components are so intricately interrelated that any change in one influences change in the others. It might be expected that the Main Street of a community, because of its economic characterizations and consequent lack of resistance to change, would be more susceptible to change than many other phenomena. Since the Negro Main Street is not only economically characterized but socio-culturally characterized

[1] Robert E. Park and Ernest W. Burgess, *Introduction to the Science of Sociology* (Chicago: University of Chicago Press, 1924), p. 163.

by sentiments, custom, social attitudes and racial factors, change occurs in it but is not as immediately apparent as in areas primarily economic. One thing that is apparent, however, is that the nature of Negro Main Street change, whatever its rate may be, is interrelated with other community changes and in turn with broader national and world changes.

The process of change which the street is undergoing is especially affected by current trends in race relations. Its continued existence is being challenged by changes in the nature of Negro-operated business, new occupational opportunities, the redistribution of people and business enterprises, increased competition, and changing attitudes toward race, reinforced by such forces as legal enactments and changing interpersonal interracial relations. Since these involve the non-material forces of attitudes, which change less readily than material forces, they are helping replace certainties with uncertainties in expected behavior in Southern culture. The result is a confused Negro personality seeking to adjust to a redefined and changing social status, for when change is occurring in a community the roles and statuses of its groups are altered.

Understanding group life is one of the basic objectives of sociological inquiry. Finding the cohesive forces that hold groups together, permit their existence through time, condition their relations with other groups, or contribute to their disintegration continues to be of sociological concern. Locating areas of study through which to view such group life broadens the sociologist's knowledge of groups and aids him in making further generalizations about universals and differentials in human behavior. Analysis of the problem of Negro Main Street development and functioning is basically a study of intergroup relations focused around behavior of the Negro consumer in relation to Negro business.

The data as analyzed in the study present several broad facts which are especially pertinent to understanding human behavior where alignments and cleavages between and within racial groups, and representatives of such groups, are of social significance. One is that intergroup relations are inseparably bound with race, one of the most sociologically significant problems of the world today. Constant redefinition of the status of racial groups evokes changing conceptions of the groups by themselves and by others. Nowhere is this more noticeable than in intergroup relations in American society, expressive of which are the changes that Negro-white relations are undergoing in the Southern city. The social forces, values, attitudes, ideologies and changes involved in group relations in the Southern urban community form a basic part of the content of human behavior in general. They may assume special connotations when connected with specific racial groups in particular localities, but they are, above all else, manifestations of the reciprocal relationships that exist between man and his social environment. They may portray unique racial cleavages, individual and group reactions, and beliefs, but they show how culture, experiences and interaction mold personality. They may be viewed through a physical reality or social datum such as a Negro Main Street, but they remain expressive of how human beings behave under given social circumstances.

This study has sought to provide answers to questions as to how such social structures as Negro Main Streets come into existence, what functions they perform, and why they persist. The answers provided have not been intended as conclusive for they have raised other questions which are suggestive of lines for further research. One such question can be stated thus: In the face of assumed differences in the patronage of Negroes by white collar and laboring classes, what variations obtain among these classes in their attitudes toward both Negro and white business? What are the attitudes of white clerks or sales people toward Negro customers of the white collar class as opposed to the laboring class? In view of existing and possible extension of patterns of white patronage of Negroes, what are the attitudes of white customers toward using Negro business? In the light of current trends, what are the attitudes of Negro businessmen toward desegregation and decreased customer discrimination? Do Negro businessmen really want white customers? Answers to these questions through further investigation would not only enhance our knowledge of Negro Main Street development as a special social phenomenon but also provide explanation of racial and cultural relations under the impact of the rapid and extensive change which is enveloping today's society.

Together They Sit

Riesman's analysis of character in *The Lonely Crowd* denotes these three types of personalities: (1) tradition-directed, (2) inner-directed, and (3) other-directed. The first type is guided by patterns established in childhood and passed on to subsequent generations. The second type, geared to a changing and mobile society, depicts elders' satisfactions with the sense of direction they have given to goals to be achieved, yet with the realization that the methods of achievement must vary from those of their predecessors. The other-directed personality, believed to be increasingly more characteristic of Americans since 1920, is one directed not by fixed goals but by others.

The Negro of the urban South today is assuredly inner-directed. This inner-direction has tended to find its most profound outlet in the so-called student movement, which is neither singular in nature nor complete with time but a web of continued protests against many Southern survivals and most vividly dramatized by attacking the eating folkways of chain stores. Sociologists define survivals as culture traits which have outlived their usefulness. The persistence in the South of segregated eating facilities, or no eating facilities for Negro shoppers, can be classified as survivals in Southern culture.

Decreeing by action that such culture traits have outlived their usefulness, Negro college students in the South initiated in 1960 a sit-in movement in protest against racial segregation and discrimination at chain variety and drugstore lunch counters. Although the movement was initiated by students, its execution ultimately involved younger and older persons and became perhaps the most totally inner-directed movement of recent times.

Among the significant features of the movement is the fact that it originated in North Carolina, where laws prohibiting integrated eating facilities are nonexistent. Started by four freshmen of Agricultural and Technical College, in Greensboro, on February 1, 1960, the movement rapidly spread to every city in North Carolina where colleges for Negroes exist, except Salisbury. So spontaneously did the movement sweep the state that within ten days demonstrations had also been staged in Durham, Winston-Salem, Charlotte, Fayetteville, and Raleigh, occurring in three of these on the same day. Once students in Elizabeth City had joined the list, this completed the college town protests; then high school students and non-students of other cities began demonstrative protests. By March 19, when Wilmington joined the ranks of sit-in protesters, sixteen cities had become involved. Just as swiftly as this city-to-city movement spread, so too did the state-to-state demonstrations. Thus did the South quickly gain world-wide attention regarding its survivals in customer discrimination.

When demonstration and negotiation failed to net immediate results, sit-in participants started picketing the stores at which lunch-counter services were sought. The South could do no more than recognize this for what it continues to be—a movement of the Negro middle class, student inspired and initiated, but adult supported. While students did the sitting-in at lunch counters, the real purchaser—the middle-class adult—executed the "selective buying" campaigns and raised the funds for bonding and legal counsel. It was this dual development, rendered effective by subsequent student-citizen organization and leadership, that made the economic impact of the movement so immediately felt. The greatest adversaries of the movement were Negroes working in the stores under attack. Such an inner-directed movement would hardly have been possible two decades earlier, for not until after World War II did the Negro really begin to assess his potential purchasing power.

The all-embracing coverage of the movement can be seen in the fact that in many cities the protest demonstrations have been extended to movie houses, libraries, and other public facilities. Many have been appalled by whites joining the demonstrations at the local level; white and Negro sympathizers in northern cities picketing branches of the discriminatory chains; local citizens' groups—interracial and other—petitioning merchants and city mayors to desegregate lunch counters; and organizations circulating lists containing names of persons willing to eat at integrated lunch counters.

An the onset of the movement, reactions of merchants took such forms as roping off lunch-counter areas and serving whites under the guise of serving "employees and guests only"; removing all lunch-counter seats and serving on a "stand up" basis; posting signs reading "Lunch Counter Temporarily Closed," "Closed in the Interest of Public Safety," "No Trespassing," "We Reserve the Right to Serve the Public as We See Fit"; and issuing proclamations of chain-store executives stating a national policy of always following local custom.

Just as overt in their actions were the white hecklers, usually teen-agers and young adults, who sought with their threats to reverse the nonviolent, passive-resistant attitudes of the apparently calm, solemn sit-in participants. Perhaps nothing attests more to the inner-direction of the movement than the tensions and fears which many sit-inners relate seeking to conquer in themselves in order not to defeat the objectives of the movement.

The voice of another group was heard declaring intentions to withdraw patronage from stores if lunch counters were integrated. This cry, re-echoed by the Raleigh merchants—even those on the Mayor's Committee, of which the writer was a part—was always verbal; no formal petitions of this nature were evidenced. One store, which receives much of its support from lower- and middle-class Negroes, removed its lunch counter altogether "rather than be coerced," it said, "by any group."

Southern cities retaliated by passing special ordinances to cope with sit-ins, arresting, jailing, using intimidating tactics, and organizing interracial committees to discuss solutions for the problems of sit-ins. In Raleigh alone, where the State Attorney General advised use of the trespass law, 41 students were arrested in one day for trespassing in privately-owned Cameron Village, a model shopping center. What the urban South was really doing was staging its last stand for the maintenance of a custom which if permitted to die would symbolize integration of the races. Pleas for survival of the custom came constantly from those who rationalized that custom does not change easily, as though it moves by its own momentum. Even "liberal" whites on Mayors' committees, as in the case of Raleigh, sought justification and not eradication of these Southern survivals. When the six Negroes on the Raleigh Mayor's Committee refused to accept the compromise solutions offered by the nine whites, the committee was disbanded as quickly as it had been formed.

What the South failed to take cognizance of in its avowed knowledge of the Negro is the latent tension, unrest, and dissatisfaction of the Negro with many Southern survivals for some time. What the Southern white has not understood is how the Negro feels as humiliation forces a quickened change in his ego-structure when he is denied a cup of coffee at a lunch counter, sent to a back door to eat, or made to stand and eat while whites sit. What the South must now realize is that the rising middle-class Negro stands equal economically to the middle-class white; that he has been maturing occupationally for at least two generations; and that the psychological resentment of the adult Negro to many of these Southern survivals has been in evidence for some time, but usually along individualized lines. Desegregation of many lunch counters—in some cities only a few weeks after the sit-ins started, in Raleigh just one week prior to the return of students to school in September—gave evidence of the value of group unity, cooperation, selective buying, and demonstration as effective weapons of helping the South see that the urban Negro stands ready to quicken the "deliberate speed" with which many surviving customs must be changed.

Whether sitting, wading, kneeling, or riding for freedom, all are part of an inner-directed movement aimed at achieving equality of status for the Negro. Through these inner-directed movements the Negro in the South, aided by those concerned with producing a functionally democratic society, seeks the use of desegregated facilities, and thus the banning of discriminatory practices whose survivals stand as insults to human dignity. Such must become the role of the South in altering America's image to other nations, as together they sit in the interest of peace.

Schedule
TRADING CHARACTERISTICS

Number ....   Address ....

The following information is for use in a research project. Your name will not be used in connection with any of the answers given. Please answer items that apply to you.

I. General Information:

A. Sex: Male ( ); Female ( ). Occupation ....
....

B. Your age group: Under 21 ( ); 21-30 ( ); 31-40 ( ); 41-50 ( ); 51-60 ( ); 61-70 ( ); 71 and over ( ).

C. Marital status: Single ( ); Married ( ); Widowed ( ); Divorced ( ).

D. Last year of school completed:.............. (Number of grade).

E. How long have you lived in the city?................................... (years, months, etc.)

F. If you are not a native of the city indicate which of these you came from: 1. Another city ( ); 2. Rural area ( ).

II. If you had all the money you desired to shop with or to secure some service for yourself, what one thing would you get first? What second? Indicate: First choice ....
.... Second choice ....

III. Do you think all Negroes should patronize Negro businesses? A. Yes ( ); B. No ( ).

IV. Do you patronize Negro businesses on East Hargett St.? (This includes doctors, lawyers, etc.) A. Yes ( ); B. No ( ).

A1. If yes, answer one of the following:
( ) Number of times per week
( ) Number of times per month
( ) Number of times per quarter
( ) Number of times per year

A2. When was the last time you were on the street?...............
....

A3. What is the name of the business or service most often used there? Name:...

A4. What is the chief reason for using this particular business or service?...

A5. Indicate how well you know the proprietor or person rendering the service by checking one of the following:
( ) Personal friend
( ) Only speaking acquaintance
( ) Know only by sight

( ) Joking relationship
( ) Business dealings only
( ) Know only by reputation
( ) Don't know him at all

B1. If you do not patronize business on East Hargett Street in-
dicate chief reason:...

V. What are the principal traits that you like for the person you
do business with to possess?..

VI. Do you consider it an *advantage* or *disadvantage* to have a
large number of Negro businesses centered on East Hargett
Street? Check which: Advantage ( ); Disadvantage ( ).
What would you say is the chief advantage or disadvantage?

....

VII. Check those among the following that you patronize on East
Hargett Street:

........Bank   ....Hardware store   ....Real estate
........Barber   ....Hotel   ....Restaurant or café
........Beautician   ....Justice of Peace   ....Shoe shop
........Dentist   ....Lawyer   ....Tailor
........Doctor   ....Notary Public   ....Theater
........Drug store   ....Photographer
Specify any not named:..

VIII. Specify types of Negro businesses with which you deal but
which are *not* located on East Hargett St. (e.g. doctor, barber,
etc.) ....

....
....
....
....
....
....

IX. Do you think it would be better if this Negro business street
(East Hargett) were located in the center of a Negro residen-
tial area, or better where it is?
Check one: A..............Better in a Negro residential area
B..............Better where it is
C. Why? ....

....

X. During the times that you have been on this street which of
the following groups of persons have you seen there most?
A...........Men   C...........Adults   E...........Rural people
B...........Women   D...........Children   F...........City people

XI. If you do business with any stores, firms, or individuals on
East Hargett Street do the following: Place a plus (+) before

the day usually used for this; a minus (−) before the day definitely avoided for this; a plus (+) for the time of day this is
usually done; and a minus (−) for the time avoided.

Days	Morning	Afternoon	Evening
..........Sunday	....	....	....
..........Monday	....	....	....
..........Tuesday	....	....	....
..........Wednesday	....	....	....
..........Thursday	....	....	....
..........Friday	....	....	....
..........Saturday	....	....	....

XII. In what groups, clubs, or organizations do you participate?
    A. ....
    B. Name the groups to which you belong that do any or all of
       these:
       1. ....Have headquarters
          on E. Hargett St.
       2. ....Hold regular meet-
          ings on this street.
       3. ....Hold occasional
          meetings on this street.
       4. ....Hold special meet-
          ings on this street.
       5. ....Arrange dinner par-
          ties on this street.
       6. ....Gather there just to
          socialize.
       7. ....Specify any other
          motive.

XIII. With which of the following do you deal most? Write (1) for
the most frequently dealt with, and (2) for the next most frequently dealt with.
    A. (   ) Negro-operated businesses on East Hargett Street.
    B. (   ) Negro businesses in other areas of the city.
    C. (   ) Non-Negro operated business on East Hargett Street.
    D. (   ) Non-Negro business in other areas of the city.
What do you like or dislike most about the businesses just
checked? 1. *Like*:...
    2. *Dislike*:...
Do you recall any pleasant or unpleasant experience you have
had in doing business with Negroes? If YES,
1. Describe experience:...
....

2. Describe any had on E. Hargett St. ....

XIV. In what major way are Negro and white businesses alike? In what way unlike? *Alike*: ....

Unlike: ....

XV. What slogans, signs, or advertisements have you noticed in Negro businesses or offices that you don't see in white ones?
....

XVI. Have you noticed any difference in the way Negroes act when trading with Negroes as against trading with whites? (   ) Yes; (   ) No. If YES, what difference? ....
....

XVII. Check the following in order of their importance to you in using or not using Negro businesses and services on E. Hargett St. Place (1) before the most important, (2) before the next most important, etc. Check only those that apply to you.

FOR USING NEGRO BUSI-
NESS AND SERVICES

(   ) To patronize Negroes
(   ) Easy to get credit
(   ) Less expensive
(   ) Wide variety of goods
(   ) Feel it my duty to use them
(   ) Open late
(   ) Convenient location
(   ) Friendly operators
(   ) Courteous operators
(   ) Satisfactory service
(   ) Absence of loiterers
(   ) Seem interested in pleasing the customer
(   ) Not crowded
(   ) Like trading with Negroes
(   ) They know me personally
(   ) Other: Specify..............

FOR NOT USING NEGRO
BUSINESS AND SERVICES

(   ) Avoid patronizing Negroes
(   ) Difficult to get credit
(   ) More expensive
(   ) Lacks variety of goods
(   ) Feel no obligation to use them
(   ) Close early
(   ) Inconvenient location
(   ) Unfriendly operators
(   ) Discourteous operators
(   ) Service not satisfactory
(   ) Presence of loiterers
(   ) Seem disinterested in pleasing the customer
(   ) Too crowded
(   ) Dislike trading with Negroes
(   ) They don't know me
(   ) Other: Specify..............

XVIII. Assuming that each of the following is available to you, place plus (+) before ones you *would definitely do*, and minus (−) before ones you *would definitely not do*.

1. ( ) Eat in a Negro café.

2. ( ) Eat in a white café with special provisions for Negroes.

3. ( ) Attend an all-Negro theater.

4. ( ) Attend a white theater with section set aside for Negroes.

5. ( ) Bank with a Negro-owned bank.

6. ( ) Bank with a white-owned bank.

7. ( ) Use restrooms or lounges marked "Colored" in white places of business.

8. ( ) Go to Negro places of business to use restrooms or lounges.

9. ( ) Use professional services of Negroes (such as doctor).

10. ( ) Use professional services of whites.

11. Specify any other that is important to you but not listed:

....

....

12. If the only place in town to do the things you *would definitely do* (XVIII above) is on the street where Negro business is centralized, would you make a special effort to go there to do them? ( ) Yes. ( ) No.

XIX. Check the income group into which your family falls *Per Month:*

A. ( ) None; ( ) $1-99; ( ) $100-199; ( ) $200-399; ( ) $400-599; ( ) $600-799; ( ) $800-999; ( ) $1,000 and over.

B. Approximately how much do you spend per month with each of the following:

1. $......................Spent with Negro business on E. Hargett Street.

2. $......................Spent with Negro business in other areas of city.

3. $......................Spent with non-Negro business on E. Hargett Street.

XX. What is your general impression of E. Hargett as a Negro business street? What do you like most about the street? What do you dislike most about it? Please use back of paper and describe.

CLASSIFICATION OF BUSINESSES*

I. PERSONAL SERVICES
   Hotels and Lodging Places
   Cleaning, Pressing, Dyeing
       Places
   Dressmaking, Tailoring
   Barber Shops, Beauty Parlors
   Shoe Repair, Shoe Shine
   Photography

II. PROFESSIONAL AND SEMI-PROFESSIONAL SERVICES
   Doctors, Dentists, Lawyers
   Nurses, Practical and
       Registered
   Consultants' Offices
   Teachers' Association
       Headquarters
   Beauty College, Barber
       College
   Funeral Directors
   Library (public)
   Trade School

III. BUSINESS SERVICES
   Notary Public, Stenographer
   Justice of the Peace
   Legal Bureau
   Employment Agency
   Advertising

IV. REPAIR SERVICES
   Automobile and Garage
   Radio, Typewriter
   Watch and Jewelry

V. AUTOMOTIVE SERVICES
   Car Sales
   Filling Stations
   Motor Oils and Accessories
   Used Car and Parking Lot

VI. EATING AND DRINKING PLACES
   Boarding Houses
   Eating Houses
   Cafés, Restaurants
   Tea Rooms
   Beer Parlors, Saloons

VII. FOOD STORES
   Butcher and Meat Markets
   Fish, Oysters, Game
   Grocers, Confectioners

VIII. CLOTHING AND DEPARTMENT STORES
   Shoe Dealers
   Milliners
   Ladies' and Men's Wear
   Children's Shops
   Clothiers and Dry Goods
   Remnants
   Toy Shops

IX. FURNITURE AND HOUSEHOLD
Furniture Stores
Electrical Appliances
Stoves and Tinware
Upholstering and Interior
Decorating
Sewing Center

X. ICE AND FUEL DEALERS

XI. FINANCE, INSURANCE, REAL ESTATE
Brokers (Loan & Pawn)
Banks
Building & Loan Companies
Investment Companies
Insurance Companies
Credit Union
Burial League
Commission Merchants
Real Estate Companies

XII. COMMUNICATION AND TRANSPORTATION
Printing Shops
Publishers
Newspaper Offices
Taxi-cab Stands
Newsstands

XIII. RECREATION AND ENTERTAINMENT
Pool and Billiard Rooms
Motion Picture Theater
Clubs and Others

XIV. CRAFTSMEN'S PLACES
Blacksmiths and Wheelwrights
Boot and Shoe Makers
Cabinet Makers
Carpenters, Painters, Plumbers,
Plasterers
Engravers
Electricians
Bottlers
Hide, Wool, Fur Dealers
Leather Dealers
Jewelry and Watchmakers
Mechanics
Gun and Locksmiths

XV. OTHER RETAIL STORES
Machinery (Boweevil, Add
Vending, Motorcycle)
Antiques
Jewelry Stores
Kodaks and Supplies
Office Supplies, Paper Company
Drug Stores
Hardware Stores
Music Shops
Florists
Carriage and Buggy Dealers

XVI. MANUFACTURING
Cabinets
Carriage and Wagon
Suspenders
Sausage
Tobacco

XVII. WHOLESALE TRADE
    Paper Dealers   Tea, Coffee and Tobacco
    Groceries

XVIII. MISCELLANEOUS
    Auction House   Organizational Headquarters
    Fire Company   (Halls)
    Office Buildings   Junk Dealers

*Specific Designations Under Classifications Were Taken Directly From Listings in City Directories.

Summary of Businesses on Hargett Street
By Race of Operator, 1875-1951

	1875-76 N*	1875-76 W*	1883 N	1883 W	1886 N	1886 W	1887 N	1887 W	1888 N	1888 W	1891 N	1891 W
I. Personal Services	0	0	1	0	1	1	1	1	2	2	2	1
II. Professional and Semi-professional Services	0	0	0	0	0	0	1	0	0	0	0	0
III. Business Services	0	0	0	0	0	0	0	0	0	0	0	0
IV. Repair Services	0	0	0	0	0	0	0	0	0	0	0	0
V. Automotive Services	0	2	0	0	0	0	0	0	0	0	0	0
VI. Eating and Drinking Places	2	6	0	3	2	2	2	0	1	2	2	1
VII. Food Stores	0	0	1	6	1	8	2	9	1	5	0	5
VIII. Clothing and Department Stores	0	1	0	3	0	4	0	2	0	3	0	3
IX. Furniture and Household	0	0	0	3	1	0	1	0	0	0	0	0
X. Ice and Fuel Dealers	0	0	0	1	0	0	0	0	0	0	0	0
XI. Finance, Insurance, Real Estate	0	0	0	1	0	1	0	1	0	3	0	3
XII. Communication and Transportation	0	0	0	0	0	0	0	0	0	0	0	0
XIII. Recreation and Entertainment	0	0	0	0	0	0	0	0	0	0	0	0
XIV. Craftsmen's Places	0	0	2	8	4	4	5	3	2	3	2	5
XV. Other Retail Stores	0	1	0	2	0	0	0	1	0	1	0	1
XVI. Manufacturing	0	1	0	0	0	2	0	2	0	2	0	3
XVII. Wholesale Trade	0	0	0	0	0	1	0	1	0	1	0	0
XVIII. Miscellaneous Places	0	0	0	0	0	0	0	0	0	0	0	1
Total	2	11	4	27	9	23	12	20	6	22	6	23

* W–White
* N–Negro

Hargett Street Businesses (Continued)

	1896-97		1899-1900		1901		1903-04		1905-06		1907-08		1909-10		1911-12		1913-14		1915-16	
	N	W	N	W	N	W	N	W	N	W	N	W	N	W	N	W	N	W	N	W
I.	1	2	2	2	2	1	2	1	3	1	3	3	2	2	2	2	3	3	1	2
II.	0	0	0	0	0	0	0	0	1	0	2	0	1	0	6	0	6	1	6	1
III.	0	1	0	0	0	0	0	0	0	0	0	0	0	0	0	0	0	0	1	1
IV.	0	0	0	0	0	0	0	0	0	0	0	0	0	0	0	0	0	0	0	0
V.	0	0	0	0	0	0	0	0	0	0	0	0	0	0	0	0	0	0	0	0
VI.	2	1	4	3	2	1	0	0	1	0	1	1	1	1	0	1	0	1	0	1
VII.	1	9	1	6	1	10	0	12	0	12	0	6	0	6	2	9	0	0	1	8
VIII.	0	3	0	0	0	2	0	2	0	2	0	2	0	2	0	2	2	1	2	6
IX.	0	0	0	0	0	0	0	2	0	1	0	1	0	1	0	1	0	0	0	4
X.	0	0	1	0	0	0	0	0	0	0	0	1	0	0	0	0	0	0	1	0
XI.	0	2	0	1	0	1	0	0	1	0	0	0	0	1	0	0	1	0	1	1
XII.	0	0	0	1	0	1	0	4	0	3	0	2	1	1	4	2	0	1	0	4
XIII.	0	0	0	0	0	0	0	0	0	0	1	0	0	1	2	0	0	0	0	0
XIV.	2	3	1	8	4	1	4	4	2	3	1	0	1	2	0	3	1	1	1	3
XV.	0	3	0	1	0	1	0	1	1	2	0	1	1	1	0	1	2	3	2	2
XVI.	0	2	0	0	0	0	0	0	0	0	0	0	0	2	1	2	0	0	0	0
XVII.	0	0	0	1	1	1	0	0	0	0	1	0	0	0	1	0	0	0	0	0
XVIII.	0	1	0	2	0	1	1	1	2	2	1	0	1	2	1	2	1	1	1	2
TOTAL	6	29	9	25	10	20	7	26	11	26	9	17	8	22	17	25	16	12	17	35

Roman Numerals Correspond To Classifications As Specified On Previous Page.

Hargett Street Businesses (Continued)

	1917 N	1917 W	1918-19 N	1918-19 W	1919-20 N	1919-20 W	1921-22 N	1921-22 W	1923-24 N	1923-24 W	1925 N	1925 W	1926 N	1926 W	1927 N	1927 W	1928 N	1928 W	1929 N	1929 W
I	4	1	6	1	6	1	6	1	10	1	10	3	8	1	10	2	13	3	10	3
II	7	1	7	1	7	1	6	0	13	0	15	0	13	0	13	0	1	1	12	2
III	1	0	1	0	1	0	1	0	0	0	0	1	2	0	1	0	1	0	1	0
IV	0	0	0	1	0	0	0	0	0	0	0	0	0	0	0	0	1	0	1	0
V	0	0	0	0	0	1	0	0	1	1	2	0	2	0	2	0	2	0	0	0
VI	0	0	0	1	0	6	0	1	1	1	0	6	0	0	0	0	0	0	4	1
VII	0	8	1	9	1	8	2	8	2	6	3	4	1	2	1	2	2	2	0	2
VIII	2	8	2	8	2	4	0	4	0	4	1	1	0	2	0	4	0	5	0	5
IX	0	4	0	4	0	0	0	4	0	3	0	4	0	5	1	0	0	0	0	0
X	1	0	0	0	2	0	3	0	6	0	6	0	4	0	0	0	0	0	0	0
XI	1	0	1	0	4	2	3	1	3	5	3	1	2	1	3	1	7	1	7	1
XII	2	3	2	1	0	1	0	2	0	3	2	3	1	3	1	2	1	2	1	2
XIII	0	0	0	3	1	5	1	1	1	1	1	1	1	1	1	1	1	1	1	1
XIV	1	3	1	0	2	1	2	4	2	3	2	3	2	3	0	0	0	0	0	0
XV	2	0	2	0	0	0	0	1	0	3	0	1	0	1	2	2	2	2	2	2
XVI	0	0	0	0	0	1	0	1	0	1	0	0	0	0	0	0	0	0	0	0
XVII	0	0	0	0	0	0	3	0	0	2	0	2	0	2	0	2	0	2	0	2
XVIII	3	1	3	1	3	0	3	0	4	0	7	0	0	0	0	0	0	0	0	0
TOTAL	24	28	28	31	30	32	29	29	43	34	52	23	36	17	34	16	38	19	39	21

Hargett Street Businesses (Continued)

	1930 N	1930 W	1931 N	1931 W	1932 N	1932 W	1933 N	1933 W	1934 N	1934 W	1935 N	1935 W	1936 N	1936 W	1937 N	1937 W	1938 N	1938 W	1939 N	1939 W
I	11	4	11	3	11	4	12	4	7	4	9	3	11	4	12	6	13	7	13	8
II	14	1	11	1	11	0	11	0	9	1	10	1	11	1	11	0	11	0	11	0
III	1	0	1	0	1	0	0	0	1	0	1	0	1	0	1	0	1	0	1	0
IV	1	0	0	0	0	0	0	0	0	0	0	0	0	0	0	0	0	0	0	0
V	0	0	0	0	0	1	0	0	0	0	0	0	0	0	0	0	0	0	0	0
VI	4	2	2	2	2	1	1	2	3	2	3	2	3	2	3	4	3	4	3	4
VII	0	3	0	3	1	4	0	1	0	2	0	2	0	3	0	3	0	2	0	2
VIII	0	2	0	2	1	2	0	5	0	5	1	3	0	3	0	3	1	3	0	3
IX	0	6	0	7	4	0	0	2	0	4	0	3	0	3	0	3	0	3	0	3
X	0	0	0	0	2	0	0	0	0	0	0	0	0	0	0	0	0	0	0	0
XI	7	0	7	0	0	1	8	1	6	1	7	1	7	1	5	2	5	1	5	5
XII	1	0	1	1	1	0	2	1	4	1	4	2	2	1	2	0	3	0	5	5
XIII	1	1	2	0	0	0	1	0	2	1	2	1	2	1	3	1	3	1	1	1
XIV	0	0	0	2	0	0	0	0	0	1	0	0	0	0	0	0	0	0	3	0
XV	2	2	2	0	2	2	2	2	2	2	2	2	2	2	2	2	2	2	2	1
XVI	0	1	0	0	0	2	0	0	0	0	0	0	0	0	0	0	0	0	0	0
XVII	0	0	0	2	0	2	0	2	0	2	0	2	0	2	0	2	0	2	0	2
XVIII	4	2	6	2	6	2	6	2	11	2	8	2	9	0	8	0	9	0	5	0
TOTAL	46	26	37	25	45	17	43	20	45	25	47	22	48	21	47	24	51	23	44	24

Hargett Street Businesses (Continued)

	1940 N	1940 W	1941 N	1941 W	1942 N	1942 W	1943 N	1943 W	1945-46 N	1945-46 W	1947 N	1947 W	1948 N	1948 W	1949 N	1949 W	1950 N	1950 W	1951* N	1951* W
I.	12	7	13	7	10	4	10	7	12	6	13	8	11	8	10	9	11	9	13	8
II.	13	0	15	0	11	0	11	0	10	0	9	0	9	0	10	0	10	0	10	0
III.	2	0	2	0	2	0	2	1	2	0	2	2	2	2	2	2	2	2	2	1
IV.	0	0	1	0	1	1	1	0	1	1	1	1	2	2	2	2	1	2	1	1
V.	0	0	0	0	0	0	0	0	0	0	0	0	0	0	0	0	0	0	0	0
VI.	3	4	3	4	3	2	3	2	3	2	3	1	3	1	3	1	3	1	3	1
VII.	0	2	0	2	0	2	0	2	0	2	1	2	1	2	1	2	1	2	1	0
VIII.	0	5	0	5	0	5	0	5	0	5	0	5	0	5	0	6	0	7	0	2
IX.	0	5	0	5	0	3	0	3	0	3	0	5	0	5	0	3	0	3	1	7
X.	0	0	0	0	0	0	0	0	0	0	0	0	0	0	0	0	0	0	0	3
XI.	6	0	6	0	5	0	5	0	5	0	5	1	5	1	5	0	6	0	6	0
XII.	5	1	5	0	4	0	4	0	4	0	3	0	5	0	3	0	3	0	2	0
XIII.	3	0	3	1	1	1	2	1	2	1	2	3	3	1	2	2	2	2	2	0
XIV.	0	1	0	0	0	0	0	0	0	0	0	1	0	1	0	1	0	0	0	2
XV.	2	0	2	1	2	1	2	2	2	1	2	2	2	2	2	2	2	2	2	0
XVI.	1	0	0	0	0	0	0	0	0	0	0	1	0	1	0	1	0	1	0	2
XVII.	0	2	2	2	5	2	5	2	7	2	11	1	8	2	6	2	6	2	6	0
XVIII.	0	0	0	0	0	0	0	0	0	0	0	1	0	0	0	0	0	0	0	0
TOTAL	51	27	55	27	44	21	45	25	48	23	52	35	50	31	47	33	48	33	49	29

(Covering Businesses on East Hargett Street From Fayetteville to Blount).

Source: Directories of the City of Raleigh, North Carolina

* 1951—Last Year For Which Indications of Color Are Given In the Directories (Previously Designations of Color Were Made By Placing "Col," C, or ° after Names of Negroes).

BIBLIOGRAPHY

Amis, Moses N. *Historical Raleigh*. Raleigh: Edwards and Broughton, 1902.

Anderson, Nels. *The Hobo*. Chicago: University of Chicago Press, 1923.

Ashe, Samuel A'Court. *History of North Carolina*. Vol. XI. Raleigh: Edwards and Broughton, 1925.

Battle, Kemp P. *The Early History of Raleigh, the Capital City of North Carolina*, A Centennial Address, Oct. 18, 1892. Raleigh: Edwards and Broughton, 1893.

.... "Raleigh and the Old Town of Bloomsbury", *North Carolina Booklet*, II (1902).

Bogue, Donald J. *The Growth of Metropolitan Areas, 1900 to 1950*. Washington: Government Printing Office, 1953.

Bonner, Hubert. *Social Psychology*. New York: American Book Co., 1953.

Boone, Irving R. (ed.). *Negro Progress in North Carolina*, V (1952).

Brown, W. O. "The Nature of Race Consciousness", *Social Forces*, X (October, 1931).

Chamberlain, Hope Summerell. *History of Wake County, North Carolina*. Raleigh: Edwards and Broughton, 1922.

City Code, Raleigh, North Carolina, 1950. (mimeographed).

City Directories, Raleigh, North Carolina, 1875-1958.

City Planning Department, Raleigh, North Carolina. *Raleigh Township Population Forecast*, August, 1953. (Monograph).

Daniels, Jonathan. *Tar Heels: A Portrait of North Carolina*. New York: Dodd, Mead and Co., 1941.

Daniels, Josephus. *Editor in Politics*. Chapel Hill: University of North Carolina Press, 1941.

Demerath, Nicholas J., and Gilmore, Harlan W. "The Ecology of Southern Cities", Rupert B. Vance and Nicholas J. Demerath (eds.). *The Urban South*. Chapel Hill: University of North Carolina Press, 1954.

Drake, St. Clair, and Cayton, Horace R. *Black Metropolis*. New York: Harcourt, Brace and Co., 1945.

Drummy, J. R. (mgr.). "Industrial Survey of Raleigh, North Carolina". Unpublished Study of the Industrial Department, Raleigh Chamber of Commerce, 1953 and 1958. (mimeographed).

Durkheim, Emile. *The Division of Labor in Society*. Translated by George Simpson, Glencoe, Ill.: The Free Press, 1947.

―――― *The Elementary Forms of Religious Life*. Translated by Joseph Ward Swain. Glencoe, Ill.: Free Press, 1947.

Eckler, A. Ross. "Census Statistics For Local Use". Talk Before Raleigh Advertising Club, Raleigh, North Carolina, November 9, 1954. (mimeographed).

Festinger, Leon, Schachter, Stanley, and Back, Kurt. *Social Pressures in Informal Groups.* New York: Harper and Brothers, 1950.

Firey, Walter. *Land Use in Central Boston.* Cambridge: Harvard University Press, 1947.

Frazer, Charles R., Sr. "The Uses of Adversity". Unpublished Autobiography. (typewritten).

Frazier, E. Franklin. *Black Bourgeoisie.* Glencoe, Ill.: The Free Press, 1957.

—— *The Negro in the United States.* New York: Macmillan Co., 1957. (revised).

General Statutes of North Carolina, XI (1943).

Gras, N.S.B. *An Introduction to Economic History.* New York: Harper and Brothers, 1922.

Hamilton, J. G. DeRoulhac. *Reconstruction in North Carolina.* New York: Columbia University, 1914.

Hankins, Frank H. "Social Discrimination", *Encyclopedia of Social Science,* Vol. XIV.

Harmon, J. H., Jr., Lindsay, Arnett G., and Woodson, Carter G. *The Negro As a Business Man.* Association For the Study of Negro Life and History, 1929.

Henderson, Archibald. *North Carolina, the Old North State and the New.* Vols. II and XI. Chicago: Lewis Publishing Co., 1941.

Hertzler, Joyce O. *Society in Action.* New York: Dryden Press, 1954.

Hughes, Everett C. "The Ecological Aspect of Institutions", *American Sociological Review.* I (April, 1936).

Hunter, Floyd. *Community Power Structure.* Chapel Hill: University of North Carolina Press, 1953.

Johnson, Charles S. *Patterns of Negro Segregation.* New York: Harper and Brothers, 1943.

Kinzer, Robert H., and Sagarin, Edward. *The Negro in American Business.* New York: Greenberg, 1950.

LaPierre, Richard T. *A Theory of Social Control.* New York: McGraw-Hill Book Co., 1954.

Larkins, John R. "The Negro Population of North Carolina, 1945-1955". Raleigh, North Carolina: State Board of Public Welfare, 1957. (monograph).

Latta, M. L. *History of My Life and Work.* Raleigh, North Carolina: Orgen Printing Co.

Lefler, Hugh T. *History of North Carolina.* Vol. XI. New York: Lewis Historical Publishing Co., 1956.

—— *North Carolina History Told By Contemporaries.* Chapel Hill: University of North Carolina Press, 1934.

Locke, Alain, and Stern, Bernhard J. *When Peoples Meet*. New York: Progressive Education Association, 1942.

Lynd, Robert S. *Knowledge For What?* Princeton: Princeton University Press, 1939.

Matherly, Walter J. "Emergence of the Metropolitan Community in the South", *Social Forces*, XIV (March, 1936).

McKenzie, R. D. *The Metropolitan Community*. New York: McGraw-Hill Book Co., 1933.

—— *The Neighborhood: A Study of Local Life in the City of Columbus, Ohio*. Chicago: University of Chicago Press, 1923.

—— "The Scope of Human Ecology", E. W. Burgess (ed.) *The Urban Community*. Chicago: University of Chicago Press, 1926.

O'Brien, Robert W. "Beale Street, A Study in Ecological Succession", *Sociology and Social Research*, XXVI (May-June, 1942).

Odum, Howard W. *Southern Regions of the United States*. Chapel Hill: University of North Carolina Press, 1936.

Olds, Fred A. "Abstract of North Carolina Laws, 1822-1830". (newspaper clippings from N.C. State Library file).

Park, Robert E. "Racial Ideologies". William F. Ogburn (ed.). *American Society in Wartime*. Chicago: University of Chicago Press, 1943.

—— and Burgess, E. W. *Introduction to the Science of Sociology*. Chicago: University of Chicago Press, 1924.

Parks, Edd Winfield. "Southern Towns and Cities", W. T. Couch (ed.) *Culture in the South*. Chapel Hill: University of North Carolina Press, 1934.

Private Laws of North Carolina, 1899 and 1909.

Quinn, James A. *Human Ecology*. New York: Prentice Hall, Inc., 1950.

—— "Hypothesis of Median Location", *American Sociological Review*, VIII (April, 1943).

Rose, Arnold M. *The Negro's Morale*. Minneapolis: University of Minnesota Press, 1949.

Stone, Gregory P. "City Shoppers and Urban Identification: Observations on the Social Psychology of City Life", *American Journal of Sociology*, LX (July, 1954).

Thompson, Lorin A. "Urbanization, Occupational Shift and Economic Progress", Rupert B. Vance (ed.) *The Urban South*. Chapel Hill: University of North Carolina Press, 1954.

Tucker, R. S. (compiler). *Early Times in Raleigh*, Addresses delivered by the Honorable David L. Swain. Raleigh: Walters, Hugh and Co., 1867.

Turner, Ralph H. and Killian, Lewis M. *Collective Behavior*. Englewood Cliffs, N.J.: Prentice Hall, Inc., 1957.

U.S. Bureau of the Census. *United States Census of Population: 1950*. Vols. I and II. Washington: Government Printing Office, 1952.

Vance, Rupert B. *All These People*. Chapel Hill: University of North Carolina Press, 1945.

Walker, Harry J. "Changes in Race Accommodation in a Southern Community". Unpublished Ph.D. dissertation, Department of Sociology, University of Chicago, 1945.

Washington, Booker T. *The Negro in Business*. Boston and Chicago: Hertel, Jenkins and Co., 1907.

Whyte, William Foote. *Street Corner Society*. Chicago: University of Chicago Press, 1943.

Williams, M. W., and Watkins, George W. *Who's Who Among North Carolina Negro Baptists*, 1940.

Woodward, C. Vann. "Origins of the New South", W. H. Stephenson and E. M. Coulter (eds.) *A History of the South*, Vol. IX. Louisiana State University Press, 1951.

Writers' Program of the Works Progress Administration. *Raleigh, Capital of North Carolina*. Raleigh Sesquicentennial Commission, 1942.

Zorbaugh, Harvey. *The Gold Coast and the Slum*. Chicago: University of Chicago Press, 1929.